'A quite fascinating piece of history, both shocking and entertaining in equal measure. I don't think we're going to see an end to the egotists and fantasists who clamour for our vote, but Debbie Kilroy has done a fabulous job in bringing 52 of the worst offenders to our notice.'
Dr Robert Lyman, author of *The Rise of the Third Reich*

'This witty and well-written book highlights 52 parliamentary rogues from 1603 to 1945 . . . It's a rattling good read.'
Professor Frank McDonough, author of *The Hitler Years*

'Relevant, informative and timely, Kilroy shows us the real unparliamentary behaviour of the past, whilst also reminding us some things never change!'
Jackson van Uden, 'History with Jackson'

MEMBERS BEHAVING BADLY

A History of Britain in 52 Parliamentary Rogues

DEBBIE KILROY

Elliott&Thompson

First published 2026 by
Elliott and Thompson Limited
2 John Street
London WC1N 2ES
www.eandtbooks.com

Represented by:
Authorised Rep Compliance Ltd
Ground Floor, 71 Lower Baggot Street
Dublin, D02 P593
Ireland
www.arccompliance.com

ISBN: 978-1-78396-938-8

Copyright © Debbie Kilroy 2026

The Author has asserted her rights under the Copyright, Designs and Patents Act, 1988, to be identified as Author of this Work. All rights reserved. No part of this publication may be reproduced, stored in or introduced into a retrieval system, or transmitted, in any form, or by any means (electronic, mechanical, photocopying, recording or otherwise) without the prior written permission of the publisher. Any person who does any unauthorised act in relation to this publication may be liable to criminal prosecution and civil claims for damages.

9 8 7 6 5 4 3 2 1

A catalogue record for this book is available from the British Library.

Typesetting: Marie Doherty

Printed by CPI Group (UK) Ltd, Croydon, CR0 4YY

For Toby, Leo and Corvus

Contents

	Author's Note	ix
	Introduction	1
One	Absolute Power (1603–37)	7
Two	What's So Civil about War? (1637–60)	27
Three	A House of Ill-Repute (1660–85)	53
Four	House Party (1685–1715)	71
Five	Capital Offence (1716–46)	95
Six	Liberty and Libertines (1746–75)	117
Seven	The Revolting Stage (1775–1806)	139
Eight	Officers and No Gentlemen (1802–32)	161
Nine	Full Steam Ahead (1832–67)	185
Ten	'Rule by Virtue' (1867–1910)	209
Eleven	Led by Donkeys (1910–45)	231
	Epilogue	253
	Acknowledgements	257
	Endnotes	259
	Bibliography	281
	Index	301

Author's Note

For the sake of easy reading, spelling, punctuation and grammar have been modernised. Dates are in the original, but the New Year begins on 1 January rather than on the traditional Lady Day (25 March), a date still mirrored, more or less, in the start of the new financial year. Where necessary, regnal numbers will reflect both the Scottish and English titles.

Introduction

Screams rent the cool night air, high-pitched, shrieking, enough to raise the hair on the necks of anyone in earshot. Eventually, to the relief of all, the noise changed to a keening, then – perhaps after minutes that felt like hours – subsided to dull, hopeless moans punctuated by the occasional whimper, a beast wounded to exhaustion. For those foolish enough to search for the source, it was easy to find. In a cell of the Bishop of Salisbury's palace, broken and naked, trussed like a chicken, the rope that circled his neck and looped around his genitals keeping him suspended in the air, were the battered and bruised remains of a Carmelite friar. Across his stomach lay a heavy stone, forcing his middle down, stretching his neck and crushing his airways, distending parts that would never work again, pushing his spine to a grotesquely angular break. Circled around him, like hyenas revelling in their catch, was a group of well-dressed men. Many wore the liveries and badges of the greatest lords of the land; all were knights, three were or would become members of Parliament.

The friar, shattered in body and in mind, died shortly after the knights had grown bored and cut him down. Nevertheless, none of the perpetrators received any punishment. One of the three MPs thereafter kept his head down, concentrating on extending his lands and serving the country as an envoy and soldier. Another, for supporting the ill-fated King Richard II, had his head cut off and put in a basket. But the remaining MP, Sir Philip Courtenay, was made of nastier stuff. Relishing 'acts of gratuitous savagery and vindictiveness', he bullied his West Country neighbours, led extortion rackets and dabbled in house-breaking and theft.[1] Despite all this, though, he kept his favoured place in both Parliament and the king's graces – for a while, at least.

The crunch came eighteen years later, in the summer of 1402, when rumours filtered through to the new king, Henry IV, about 'evildoers and children of iniquity arrayed in manner of war', all commanded by Courtenay, laying siege to Newenham Abbey in Devon.[2] As representatives of the abbot complained:

> Philip de Courtenay, knight, with a very large number of men assembled under his command . . . made an assault on the said supplicant and forcibly removed him from his aforesaid abbey . . . [T]hey took him away and threatened him with harsh words as far as the town of Honiton, and there by threats and harsh words they made the said supplicant pay for their expenses against his wish, and from there they . . . imprisoned and detained the said supplicant in prison there for the next fifteen days, on account of which the said supplicant was in despair of his life.

In response, Henry sent for Courtenay to explain himself, but the errant knight refused to show. Instead, 'with a large number of men, armed and arrayed' he once again attacked the abbey, terrifying yet another abbot and forcing the monks to seek protection in the surrounding woods. Two, however, were caught, taken to Courtenay's estate and forced into service as 'hunters and falconers'.[3]

Enough was enough. It was one thing to trample on lowly friars and commoners, but quite a different story to attack the upper echelons of society. Courtenay was sent to the Tower of London, there to remain at the king's pleasure. That pleasure was to last two weeks. Before the end of the month, 'the lords spiritual and temporal asked the king to have mercy on Sir Philip Courtenay, and to make order for him to be released from prison'.[4] With sureties granted by his friends, he was once again free to terrorise the county. And although he would never again attend Parliament, his service to the Crown continued. He was, first and foremost, a warrior, and in a time when England was constantly at war, he was simply too necessary, too rich and too favoured to be punished.

Introduction

❋

When the friar was murdered in May 1384, Parliament was no longer in its infancy. The great lords and other representatives of the land had been called on an ad hoc basis for over a century, with more formal structures crystallising for at least fifty years. But it had a lot more growing to do before it could reach full maturity. It was still under the control of the Powers That Be and would have to wait centuries to become an institution, rather than a sporadic event. Until that point – the last unilateral dissolution by the sovereign was in the nineteenth century – the true running of the country was conducted by a small coterie of Privy Councillors and favourites surrounding the monarch. Indeed, there was no other way. Up until the end of the seventeenth century, Parliament met infrequently, with sessions – when they happened – lasting a tiny portion of the calendar year, and usually only when the government coffers were empty (the House of Commons being the only body able to grant taxes). Over the succeeding centuries, through wars and compromise, popular pressure and individual action, Parliament slowly, haltingly extended its remit and importance until it became pre-eminent. But in 1384 that was a long way off: Parliament was very much still the adolescent and, like any teenager, it could be erratic and impulsive and volatile. Members tested, stretched and sometimes overstepped their boundaries. They lacked the wisdom and experience always to make the correct decisions and were all too often swayed by the 'influencers' of the day. And as the Carmelite friar found to his disadvantage, their parties could ruin life and limb.

But surely, over the course of the next six-and-a-half centuries, during its metamorphosis from advisory body to controlling influence, Parliament and its members grew up? MPs learned from their mistakes and became the dependable, honest and honourable representatives that they are today? After all, we have been taught to glory in this great British institution, to celebrate the gradual lessening of absolutism and the ascendancy of a representative democracy that is now the epicentre of civic life. The political, and very often physical, ancestors of our current MPs made Britain not only powerful, with an empire stretching the globe, but proud: they stood up against tyranny; they brought unimagined wealth and success to the small island that, for so long, seemed to mark the edge of the world; they educated it and they improved it; they made it safe and prosperous. Through their diligence and dedication, these forebears brought light to the darkness. Even if some portion of their politics seems alien to modern eyes, these were remarkable men doing remarkable deeds, and in their spare time they were 'inventing' science, ensuring basic freedoms, literally building our national monuments and winning wars.

These are the legends on which Britain was built. But for as long as the House of Commons has existed, within its walls there have also been miscreants and marauders, serving themselves rather than the people. There have been cheats and liars, playing games, playing the markets, playing the people who trust them. Beyond that, there have been abusers and kidnappers and murderers, violent men doing violent deeds, often using Parliament as a front and excuse. And they were not a small minority; they were not the exception that proves the rule; they were not just the odd – in either definition – backbencher. Instead, they were government ministers, leaders, men who down the centuries have been remembered with respect, if not fondness. And they were many. Although only fifty-two of their number are featured within these pages – and handily listed, with dates and constituencies, at the start of their relevant chapters – hundreds more could have been included. But that would have produced an encyclopaedia, not a story, and it is the story that fascinates me: where did these men come from, what did they do and how on earth did they get away with it? So, this becomes an alternative history of Britain, told through the actions and misdeeds of the chosen few.

In writing this way, I might well be upsetting the apple cart. Firstly, because although the events themselves haven't changed, my perspective is different from the famous histories that have gone before. The big moments in this archipelago's tale become the background to the narrative, which instead is – as much as possible – told through the eyes of misbehaving MPs and their victims. Greater emphasis is therefore placed on their faults and frailties than on their more respectable occupations, and more reliance placed on gossip and rumour than would be expected in the average history book. Some of these men – and, up until one hundred years ago, they were all men – have never made much of an impact on the national consciousness; others have since been swept under the carpet. A number, however, are still considered the 'great men' of history. And why not? Does being an awful person stop one from being a brilliant politician? Equally, can someone be a terrible politician but a genuinely decent human being?

Whether great or small, the fifty-two men selected embody some aspect of British history, be it a time, an ideal, a place, a party, or an event. Occasionally, they're included because, despite all their faults, they are fabulous. They were alive and engaging in their various roguish undertakings from the first point at which it is possible to consider 'Britain' a political entity – the union of the crowns of Scotland and England under James VI and I – until the end of the Second World War. All of them were Commoners – sitting in the English, and then British, House of Commons – for at least part of their life. But they were not necessarily career politicians, a relatively modern phenomenon that would have made little sense to many of the men in these pages, who flitted in and out of the Commons in their pursuit of riches and glory, but who rarely saw becoming an MP as an end in itself. There were, of course, plenty of ne'er-do-wells in the House of Lords too, but MPs are elected: constituents chose these men as their representatives, and often – although not always – there were alternatives. What, then, does it say about society's expectations if it returns the same rotten politicians again and again?

Secondly, this is a book about bad behaviour. This is therefore a trigger warning: many of the politicians contained within these pages committed heinous crimes. Some abused animals and children and wives; some perpetrated acts of cruelty and malice upon individuals and groups; some met sticky ends, including at their own hands. And, while there are a few sailors featured here, many more could swear like them – or like Restoration poets.

Thirdly, I am not reading morality backwards, bringing current opinions down as judgement on the past. Instead, as far as logic allows, the

MPs' contemporaries will be my guide. This in itself presents problems. There are some crimes that will always be crimes: premeditated murder is generally taken as illegal, or at least something to be condemned, as is rape, theft and extortion. The trouble even with these, however, is the hazy edge of definition. If someone is killed in a duel – which is premeditated but which is also, in a way, consensual – should that be given equal weighting to murder by poisoning? In addition, there are 'crimes' towards which we wouldn't bat an eyelid now, but in the past could lead to imprisonment, maiming or, in extreme cases, execution by way of punishment. And then there are acts and behaviours that today are considered despicable, but at the time would not even provoke a shrug of the shoulders – the brutal and bloody business of slavery being an obvious example. Nevertheless, despite the limits to a contemporary approach, the rule of thumb for inclusion is that members' behaviour must not only be shocking now, but also in the MPs' own times.

So what are we left with? A rip-roaring romp through British history taking in a whole range of bad behaviour, stretching from the idiotic and mildly embarrassing to the horrendous and life-changing. Some stories might prompt a wry smile, others will astonish, perhaps a few will leave you dumbfounded. But all will make you question the very foundations of our political system. For this is a sensational history of members behaving badly.

Chapter One

Absolute Power
1603–37

Dramatis Personae

1. Sir Robert Carey (*c.*1560–1639)

> Morpeth (Northumberland) 1586–87
> Morpeth (Northumberland) 1589
> Callington (Cornwall) 1593
> Northumberland 1597–98
> Northumberland 1601
> Grampound (Cornwall) 1621

2. Sir Francis Bacon (1561–1626)

> Bossiney (Devon) 1581
> Weymouth and Melcombe Regis (Dorset) 1584–86
> Taunton (Somerset) 1586–87
> Liverpool (Lancashire) 1589
> Middlesex 1593
> Ipswich (Suffolk) 1597–98
> Ipswich (Suffolk) 1601
> Ipswich (Suffolk) 1604–10
> Cambridge University 1614

3. Giles Mompesson (1584–c.1651)

    Great Bedwyn (Wiltshire) … … … … … … … … … 1614
    Great Bedwyn (Wiltshire) … … … … … … … … … 1621

4. Sir Edward Villiers (1585–1626)

    Westminster (Middlesex) … … … … … … … … … 1621
    Westminster (Middlesex) … … … … … … … … … 1624
    Westminster (Middlesex) … … … … … … … … … 1625

5. Sir Edward Coke (1552–1634)

    Aldeburgh (Suffolk) … … … … … … … … … … 1589
    Norfolk … … … … … … … … … … … … … 1593
    Liskeard (Cornwall) … … … … … … … … … … 1621
    Coventry (Warwickshire) … … … … … … … … … 1624
    Norfolk … … … … … … … … … … … … … 1625
    Norfolk … … … … … … … … … … … … … 1626
    Buckinghamshire… … … … … … … … … … … 1628–29

6. Clement Coke (1594–1630)

    Clitheroe (Lancashire) … … … … … … … … … 1614
    Dunwich (Suffolk) … … … … … … … … … … 1621
    Aylesbury (Buckinghamshire) … … … … … … … 1626
    Aylesbury (Buckinghamshire) … … … … … … … 1628–29

There was a clamour at the gates of Holyroodhouse. Too late in the evening for any but the most important tidings, it immediately caused a stir – as did the appearance of the messenger, dirty, bruised and bleeding from a head wound. It was obvious the man needed medical assistance, but that would have to wait as he was shown post-haste to the king's bedchamber. Once there, the new arrival, Sir Robert Carey, English courtier and former MP, dropped to his knees and addressed James VI by his new and much extended title: King of England, Scotland and Ireland. For the date was 26 March 1603. Elizabeth I, Queen of England – not yet the Gloriana of legend, but the ageing and ailing curse of many an ambition – had died two days before.

This news would change the world, and Carey had arranged matters well to be the one to deliver it. For Carey was a gambling man, and this arduous four-hundred-mile trip north from Richmond Palace near London to Holyroodhouse in Edinburgh, Scotland, was both a symptom and remedy of his addiction. The younger son of a well-to-do family with little inheritance of his own, his path to prosperity had led him to Court. He was charming and witty and had quickly ingratiated himself with the late queen. But to live at Court meant a certain level of keeping up appearances in both wardrobe and behaviour. And as so often happened to gentlemen of limited means, he fell into debt to do so.

Very often Carey's bets provided a sticking plaster. Taking up a wager in 1589 to walk from London to Berwick on the Scottish border, he had arrived twelve days later with sore feet but £2,000 (about half a million today) richer.[1] Now, fourteen years after that initial bet, he was gambling for the highest stakes of his life, because this latest little jaunt had been expressly forbidden by the English Privy Council. But he had ambition, and this time he had a horse. Risking all, Carey circumvented the restrictions, using friends and family to smuggle him out of the locked gates of Richmond Palace while the queen's body was still warm. If his gamble failed, it would spell the end of his political career; if he succeeded, the new monarch's favour would go a long way to alleviating every want of Carey's for good.

So Carey put up with a pounding, bleeding head, caused by a kick from his blown horse. He ignored the exhaustion of travelling four hundred miles non-stop over two days. He tried not to think too deeply about his return to London. He even remained attentive during one of his new king's famed rambling speeches. And he was duly compensated, for a while. A pleased James allowed Carey to kiss his hand before summoning doctors to tend to his bloody guest, and as a further gift the following morning swore Carey in as a gentleman of the bedchamber. Sadly for Carey, James's wish to honour his own Scottish nobles soon led to his demotion. His position was reduced to the much less important role of gentleman of the privy chamber, and to add insult to head injury, he lost his offices and estates on the border. When he died, still profligate, in 1639, he was buried with as much 'thrift as will stand with decency'.[2]

Despite Carey's personal loss, the transition to a new dynasty was surprisingly smooth: there were no wars, there was no great lurch in religion, and there were only a few executions. Many had predicted otherwise. Although the official story insisted that Elizabeth 'named' her successor in her final hours, signalling her preference with a raised hand long after her voice had given out, the truth was that James was not the only possible choice of monarch. There were other powerful people both foreign and domestic who had a claim to the throne; more so, as the will of King Henry VIII – Elizabeth I's father – specifically excluded his Scottish relations from the English Crown. Nor did it help that James was, indeed, Scottish: after centuries of war, no Englishman really liked anyone from Scotland, and the feeling was mutual. Yet James's accession as king of England, despite the legal and social issues, was convenient for the Privy Councillors who had been in secret – and therefore treasonous – correspondence with the northern monarch for years, and who remained desperate to protect their position, power and particular brand of Protestantism.

Nevertheless, a new style of kingship was required. James knew he couldn't rule through right of statute, let alone conquest, so he needed another route: divine right. Henry VIII might not have signed off on the new arrangement but, helpfully, God had. Still, while in early Stuart Britain there were as yet few to gainsay the Almighty, there were those eager to (mis)interpret Him. So, to put the right spin on it, James turned to liberality. On his leisurely progress from Edinburgh to London, the new king handed out so many knighthoods that they fell out of fashion: one account suggests that 906 men were knighted in the first four months of his reign alone, including Thomas Gerard, brother of the infamous Jesuit and future Gunpowder Plotter John Gerard. Some were raised to the peerage, with so many Irish and Scottish earldoms created that purchasers sent land agents to check the places actually existed. Others were given sinecures or simple random pay-outs from the Treasury in the form of gifts and grants, while monopolies were dispensed to favourites and their families.

This, then, was to become the nature of James I's reign in England over the next twenty years: ambitious men scrambling over each other, stepping on the heads of rivals – and everyone else – for the rich pickings sloshed from James's table. Nepotism, bribery and corruption were an unavoidable fact of life. To a country used to the frugality and virtue of the Virgin Queen, it was a shock to the system, encouraging chancers and complainants in equal measure.

✱

Lord St Alban, once merely Francis Bacon, had risen from the lowly place of younger son to the heights of power in government and the courts through grit, determination and a razor-sharp mind. He had served in nine Parliaments, stretching all the way back to 1581, being elevated first to a knighthood, then to the peerage, and on 27 January 1621, just weeks before he sat labouring to find the right words to describe his wrong behaviour, created a viscount. He had gained a seat on the Privy Council and been appointed lord chancellor, the head of the judiciary in England, famed for prosecuting some of the most noteworthy cases of his day and sitting in judgement on many more, using his intellect to sniff out lies, injustice and malicious behaviour wherever it was to be found. His advice was sought by royalty, his influence felt in every corner of the land. Even the 1621 Parliament, the very one now determined to ruin him, had been called at his suggestion.

Throughout his career, Bacon had authored hundreds of letters, speeches in both the Lower and Upper Houses of Parliament, case summaries, treatises and essays; he had been read and admired by the very highest in the land and beyond; he believed, if he didn't flatter himself, that some of his work would be handed down to posterity: words of wisdom, of history, of natural philosophy, that would enhance humanity's store of knowledge forever. Now, gripping his pen, racked with pain from another bout of the recurrent 'illness' that this time would surely be the death of him, he turned his attention to perhaps the hardest thing he had ever had to compose.

He took a breath and began to write: 'Upon advised consideration of the charge, descending into my own conscience, and calling my memory to account so far as I am able, I do plainly and ingenuously confess, that I am guilty of corruption; and do renounce all defence, and put myself upon the grace and mercy of your lordships.'[3]

This was as plain as he could express, and no less true for it. For, if truth be acknowledged, he was guilty: not in his heart – his intentions had always been proper – but in action and deed; he had been bribed. He had, in his innocence – or was it arrogance? – accepted gifts as a representative of the king and as a judge, when cases were still open, suits unsolved. Not that this had affected the outcome. The irony was that the first two witnesses to come forward against him had done so complaining their bribes had not worked.

One claimant, seeking favour in a land dispute, had paid Bacon £400 after assuring him that it was 'for favours past, and not in respect to favours to come'.[4] Yet the case had not been fully closed when Bacon accepted the money so, despite the fact that Bacon's decision left the briber unsatisfied, it was a corrupt payment. The other came from an equally dissatisfied claimant who, via Bacon's assistant, had put £100 in the lord chancellor's hands in the hopes of a desirable outcome. Shortly afterwards, judgement went against the claimant. After two years of to-ing and fro-ing, the decision was altered somewhat in his favour, although apparently not enough.

After that, the charges came thick and fast, encouraged by Bacon's arch-rival, the MP and lawyer Sir Edward Coke. It was twenty years since

Coke had publicly warned Bacon, 'if you have any tooth against me, pluck it out; for it will do you more hurt than all the teeth in your head will do you good'. Bacon's riposte, while brilliant, had merely entrenched Coke's dislike: 'I respect you, I fear you not; and the less you speak of your own greatness, the more I will think of it.'[5] Now it seemed that, having festered, it was too late to pull the tooth. Twenty-eight different instances of bribery were discovered, with evidence provided by forty-one witnesses. Even after the vexatious and opportunistic were removed, twelve charges remained, totalling – through objects, cash and easy loans – above £10,000 (over £2 million today).

Punishment was inevitable. A £40,000 fine was levied, along with an indefinite spell in the Tower. Bacon was banned from ever holding another state or Court position – or even coming within twelve miles of the Court – and although he managed to keep his title, he would never again be allowed to sit in Parliament. But the reality of the punishment was not so harsh, and it wasn't the feared early death that saved him, but the measure of the times. Thanks to, for once, some careful financial management, the fine was held in trust and never paid, while Bacon was released after spending just three days in prison. And the withdrawal from public life would, in the end, allow him to concentrate on his greatest passion: science and the advancement of learning. In the eyes of posterity it would, ultimately, be his philosophy that redeemed him. For the remaining five years of his life, he threw himself into all manner of thought and actual experiments, eventually succumbing to a chill caught while investigating methods for freezing chicken, leading to the observation that frozen chicken does, indeed, last longer than bacon.*

---

* Thanks to Sally Coulthard for this one: *Fowl Play* (London: Head of Zeus, 2022), p. 236. There is, however, another theory about Bacon's death, posited by Lisa Jardine and Alan Stewart, that suggests he died following inhaling an overdose of either nitre or opium to alleviate his ill health. Lisa Jardine and Alan Stewart, *Hostage to Fortune: The Troubled Life of Sir Francis Bacon* (New York: Hill and Wang, 1998), pp. 504–11.

Yet, to contemporaries, Bacon's reputation was ruined, his career destroyed. This man, peer, lord chancellor, judge, had fallen quickly and without repair. His name was mud, with 'many indignities... said and done against him, and divers libels cast abroad to his disgrace'.[6] For not only had he been caught in his crimes, but he had lost the king's favour in the process. The men who had grovelled at his feet when he was riding high now hurried away, eager to distance themselves from any whiff of failure. To make it worse, there was little Bacon could say in his defence. The only excuse – for it was no good reason – was 'I shall not be found to have the troubled fountain of a corrupt heart in a depraved habit of taking rewards to pervert justice; howsoever I may be frail and partake of the abuse of the times.'[7]

And what times they were, when men in positions of power were expected to skim a portion off the top – and would often pay an upfront lump sum for the privilege. This is what oiled the machinery of government in a time when inflation had diminished many official salaries to a peppercorn, and the government itself was too stretched, and disorganised, to rationalise its accounts. Everything that could be – from rents to taxes – was farmed out to freelancers to collect on behalf of the Crown, always at a significant loss. And this was assuming that those revenues were honestly declared in the first place: Elizabeth I's lord high treasurer, who should have known better, had self-assessed himself for tax at a measly £133 per annum, despite having an income of thousands.[8] It was therefore viewed as only natural for officials to accept whatever payments they were offered: a side of venison here; some linen there. Generally, problems arose only when the expense of gifts, or levels of embezzlement, interfered with the running of government.

✼

In 1606 or 1607 the relatively poor country lad Giles Mompesson had eagerly married the daughter of a much more socially acceptable Wiltshire family. It was a giant step up the ladder, his world expanding to the point that, by 1614, he was even considered worthy for nomination as an MP.

But more than that, his in-laws had other marriageable daughters, making important connections with ambitious and wealthy families across the country. In a world where nepotism and patronage ruled, the possibilities seemed endless, and Mompesson quickly made the most of this new network.

Take Edward Villiers, for example, the Leicestershire gentleman who was now his brother-in-law. It didn't matter that Edward was a bad egg who had been forced to resign his position in the militia for diverting funds to his own pocket. What mattered was that Edward had a secret weapon: his half-brother was George Villiers, newly appointed Lord Admiral, future Duke of Buckingham and latest good-looking royal favourite with the ear, and heart, of the king. In no time at all, George had hushed up the militia affair so that Edward could carry merrily on, accusing innocents of non-existent misdemeanours in order to gobble up their estates and accepting bribes to encourage George to overlook underlings' crimes and thus pervert the course of justice. So, despite everything, Edward was the perfect brother-in-law to consult when Mompesson essentially invented the public health racket.

The inns of England were notorious places, encouraging drunkenness and lechery in equal measure. They were a danger to the individual and thus, allegedly, to the spiritual and material health of all England. For years, feeble attempts had been made to curb the inns' excesses, but no matter the firmness of the stick used by the authorities, every effort had ended in brewer's droop. Mompesson, however, would take it all in hand; he just needed a patent granting him responsibility for the licensing and controlling of inns, which included the fixing of prices and amenities, thereby removing the task from 'idle' judges and local justices of the peace. The Crown would receive 80 per cent of the income derived from fees and fines, Mompesson would keep the rest, disreputable inns would be closed, and England would be a more sober place. Edward Villiers liked the idea and, along with another brother, agreed to present it to George, who in turn took it to the king in return for a share of the profits. Negotiations followed, and Francis Bacon – acting as one of the four legal opinions – agreed to it.

By March 1617 the patent, sealed by James on the advice of his favourite, was granted and Mompesson was knighted, 'the better [to] fight with the Bull and the Bear, and the Saracen's Heads, and such fearful creatures'.[9]

Within a few weeks, the reign of terror had begun. It started with new extortionate licences, bought by 1,200 innkeepers at an official price of between £5 and £10, but which could cost up to £30 each, with the difference pocketed by Mompesson.[10] Next came the informers, homing pigeons homing in, checking everything from establishment staircases to inn hay bales, dolling out fines for renovations or for charging above the inflation-busting price, set in 1390, for a pint of beer. Not content with haranguing, bullying and threatening the listed innkeepers in the country, the role's definition was extended beyond all sense. Bath, which previously had six inns, suddenly had twenty, 'whereof some of them have scarcely a stable for a horse, or lodging for a man'.[11]

Entrapment was positively encouraged. One agent, Ferrett by name and ferret by nature, arrived at the inn-less Brewood in Staffordshire late at night. Seeking out the octogenarian Cooke, a former innkeeper who still made a bit of cash selling ale during the day, Ferrett wove together a tale of pity and woe, convincing the kindly old man to give over his own bed. Cooke even turfed out his cow from the shed to make room for Ferrett's horse. The weasel then turned on him: 'This is well,' he said. 'You are one of those that I look for. You keep an inn, you receive a horse and man.'[12] For his troubles, Cooke was fined and made to appear before the commissioners in London – a journey of over a hundred miles. Others were thrilled to have the chance to acquire inn status, particularly when they had been denied it by the local justices of the peace. And when officials attempted to rectify the situation, they too were threatened.

Yet this was not the sum of Mompesson's crimes. Other, equally lucrative, patents were snaffled up by him. One was to search for concealed Crown lands – lands used by others but that belonged to the monarch – passing the large plots back to the state but keeping any worth less than £200 for himself. Happily, it fell to Mompesson's lot to rate the discovered land, and he did a superb job. In one instance, 700 acres, previously worth

£300 per annum, were valued at just 10s. – a downgrade of 98 per cent – meaning that this, too, could be gobbled up by his rapacious greed.[13] Then there was the notorious acquisition of a monopoly for manufacturing gold and silver thread, with Mompesson and Edward Villiers committing gold- and silversmiths to prison without examination or trial for refusing to give up their profession.

All of this was prime fodder for a Commons investigation. As the complaints mounted, Mompesson was committed to the care of the serjeant-at-arms and ordered specifically to attend the House every morning. Under the glare of his fellow MPs, he squirmed and sweated, defending himself where possible, excusing the inexcusable, and flat-out denying what couldn't be explained away. As the evidence built against him, options were running out. Bacon was under investigation himself; Buckingham had decided to save his own skin; and rumours were flying that the careers of those impeached might end on the block. There was only one option left to Mompesson. After a gruelling session of grilling, he begged to be allowed to return home to fetch some papers to support his case. There, he made a show of going into his wife's chamber where the watchful accompanying serjeant could not follow. Quick agility gave him his escape through a window, racing from his house to the river and aboard a boat bound for France. He was safely out of harm's way before the alarm was raised.

The House was livid. Too late, a warrant was sent to apprehend Mompesson at the ports, a proclamation was issued for his arrest, and he was expelled from Parliament. More was to follow. Tried *in absentia*, the Lords concluded 'That the said Sir Giles Mompesson had erected a court without warrant; and also that he imprisoned the king's subjects, and exacted bonds from them by threats, without warrant; and afterwards, by undue practices, procured a proclamation, and other warrants, to colour such his doings; and yet executed all those ills, and seized the goods of divers persons, contrary to such authority so unduly procured by him.' His punishment went further than Bacon's: he was degraded from his knighthood, outlawed, exempted from all general pardons, his goods and lands forfeited, and he would 'be ever held an Infamous Person'.[14]

Yet as with Bacon, the wording of the sentence was worse than its reality. Within a month of Parliament's adjournment, Mompesson's family was granted use of his fines and confiscated lands, and less than two years later he was allowed to return temporarily to England. By 1628, he was permanently back in the country. Although never allowed back to Court, he kept his hands in various ventures and even undertook odd jobs for the state. It seems he must have felt some level of gratitude to the new king, Charles I, for he fought as a Royalist during the civil wars and died in 1651, still complaining of his 'small estate . . . after so many and grievous crosses, afflictions and calamities' endured.[15]

Punishment was even shorter for Sir Edward Villiers: he was cleared of all offences and compensated for the loss of the gold- and silver-thread patent with a number of other lucrative contracts, eventually ending up as lord president of Munster. It was in this role that he found a small measure of redemption, paying from his own pocket 'for the maintenance of these miserable fleet soldiers' limping back from a failed military expedition to Cadiz.[16] It is likely that he caught dysentery from this wretched group, dying from the disease in 1626. The monopoly on gold and silver thread, so much decried in Parliament, was 'set up again under colour of a new corporation' through the nod of the king.[17] Little had changed.

But perhaps the greatest villain in the 1621 Parliament was the member leading the charge against the scandals of that year: Bacon's enemy, Sir Edward Coke, whose name has travelled down the generations as the stout defender of the common law. Coke's enduring influence is such that in books of legal maxims today, about half can still be directly attributed to his work.[18] For his pen was a sharp instrument and could cut through opponents like a knife through butter. With it he could dismay kings, convict felons and change lives. If only it was always for the better.

※

Lady Elizabeth Hatton was a delightful woman. Intelligent and quick-witted, she was also well connected, elegant and attractive – particularly so once her first husband died, bequeathing her large estates across London and the south of England. So it was something of a surprise when, with significant 'guidance' from male relatives, she chose Sir Edward Coke for her second, just a few weeks after Coke had become a widower. Indeed, it was perceived 'to the great admiration [i.e., wonder] of all men that after so many large and likely offers she should decline to a man of his quality, and the world will not believe that it was without a mistake'.[19] No one was more mystified than Bacon, who had been rejected by the good lady just a year before, but very few were surprised when the relationship proved particularly stormy. Within two years of the wedding, Lady Hatton – for she never took Coke's name – had secured a temporary separation. Various efforts at mediation over the next two decades, while producing two daughters, failed to make any permanent headway, and the estranged couple lived apart in mutual dislike for the rest of Coke's life.

The cause of the problems was not just that Coke hated being outclassed by his feisty, intellectually superior wife, but that he was grasping, self-centred and concerned only with his own advancement, utilising his extensive knowledge of the law always to put himself first. He thought nothing, for example, of taking all his wife's land, including her jointure (the portion set aside specifically for her support), and putting it to his own use while leaving her to live as a mere indentured tenant. He broke into his wife's houses 'to inventory, seize, ship, and carry away all the goods' – even her clothes weren't safe from his acquisitive hands.[20] If his wife dared protest too much, 'his rage was such that he came violently into my chamber, rent my ruff from my neck, offering unworthy blows', as she described.[21] Lady Hatton begged the Privy Council to 'Stop, then, his high tyrannical courses; for I have suffered beyond measure of any wife, mother, nay of any ordinary woman in this kingdom'.[22] When her pleas had no lasting impact, she used her connections to introduce a bill in Parliament to recover the estates. But Coke, being a parliamentarian himself, bullied and berated his fellow MPs until the bill was 'thought fit to sleep'.[23]

Coke's approach to his wife's daughters mirrored his attitude to her money: they should be entirely at his disposal. Lady Hatton's stepdaughter from her first marriage was 'sold away' into a marriage to strengthen his relationship with the earls of Warwick, but at least in this case the groom had all his marbles, which was not something that could be said of the partner Coke would choose for one of his own daughters with Lady Hatton.[24]

Sir John Villiers was plagued by bouts of insanity. He was also poorer and older than his intended bride. But he was the brother of Buckingham, and by 1617 Coke had been more forthright than usual in irritating the royal favourite. He therefore needed to find a way to worm his way back into Buckingham's good graces, and what better method than to cement an alliance through marriage to the one Villiers brother whom no one else would touch with a very long stick? It seemed a perfect plan to Coke, although even Buckingham needed convincing with the promise of a super-large dowry. When the fourteen-year-old Frances Coke and her mother were informed of the already agreed match, however, they were horrified. They attempted to change Coke's mind, Frances weeping and begging, Lady Hatton arguing and cajoling. All to no effect. There was, therefore, only one thing to be done.

Lady Hatton laid her plans carefully, for there was so much to arrange secretly. Yet they managed it magnificently, Frances and her, waiting until Sir Edward had departed for bed at his usual early hour of nine o'clock, sneaking down the stairs, creeping across the threshold and away from the house into a waiting carriage. The twenty-mile, night-time journey from the home-cum-prison at Holborn to sanctuary at Weybridge was wearying and dangerous – despite their armed escort – particularly as they'd taken a circuitous route to avoid pursuit. But they reached Lady Hatton's cousins shaken yet safe, just as day was dawning. Hurried into private rooms, they were fed and watered, and well concealed. And there they remained, hatching a plan to make this huge problem go away.

Hidden they might have been, but Coke was not stupid. Catching whispers on the wind, and putting two and two together, he obtained a warrant for their hideaway and set off in breastplate and sword, collecting heavies, ne'er-do-wells and weapons along the way. Reaching Weybridge, he found the door barred to Lady Hatton's impromptu fort. Yet with Coke armed with a makeshift battering ram and pistols, this provided no barrier.

Smashing gates and breaking windows, he forced his entry, shouting, 'If we should kill any of you it would be justified homicide; but if you kill any of us it would be murder.'[25] Intimidated and wrong-footed, the defenders hesitated, and Coke and his goons spread out through the house.

Frances and her mother were discovered, trembling in each other's arms, hiding in a dark closet. Ripping the weeping child kicking and screaming from her mother's clutches, Coke dragged Frances out and, slinging her behind him on a horse, set off at a gallop, surrounded by his 'honour' guard. Lady Hatton would not give up that easily, however, hailing her driver as she hurried out of the house and into her carriage. It was nigh on impossible to catch up with the band, but they gave it their best shot, driving the horses to exhaustion, ignoring the furrows and grooves of the perilous unmetalled roads. But the bumpy lanes proved too much. Catching a wheel in a rut, the rapid motion was brought to a sudden stop. The horses lurched; the coach flipped. The pursuit was over, for the time being.

Lady Hatton did not take long in appealing to the Privy Council. Laying the case before them, detailing the house-breaking and assault and kidnap, the council was horrified and immediately began a prosecution for riot. Coke, however, had himself covered. He had contacted King James, who was then visiting Scotland, and accused Lady Hatton of kidnapping her own daughter. James, of course, did not want to upset his darling Buckingham and so overruled the Privy Council, but Lady Hatton had one more trick up her sleeve. Her time in hiding had not been wasted. Instead, she had busied herself arranging a more suitable marriage for Frances, with the Earl of Oxford, who was then resident in Venice. As evidence, Lady Hatton submitted a contract between the two parties, which Coke promptly claimed to be a forgery. Suddenly finding herself charged with conspiracy, Lady Hatton was confined in the house of a London alderman until after her daughter's marriage. Thereafter, she refused to be in the same room as her husband, 'saying if he came in at one door she would go out at another'.[26] Frances, meanwhile, was left to suffer decades of unhappy marriage, scandal – thanks to her ongoing relationship with another MP – and exile, all for her father's glory.

✽

While the father's favourite weapon was the pen, Sir Edward Coke's son by his first marriage, Clement, preferred the sword. Already experienced in the Commons, elected underage on his father's gentle persuasions, Clement continued his education in 1616 by travelling to the Netherlands, supplementing his curriculum by killing a Catholic exile in a duel. Aware that the duel could quickly grow into an international incident, and a personal embarrassment, Sir Edward asked the English ambassador to intervene and ensure that the cause of death was listed as a fault of the unfortunate victim's surgeons rather 'than the danger of his hurt'.[27] The matter did not rest, however, for although the authorities were content, the victim's friends were less so and a line of challengers started to form. Having decided the order in which they would fight Clement, they sent a note demanding satisfaction, only for the knave to attack the messenger. This time, however, Clement had met his match: despite being wrong-footed by such an ungentlemanly act, the messenger came off better, and 'ran him almost through the body in the midst of the breast'.[28] It was hardly surprising, then, that as soon as Clement was enough recovered, he was escorted back to England, the better 'to be delivered of many quarrels, wherein he is engaged'.[29]

If these early events could be put down to youthful exuberance, later actions had no such excuse. Thanks once again to the efforts of his father, Clement was elected to the 1621 Parliament. Whiling away the many hours during which Sir Edward harangued his fellow MPs, Clement allowed his attention to drift, eavesdropping on the conversations around him. When he heard MP Sir Charles Morrison make a joke about his father's honour he was not happy. Clement bided his time, waiting for the day's session to finish to take his revenge. Later, as a stretching Morrison made his way down the stairs from the Commons chamber, Clement pounced, hitting the unsuspecting man on the neck and pushing. Morrison, losing his footing, tumbled down the remaining steps, but luckily – for him at least – he collided near the bottom with another member who usefully cushioned his fall.

It took a minute for Morrison to catch his breath and for the world to stop spinning, but steadying himself he brandished his sword, aiming, so he later claimed, to give Clement a little tap with the scabbard. But Clement had followed Morrison down, readying himself with someone else's blade in hand. With any advantage gone, indeed with the advantage resting with the enemy, Morrison took the wiser route of walking away. Still, the brawl could hardly escape the notice of the wider Commons, and it was raised the very next day in the House. Both men were placed in custody, although the House's sympathy clearly lay with Morrison, who was released in just over a week. Clement, by contrast, was sent to the Tower and freed only after submitting a grovelling apology.

As with every other scandal, Sir Edward managed to avoid the censure heaped on Clement. Perhaps it was thanks to his initial refusal to have anything to do with his son; perhaps it was because he then made amends by delivering an emotional plea for Clement, employing tears and oratory in equal measure. Or perhaps he was simply too valuable a tool, for his style certainly suited the Parliaments that would meet during the 1620s.

Bellicose and jealous of its liberties, by the end of the decade Parliament was locked in a verbal battle with the new king, Charles I. It had not started as such. When James died of fever, stroke and dysentery (in that order) in March 1625, the first Parliament of Charles I welcomed his heir with open arms. Indeed, one MP optimistically stated that Charles had been 'bred in parliaments', and 'did us so many good offices, so many gracious favours' that 'we may well trust him'.[30] It was downhill from there. In 1626 members tried to impeach Buckingham, once the favourite of the late king and now favourite of the new, forcing Charles into an early dissolution. The new Parliament in 1628 was no better. In the intervening years Charles had attempted to raise a deeply unpopular extra-parliamentary tax, the Forced Loan, which was liked as well as any new tax then or since, with many former MPs leading the dissent and being imprisoned without trial for their pains. Despite the Loan, by 1628 the Crown desperately needed more money. But the summoned Parliament was unwilling to cough up without redress of grievances and written assurances of its rights. By June,

Charles had relented, agreeing to a list of basic civil rights that went down in the statute book and in constitutional history as the Petition of Right – drafted in the main by the one and only Sir Edward Coke.

This, and the subsequent granting of a subsidy by Parliament, should have been a cause for celebration for the political nation, but more was to come. For centuries an import tax had been levied on certain goods, and for centuries the right to collect that tax in perpetuity had been granted by Parliament every time a new monarch came to the throne. In 1625, however, Parliament had conspicuously failed to do so, leaving Charles without a large portion of the Crown's customary revenue. Without any other option, and having already pawned the crown jewels, Charles was forced to collect the duty on his own authority, which went directly against the Petition of Right. Just as Parliament was drafting another complaint, the king hastily prorogued the session. The following year was no better, even though Buckingham had been assassinated by a disgruntled army officer in the intervening period, with the king's ill-judged reforms of the Church of England, and tax, taking centre stage.

The Elizabethan religious settlement, established by the late queen in 1559 after the back and forth between Catholicism and Protestantism of the previous three reigns, was a mongrel beast. Technically Calvinist – a fundamentalist, Bible-based Protestantism – it tried to make the state religion palatable to everyone, making outward conformity the key but 'not liking to make windows into men's hearts and secret thoughts'.[31] By 1625 that settlement was breaking apart. A vocal minority – the 'Elect', or godly, who considered themselves separate from, and above, the wider Christian community – believed that the Reformation had not gone far enough. Others, including Charles, found elements of the Calvinist doctrine unhelpful and instead looked to 'beautify' religion with an increase in 'popish' ceremony and ritual. So, while never even slightly preferring Catholicism, Charles made attempts to bring the state religion more to his way of thinking – the communion table was moved and became the altar (again), towards which worshippers were encouraged to bow; surplices were compulsory; and space was found for religious ornament. All of this was undertaken to the disquiet of that godly minority, many of whom loudly jumped up and down in the Commons. With dissent mounting, and the promise of an amicable compromise rapidly disappearing, Charles dissolved Parliament – but not before three MPs held the Speaker in his chair while the House passed a number of resolutions against the king.

So started eleven years of what became known as the Personal Rule, in which Charles refused to call Parliament and instead turned to 'other courses' for the income that the state required 'both for the defence of ourselves and [our] allies'.[32] For the majority of the time, it worked well. Old feudal duties and taxes were demanded on Charles's own authority and grudgingly paid by his subjects. Enough money came in to cover the day-to-day costs of running the country, and the Court had room to indulge in the visual arts and their artists, strengthening regality through ritual and ceremony. All might have been well if only Charles hadn't felt the need to continue fiddling with religion across all of his kingdoms. But in Scotland, trouble was brewing.

Sir Edward Coke saw only some of this. Having been Parliament's leading voice for much of the previous decade, he retired to his country mansion and concentrated on his writing and finding 'pockets' of money to pay off Clement's debts or – after his son's death in 1630 – portions for his granddaughters' dowries. Still, by now he was in his eighties and death would not wait forever. As he ailed, government officers were sent to his estate to confiscate papers while Lady Hatton rummaged for movables she could claim as her own. Coke died in his bed, 'quietly, like a lamb', on 3 September 1634.[33] As Lady Hatton quipped with relief, 'We shall never see his like again, praises be to God.'[34]

Chapter Two

What's So Civil about War? 1637–60

Dramatis Personae

7. Sir Richard Grenville (1600–59)

    Fowey (Cornwall) 1628–29

8. Sir Henry Slingsby (1602–58)

    Knaresborough (Yorkshire) 1625
    Knaresborough (Yorkshire) ... ... 1640 (I)*
    Knaresborough (Yorkshire) 1640–42

9. Daniel Axtell (*c.*1622–60)

    Kilkenny 1654–55

10. George Monck (1608–70)

    Devon 1653
    Devon 1660

---

* Roman numerals here and elsewhere are used to differentiate between separate Parliaments that sat in the same year.

Members Behaving Badly

The mud was thick, sucking horses' hooves and worn-through boots, caking everyone to such a dull beige-brown that it was impossible to tell the colour of the tattered clothes beneath. The one silver lining, if it could be called that, was that the upward-reaching filth disguised the similarly coloured evidence of dysentery, dribbling down the legs of far too many soldiers. Not that it smelt much different.

The least the incessant rain could do, Sir Richard Grenville, the king's general in the West, thought with a wry smile, would be to wash the pitiful army clean. Instead it added another layer of misery to the sodden motley crew, with their soaked powder and prune-wrinkled skin. Casting his eyes heaven-wise – as if that would help! – he saw no end to the interminable sheeting rain that plagued his ragged army, camped out in the open while the enemy took refuge in proper buildings, with proper roofs. The grey sky was as lacklustre as the hopes of the band who had been besieging this wretched place for a year. For no matter what he did, no matter how many land-side attacks he threw at the defended port, no matter what stratagems and tricks he employed, the ships still rolled in and out of Plymouth harbour, as sure as the tide itself.

Sir Richard, former member of Parliament, now fighting Parliamentarians, was used to such stalemates. As a younger son, he had needed to make his own way in the world, and that way had been the army. From the age of eighteen he had been a fighting man, serving as an English volunteer in almost every ill-managed, ill-fated, costly campaign of the Thirty Years' War that was engulfing the Continent. Yet despite the pronounced failures of these expeditions, he had avoided censure – at least on the field.

His time in Parliament, however, had not been an unalloyed success. The one time he had been a member, during the stormy years of 1628 and '29, he had only just escaped punishment for insolent and disrespectful speeches. Excused on the grounds that he was a gruff soldier rather than a polite politician, he had been spared the embarrassment of expulsion but had never entered Parliament again.

His marriage to Mary Howard had likewise been an abject and costly failure. Having entered into the contract with the strong-willed, three-times widow, Grenville had hoped her fortune would ease him out of the debts he'd accrued through high and fast living. Instead, she had locked away her estates, and 'by not being enough pleased with her fortune, he grew less pleased with his wife'.[1] Years of lawsuits followed, as Grenville tried to circumvent the pre-nup while still spending lavishly on lifestyle and show. This merely compounded the personality clashes between the couple, who flung claim and counterclaim of sexual impropriety and domestic abuse at one another as their dirty laundry was aired in public. It was little wonder that for years they had been living separately, but to add injury to the insult, Grenville had been ordered to pay alimony out of estates that he had never managed to possess. The sum result was more debt, violent threats against George Cutteford, his wife's steward and former lover, ruinous fines for slander and a stint in the Fleet prison, from which he'd escaped and fled to Europe, returning six years later in 1639, just as Charles I's three kingdoms of England, Scotland and Ireland descended into rebellion and war.

Casting his mind back, Grenville looked for the trigger to the current problems. If a turning point towards disaster could be placed with any certainty, 1637 – eight years before this cursed, crippled siege – would have marked it. In frustration at the continuing onslaught of criticism and insubordination, the English government had given three puritans – a gentleman, a lawyer and an independent preacher – who had been campaigning about the 'Catholicisation' of the Church of England exactly what they had sought: fame and martyrdom. Although their lives were spared, these three loud, self-righteous fanatics were given the shocking platform of the pillory and mutilation. With ears cut off and blood pouring down their necks, pooling on the floor as they remained tied and tethered like common criminals, they showed the patience of the saints. And the public revered them as such, supplicants rushing forward to dip handkerchiefs in the red puddles, the relics cherished as much as any of the superstitious Catholic faith.

Perhaps, given time, memories of that day would have faded, combined with other scenes of brutal punishment that were viewed as a necessary part of Stuart education and entertainment. But other problems were piling up. Charles I, a king of Scotland who had taken eight years even to visit the place to receive his coronation, wasn't especially enamoured of his northern kingdom. They did things differently there. The Court was informal, with drinking, and touching, and no sense of structured space. Quite simply, as Charles saw it, it was not at all couth. But if the Court were strange to him, the Scottish Church, the Kirk, was positively alien, with its distrust of bishops, its spartan services and its emphasis on preaching and personal, as opposed to communal, experience. So, as was the early-modern way, Charles had sought uniformity in religion, with a suspiciously English, ritualised slant. Yet if the puritans of England were dismayed by his reforms, this was nothing to the more precise Scots. Where bishops in surplices had occasionally merited muttering in the southern country, where disdain for the 'altar' and for bowing had sometimes led to an uncontrollable need to relieve oneself within a church's sanctified walls, where a prayer book had prompted a few severed body parts, in Scotland it provoked war.

The Covenanters, those thousands of protestors who signed the 4,300-word pact against religious 'innovation', had organised. As word and support spread across Scotland, they had formed an alternative government, threatening to summon Parliament on their own authority, and attracting the backing of some of Charles's own Scottish Privy Councillors. There was no way Charles could have backed down while saving face and dignity. So he hadn't. At great expense to his own slowly recovering coffers, and to the English localities, in 1639 an army was mustered and marched to the border. With it had gone Grenville, but if he was looking for a fight as well as forgiveness, he was to be disappointed. The extent of the First Bishops' 'War' was the two armies sitting on each side of the River Tweed, looking threatening until a truce was agreed. But the Covenanters had won a propaganda victory, 'Their remonstrances, declarations and pamphlets were dispersed, and their emissaries and agents insinuated into the company of all who were anyway discontented or galled at the proceedings of the state of England.'[2]

The results were quick to be seen. At the start of 1640, for the first time in eleven years Charles had been forced to summon a Parliament to beg for money – and fast. The 'Short Parliament', however, had other ideas. Led by a few 'tumultuous and popular spirits'* loudly enjoying their platforms, the Commons turned first to consider its members' grievances rather than the king's plea. Even when Charles personally implored them, just for once, to put aside their differences and concentrate on the clear and present danger from the north, they ignored him. With seemingly no hope of extra funds, but potentially with a highly treasonous inquest into the king's responsibility for causing the war, Charles again abandoned Parliament.

The dissolution unleashed a tsunami of problems. Catholic plots were suspected, many thought to have popish leanings beaten and killed. Iconoclasm reached new heights – or depths. Trade crumbled and debts were called in. Soldiers, temporarily raised to protect the country, instead turned on their officers and the towns through which they passed, venting their frustration on any in their way. The population groaned under local levies and grieved for suppressed rights. Mobs ruled; the country was polarised. In an age when many believed in the literal truth of the Second Coming, Christ seemed to be knocking at the door. As one pessimistic letter writer observed, 'Death's harbinger, the sword, famine and other plagues that hang over us are ready to swallow up the wicked age.'[3]

The Scots, sensing weakness and conspiring with the king's enemies – including the noisy MPs – took the initiative. A skirmish at Newburn had turned into a rout for the English, where Grenville was one of the few men who managed to hold his company together long enough to protect the retreating rear – although complaints of abuse, and withholding of pay to line his own pockets, were quick to follow. Newcastle was shortly thereafter abandoned, left to the northern army who took it without a shot being fired. With tribute to the Scottish army, designed to keep the invaders at bay, thereafter costing £25,000 a month, complaints from the country rolling in, and disaffection from all quarters growing, it had seemed that

---

* 'Popular' was not a compliment at this point. It was used to describe the radical looney fringe of politicians who relied on, and stirred up, the mob. Thomas Peyton to Henry Oxinden, 6 May 1640, in Dorothy Gardiner (ed.), *The Oxinden Letters, 1607–1642* (London: Constable & Co., 1933), p. 172.

calling another Parliament – known to history as the 'Long Parliament' – was the only way forward. It was the wrong decision.

With leaders of the Commons working in cahoots with the Scots, cleverly manipulating fears and misrepresenting rumour as fact, they had created an atmosphere of panic. Parliament had gone after the king's advisors, using impeachment to commit 'murder with the sword of justice'.[4] Then it went after Charles himself, limiting his prerogative in ways that were undoubtedly unconstitutional, cutting his funding, attempting to take control of the militia and attacking him in the newly uncensored, emergent press. By the beginning of 1642, Charles had had enough. After a failed attempt to arrest five MPs and one peer, he moved first to Hampton Court and then to Windsor. By March 1642 he had retreated to York, and eventually raised his standard against Parliament at Nottingham in August.

To compound the king's problems, in 1641 Ireland had erupted in rebellion. It was hardly surprising. For centuries Ireland had strained under the weight of an imposed regime, its oppression exacerbated by the failed imposition of Protestantism on the bulk of the determinedly Catholic population, and by the heavy-handed attempts of the king's representatives in the country to enforce a novel, and demanding, obedience on the entire population. As fears of an English, Protestant takeover of Ireland increased, the native Irish turned on the small elite centred around Dublin and the settlers in the new plantations. And when the old ruling class, the Old English, were treated with as much disdain by the London Parliament as the rebels, they began to find common cause. The one positive from all this was that it united king and Parliament in Ireland, as future Royalists served alongside future Parliamentarians in the bloody suppression of a common enemy – even though many Irish rebels remained loyal to the Crown itself.

Right in the middle had been Grenville. Appointed governor of Trim in Co. Meath, 'the signal acts of cruelty he did every day commit upon the Irish' became notorious – even by the brutal standards of the day. 'Trim Law' was the only law. Civilians, 'eighty men, women and children, who lived under protection', were slaughtered while going about their business; forty-two more, and eighteen infants, simply for being in the wrong place at the wrong time.⁵ Others, fleeing the fighting, or seeking protection, or bringing in the harvest, were butchered likewise. Infirmity was no protection: along with babies and the aged, men with palsy, the bedridden and immobile, a blind couple, all suffered the wrath of the Trim Law. The lucky among those avoiding the gallows lost their lives quickly, by the sword. Others bled out like pigs, their necks a ghastly, gaping smile, or were bound, smothered with straw and torched.

But aside from slaughter, what were the aims in Ireland? Charles had been keen to come to terms quickly, hoping to free his soldiers to fight in England. The English Parliament, understandably, thought little of his plan. For very different reasons, so too had Grenville. Returning to England in frustration, he had docked in Parliament-held Liverpool in the summer of 1643 and was promptly taken into custody. Transported to London, over three months he convinced the 'Roundhead', Parliamentarian leaders of his earnest desire to serve their cause, declaring that 'he would never take up arms against but for the Parliament and die for the defence of them with his last drop of blood'.⁶ Naively believing his avowals, they loaded him with cash, horses, supplies and military plans for the next year, and sent him on his way in a coach and six. But instead of following orders, he had proudly led his troops to the king's headquarters at Oxford. Parliament never forgave him, erecting empty gibbets reserved specifically for 'Skellum' – 'scoundrel' – Grenville.

Despatched to his family's base in the West Country, with the aim of recruiting men to the king's cause, Grenville had instead begun 'his war first upon his wife'.⁷ With slight excuses, Mary's former lover, George Cutteford, and Cutteford's long-suffering legal wife were locked behind bars, their children and staff turfed out of the house, and £500 worth of their goods 'distrained'. Not content with that alone, upon the weak pretence of spying, Grenville had Mary's solicitor hanged.

That business successfully resolved, Grenville had set himself about the business of enhancing his newly acquired estates. As his critic Edward Hyde complained, 'he was in truth himself the greatest plunderer of this war, for whenever any person had disobeyed or neglected any of his warrants . . .

he sent presently a party of horse to apprehend their persons and to drive their grounds . . . so that he had a greater stock of cattle of all sorts upon his grounds than any person whatsoever in the west of England.'

If Parliamentarians dared to hold any land near his command, 'he seized . . . all the furniture in the several houses, and compelled the tenants to pay to him all the rents due from the beginning of the rebellion', despite such sequestrations belonging to the king. 'By these and such like means', Hyde continued, 'he had not only a vast stock, but received great sums of money, and had as great store of good household stuff as would furnish well those houses he looked upon as his own.' If that were not enough, he received taxes, 'which would always pay double the men he had, and were exactly levied'.[8] By 1645 Grenville had grubbed more 'than his majesty bestowed upon all his general commanders of armies, and upon all his officers of state, since the beginning of the rebellion to that time'.

It was against this complex and lamentable backdrop that Grenville now found himself placed in a damnable position of trust, directing the siege of Plymouth under a sky as dark as his mood. Having promised that it would fall to the Crown, and fast, the city's resolute defence seemed determined to humiliate him. Frustrated with the miserable conditions and palpable failure, he vented his emotions on any enemies who came his way. And his cruelty knew no bounds. On patrol he surprised two Parliamentarians foraging for food, but instead of simply killing them – or capturing them for information – he 'enforced one to hang the other presently at the next tree they came to, the Cavaliers dispatching the survivor, Skellum Grenville sitting on his horse beholding the spectacle'.[9] Those promised quarter could expect no better. Prisoners of war were despatched to, and then often in, Lydford castle in the bleak Devonian moors. Lydford Law became the new Trim Law, with scores of prisoners executed without trial, their more fortunate companions left to starve and rot. As a contemporary poet recorded:

> I oft have heard of Lydford law;
> How in the morn they hang and draw,

And sit in judgment after;
At first I wondered at it much,
But since I find the matter such
As it deserves no laughter.[10]

Yet while Grenville was exercising his own form of majesty, the Royalist cause was falling apart. Battles were lost, soldiers – if they could be recruited at all – deserted, and the countryside and its occupants lay ravaged. Intrigue, sustained by a replication of commands, ruled; chaos and confusion reigned. Royalist commanders spent more time fighting each other than the enemy. When one former MP, Sir Henry Slingsby, took offence at a fellow drunken Royalist commander, Lord Culpeper, there fell out:

> a quarrel betwixt them two only, and at bare fisticuffs they were a good space, till the company parted them, and then Culpepper [sic] and Slingsby, in the moonshine, got them into the garden and like two cocks at the end of a battle, not able to stand well, offered and pecked at one another till the weight of Slingsby's head drew him to the ground, which advantage Culpepper took hold of, and by it got Slingsby's sword . . . But by good fortune the rest of the associates came in, and easily persuaded the duellists to end the quarrel by the cup again, which service continued till the next day, with divers and several bouts at fisticuffs.*[11]

The proud Grenville was no better. Accused of rashness in one council of war, Grenville flung back the charge of cowardice. With honour at stake, the subordinate officer raised his pistol and in typical Royalist fashion aimed at, and missed, his commander. Grenville, at last proving his military ability, 'fired his own pistol upon the colonel and slew him dead upon

---

* Slingsby was beheaded on 8 June 1658 for conspiring with the Royalist underground.

the place'. Dismayed and distraught, the unfortunate man's brother 'fired off his own pistol upon Grenville and missed him, whereat Grenville drew his sword and ran him through'.[12] At this point, it could be said that all the disciplined and dedicated Parliamentarian New Model Army need do was sit back and watch.

Instead, they pressed their advantage, advancing further and further into Royalist territory. In a vain attempt to turn the tide, and believed to be at his own suggestion – a surmise he later determinedly denied – Grenville was ordered to abandon Plymouth and lead the sodden foot soldiers upcountry. But bravely bold Sir Richard outright refused, it being 'inferior to his late former command'.[13] Committed as a close prisoner for disobedience, his petitions to fly into exile were eventually heeded. As the last vestiges of the Royalist cause collapsed in the spring of 1646, and the First English Civil War came to an end in their bitter defeat,* Grenville made good his escape – but not before his remaining portable possessions were plundered by both sides. He would spend the next decade and a half on the Continent, hounded by his reputation and still pursuing claims to his wife's property through foreign courts. In 1654 he was at last expelled permanently from the exiled royal presence, but his wish, 'to find me a quiet dying-place in my native country, never again to touch with any worldly affairs', did not come to pass: he died just a year before the restoration of the monarchy, in Ghent.[14]

Grenville's wife, Mary, long outlived him, dying in 1671. Her spirit, however, lasted even longer. According to Dartmoor legend, 'She was supposed to ride every night for her sins in a coach made of the bones of her four dead husbands . . . drawn by headless horses, and in front of the carriage runs a sable hound, with one eye in the middle of his forehead. Arrived at Okehampton, the hound plucks a blade of grass, and the cortège returns to Fitzford, where the blade of grass is laid on a certain stone . . . it will last until every blade of grass in Okehampton Park is plucked, or the world comes to an end.'[15]

---

* The last Royalist 'stronghold', Harlech, held out until March 1647.

What's So Civil about War? (1637–60)

※

At the beginning of 1649, less than three years after the First English Civil War had finished, and mere months after the ending of the Second, the world was once more turned upside down. Daniel Axtell, a former London grocer's apprentice turned Parliamentarian captain, major and then lieutenant-colonel, had been in the thick of it all. It was, he admitted to himself, a strange path that had led him here, guarding a platform outside Banqueting House in Whitehall on a cold day in January in 1649. So strange, indeed, that it must be Providence, the work of God directing his steps, helping him make history.

Back in August 1648, he had been commended to the Commons as being 'extraordinary active and diligent' in his storming of Deal castle during the Second English Civil War.[16] Then, on 6 December, he had stood strong, his back erect with the righteousness of the Elect, as he blocked members of Parliament from taking their seats in what became known as Colonel Pride's Purge. In one fell swoop, this act of political cleansing by the New Model Army and their hero, Oliver Cromwell, had purified the Commons of the dithering, timid supporters of reconciliation with the former king. It had almost halved the number of MPs. Those that remained were the committed, courageous and godly men who formed the 'Rump'. Scores more members, through fear for themselves and their estates, had chosen to abstain from Parliament of their own volition. From now on, Parliament would only be for the worthy: for those blessed by God, for those who knew what the country truly needed far better than the silenced electorate.

Next, on 20 January – the Day of Judgement, as Axtell liked to term it – he had stood guard at the trial of Charles Stuart. And he had helped the sentence pass, encouraging, cajoling and where necessary beating the soldiers under his command until they cried out for the execution of the former king. All of that had led to this day, the most momentous day in history. For surely it would change the world.

Before him, the multitude jostled. London had once been friendly to the Parliamentarian cause, but in the last few years weaknesses and cracks had started to appear as its citizens had chafed at further taxes and impositions, necessary for winning the war, and controls on debauchery, essential for saving souls. And now, for over three hours, the mob had been made to wait as men were found to sign the order to behead the king and as the Rump scurried around, hurriedly passing a law to make the proclamation of a replacement illegal. Before Axtell was a sea of pinched, unimpressed faces. Feet shuffled or stamped, depending on whether impatience or cold predominated, and Axtell couldn't be too careful. Just then, his eye was caught as a schoolboy – or perhaps a rowdy apprentice – pushed his way to the front, ducking and diving his gangly body through the crush. Yet there were no projectiles in the boy's hands, his expression one of excited anticipation rather than scorn.

The boy and the crowd didn't have much longer to wait for the spectacle to start. Necks strained, backbones stretched, as men, women and the occasional child craned to catch a glimpse of the dark-haired, bareheaded figure appearing in an upper-storey window of Banqueting House. All eyes focused on this new person, waiting for his words, reading his responses. Physically, the draw was surprising: so much attention for such a small individual. A diminutive man, barely reaching five feet tall and dwarfed further by the looming guards surrounding him, he stepped through the window onto the prepared, black-draped platform, dignified and composed – at least until he saw the height of the block, a mere six inches above the stage.

'Is there no higher?' those close to him heard him ask.

The condemned man received a polite but firm negative in response, so with nothing else to do, he gathered his courage once more and turned his attention to the crowd.

✽

Lo! It was enormous! Stretching all the way from Whitehall to Charing Cross, a heaving horde of humanity. Between him and them, however, was the bristling mass of soldiery, a steely wall of weaponry and determination. There was no way the people, his people, would be able to hear his final words.

Yet they must be spoken. And without his characteristic stutter. Turning instead to the armed men around him, Charles Stuart, formerly King of England, Scotland and Ireland, addressed his words to them.

'I shall be very little heard of anybody here, I shall therefore speak a word unto you here; indeed I could hold my peace very well, if I did not think that holding my peace would make some men think that I did submit to the guilt, as well as to the punishment.'

As much as these things were set pieces, the condemned man still needed to break with tradition. This speech, now, was the chance he never took during his travesty of a trial. Then, for the sake of every monarch who might succeed him, he had remained silent and refused to accept the legitimacy of the court. Now, he was facing the worst. Now, all he could do was protect the future of the monarchy. Establishing his innocence was compelling; securing the throne for his successors was essential.

'[A]ll the world knows that I never did begin a war with the two houses of parliament, and I call God to witness ... that I never did intend for to encroach upon their privileges; they began upon me.' Instead, 'I do believe that ill instruments between them and me have been the chief cause of all this bloodshed.'

While he might be innocent of the charge, however, 'God forbid that I should be so ill a Christian as not to say that God's judgements are just upon me. Many times he does pay justice by an unjust sentence, that is ordinary. I will only say this, that an unjust sentence that I suffered for to take effect, is punished now by an unjust sentence upon me.' It was that fateful day in 1641 when he had signed, against honour and every instinct, the death sentence of his counsellor and former Irish viceroy, Thomas Wentworth, Lord Strafford, in a futile effort to stay war, that weighed heavily on him – still.* He should have known – he did know – that good could never come

---

* History works with terrible irony: in the 1620s Wentworth had been a proponent of the liberties of Parliament and was one of the refusers of the Forced Loan, for which he was imprisoned. In 1621, he had even been the one to suggest that the abusers of monopolies and patents should be impeached. It was an awful twist,

from so wicked a deed. That, that very moment, is what had preceded all the rest.

From unjust cause it was a simple step to unjust government, and his next statement had the ring of prophecy. 'You will never do right, nor God will never prosper you, until you give God his due, the king his due (that is, my successors) and the people their due.' 'It was for this that now I am come here,' the former king continued. 'If I would have given way to an arbitrary way, for to have all laws changed according to the power of the sword, I needed not to have come here; and therefore, I tell you . . . that I am the martyr of the people.'

Charles Stuart, nervous but resolute, finished his speech. Turning to his guard, he requested, 'Take care that they do not put me to pain.' The dread of that, and the awful spectre of a messy death, almost confounded him. Might it be easier if his hair were out of the way? There was a nod from the masked executioner and a cap was produced. He stuffed his long hair under it, exposing his neck. But his clothes might also prevent a clean cut. He stripped off his cloak and medals, then his waistcoat, but reached to put his cloak back on. The two shirts he'd worn had provided less protection from the cold than he'd hoped: he could not be seen to be shivering.

Finally prepared, he turned again to face the crowd, the hostile, the curious, the sympathetic. 'I go from a corruptible to an incorruptible crown, where no disturbance can be, no disturbance in the world,' he stated with certainty, and perhaps a little relief, as he lowered his body to the floor, his neck to the block.

Almost prostrate, he turned his last thoughts to silent prayer. After a brief pause, he stretched out his hands, a predetermined sign. The axe was raised. It held an eternal moment in the air. Then the blade dropped. Charles Stuart's head was separated from his body in one swift, clean swing.[17]

As was normal in this highly abnormal time, the executioner stooped to pick up the grisly trophy. Gripping it by the hair, gore dripping to the

---

then, when he was tried under the very process – and through the demands of the very body – that years before he had supported so vehemently.

ground, he shouted the standard line: 'Behold the head of a traitor.' But there was no customary cheer. A collective groan had escaped the lips of the throng as the axe had touched the late king's neck, followed by silence, a hush so absolute it seemed possible to hear the drip, drip, drip of blood spattering on the frozen ground.

This was not the way it should have been. Those who had pushed for the king's death had envisioned a celebration of freedom and liberty of conscience. Orders were quickly given. Axtell directed his men. Troops of horse, stationed at Charing Cross and King Street, rode towards the crowd as they pushed to dip handkerchiefs, bits of cloth, anything, in the sacred blood of the martyr of the people. But to remain there, at the scene of the ... event, was to follow Charles to the grave. So they left. Within minutes the street outside Banqueting House was once again unnaturally silent.

❋

Axtell was not to remain long in London. Within months he was on his way to Ireland, sent by Parliament to lay the vengeance of God upon the rebels there. And what vengeance they received. The situation in Ireland had not improved in the years since Grenville had implemented his Trim Law. Following the truce, Ireland had drifted into two opposing camps, neither strong enough to deliver a killer blow. On the one side, supported by the Parliamentarians, were the collected Protestant settlers and Scottish Presbyterian army units and their English and Irish friends; on the other was a loose alliance between the Confederation – Catholics who were resolutely Royalist but also occasionally financially and politically 'supported' by Rome – and Irish Protestant Royalists. Both occupied land, both struggled to control it. And each of their underfunded administrations struggled on against a background of low-level violence. But, with the king dead, the former Irish enemies had come together, declaring for Charles I's son, Charles II, a situation unpardonable to the remnants of the English Parliament.

So Axtell, as the hottest sort of Protestant and Parliamentarian, with 'more than ordinary zeal in punishing those Irish', unleashed Hell.[18] Feared and loathed by the entire population, he 'killed forty times more in cold blood than in hot'.[19] A major who surrendered Ballimay castle in return for the lives of his men 'was run through the body by the said colonel', along with 190 of the supposedly spared soldiers. '[F]ifty of the inhabitants near Thomas Town living under his protection, for no other reason but that a party of [Lieutenant General Oliver] Cromwell's army was defeated the day before' were hanged.[20] But it was Axtell's actions at Meelick Island in the River Shannon that gave him most notoriety. Under cover of darkness, the light of the Lord guiding his way, Axtell had stormed a garrison of three thousand men, who, taken by surprise, had fallen into panic. About eight hundred struggled to swim for safety across the river; only three hundred made it. Those remaining surrendered on promise of clemency but, true to form, were massacred on Axtell's orders.* The overall Parliamentary commander in Ireland was not impressed: Axtell was court-martialled and recalled. But his exile lasted no longer than the commander and, when the commander died a year later, the remorseless Axtell returned.

It was not the heat of the battle, that adrenalin-fuelled vindictiveness, that spurred Axtell on. It was instead his God who 'did use me as an instrument in my place, for the suppressing of that bloody enemy'.[21] Axtell believed that it was he who had been instructed to 'pour out the vials of the wrath of God upon the earth . . . for they have shed the blood of saints and prophets, and Thou hast given them blood to drink'.[22] So, there was no reasoning with him when, for example, in 1650, 'as matter of recreation', he 'commanded his troops to gather together a great number of the protected people near Kilkenny and, being all in a cluster, bid the troopers rush through them and to kill as many as happened on the left hand of the troop and to spare the rest. Thirty persons were murdered then on that account.'[23]

Still, there were other, less 'noble', factors at work. A 'captain of horse . . . coming to Kilkenny upon a safe conduct was hanged by the said Axtell because he had a good estate within two miles of Kilkenny.' The butler to

---

* It is possible that these actions, at least, were taken on direct orders from Oliver Cromwell.

the Duke of Ormond, who surrendered to Axtell on promise of quarter, was 'tortured to death by burning matches between his fingers, in the castle of Kilkenny'.[24] His crime was refusing to say where he had stashed his employer's plate. Where victims were too poor to possess moveable wealth, their bodies could still earn Axtell a pretty penny. When some rebels were found hiding in a village, all the villagers were rounded up and three – those deemed most likely to have collaborated – were hanged. The others, however, did not escape punishment: they were sold into servitude and transported to the new plantations in Barbados, there to sweat and toil for the rest of their lives.

The acquisition of goods and estates brought Axtell more power and prestige. Enough, indeed, for him to be nominated to the First Protectorate Parliament of 1654 as one of thirty representatives for Ireland. But he couldn't make the most of this new-found glory: the Parliament was dissolved as soon as legally possible – thanks to a creative reading of 'month' to mean lunar rather than calendar – by the alleged lover of parliaments, Lord Protector Oliver Cromwell, who found MPs to be just as obstinately infuriating as his predecessor had. By this point, Axtell was falling out of love with the regime he'd helped to create anyway. Cast aside, over the next few years, he grew more and more uneasy about the government's conservative drift until, in 1656, he returned his army commission because 'the godly were discouraged, and wicked men countenanced'.[25] He retired with his disillusionment to his estates, though would later re-emerge to make one last stand.

The Good Old Cause – the cause that had brought the Rump and army together, that had led Charles Stuart to the scaffold, that had worked for freedom of puritan conscience – was a thorny issue for those trying to make the state a functioning, workable entity. Cromwell soon discovered that it was all well and good to spout conflicting idealistic nonsense, but when those ideals weren't shared by a majority of the population, most of whom simply wanted peace and lower taxes, *realpolitik* had to take control. The forceful personality of Cromwell kept the country steady for several years through a powerful combination of fear and wonder. But malaria and kidney stones shortened his life and, on 3 September 1658, rule passed to his eldest surviving son, Richard.

So started one of the most convoluted periods of English history. Despite the fact that Cromwell Junior was liked by everyone – perhaps *because* he was so well liked – he simply could not rule to the satisfaction of all. With a new parliament tying itself in knots over the constitution and control of the army, the latter once again stepped in, expelling Parliament and Richard to boot. But the army still needed a parliament, thanks to the ever-increasing gap between salaries owed and salaries paid, so they turned to the supporters of the Good Old Cause, the republicans of the Rump dismissed by Oliver years before. The civilian Rumpers, however, were no happier to accept military rule than any parliament that went before them and, with more passion than sense, started making moves to reduce army power. In response, the army did what it did best: it closed Parliament, again. But one army grandee was less than impressed by this turn of events. At Dalkeith, in Scotland, General George Monck had been tending his ruinously expensive rented estate and making plans to retire to Ireland. With the expulsion of the Rump in October 1659, all that changed.

George Monck was not the likeliest man to weigh in on national politics. Yes, he had been nominated to Parliament in 1653, and yes, his roots were impressive: the Monck family were alleged to have landed with the Conquest, establishing a base for themselves in Devon and connecting with other great local families – including their Grenville cousins. But a family feud had led to the discomfiture of his father, Sir Thomas. Embroiled in debt and embarrassed in front of the king, Sir Thomas had languished in gaol, working to his death to clear his name through the courts – and launching a vexatious claim against Francis Bacon in the process.

George, however, preferred more direct means. Drowning his sorrows in an Exeter inn one September evening in 1626, he, his brother and a friend had espied the man, Nicholas Battyn, whom they held chiefly responsible for Sir Thomas's humiliation. Picking up cudgels, they crept after Battyn, who, unawares, was making his way to the kitchen. When out of sight of the majority of customers, they sprang. The eager seventeen-year-old George 'struck [Battyn] with his cudgel upon the head whereby his head stooped towards the table, and forthwith the said George ... gave him two blows more, then they all three fell on him with their cudgels and gave him near twenty blows'.

Not yet satisfied, they drew their swords to run the downed man through. Enough was enough for Anna Barons, the innkeeper's wife: a sound beating could be ignored, but murder under her roof would only lead to trouble. Wrapping her beefy arms around George's brother, she heaved him away while her husband half carried the bruised and bloodied victim from the room. Caring nothing for the attackers' swords, Anna blocked their path to follow, ignoring threats to 'kill her if she would not let them go forth'. But George was too quick for her. While his companions kept Anna's attention, he slipped past; they were left to make an ungainly exit out of the window.

Monck's quarry was still at the inn. Not waiting a minute longer, Monck advanced, his cudgel landing three more blows before the man managed to stumble away. But as with any terrible horror movie, he ran in the wrong direction. Now cornered in a courtyard, he was easy pickings for George. BAM, BAM, BAM. Three blows more and the cudgel broke. Onlookers, taking advantage of the pause, tried to help. They couldn't restrain Monck for long, but it gave Battyn the chance he needed. Staggering past his attacker and out into South Street, he took a moment to catch his breath, 'standing at the door, and holding at a post'. Battyn then tried to run once more, but his injuries were too great: his head swam, his legs gave out, he fell. Monck, 'following him with his sword drawn, thrust at the said Battyn with his sword ... insomuch that his sword turned almost double'.[26]

Leaving his victim a bloody mess, Monck fled. But not quickly enough. Almost immediately he was caught and thrown into gaol, along with his abettors. The other two were granted bail the same day, but it was denied Monck while the court awaited medical opinion. Unbelievably, the surgeon reported that Battyn would survive. In less than a month, Monck was free to stalk the streets again. Yet the surgeon had been overly optimistic, and Battyn eventually died from his wounds. Not that it mattered to Monck. Aware that he could face the gallows, he had done what so many other impoverished 'gentle' sons had done before him: joined the army.

Initially serving under his cousin, Sir Richard Grenville, Monck won distinction where almost no distinction could be found in the failed English interventions during the Thirty Years' War, before turning his attention first to Scotland and then to Ireland. Grudgingly joining the Royalists on his return to England, he was almost immediately taken prisoner and sent first to Hull and then to the Tower of London, where he remained, largely forgotten for the duration of the First English Civil War.

The cloud had a silver lining, though. For while Monck was whiling away his time in the Tower writing a manual on military tactics, he met a woman who captivated him. Anne Clarges wasn't what one would call the normal catch: she was not particularly attractive – when Samuel Pepys was feeling kindly, he would later describe her as 'ever a plain, homely dowdy'; when less kindly, 'a damned ill-looked woman' – and, worse still, she came from common stock.[27] Anne was the daughter of an obscure farrier, and had married a haberdasher with a shop in London. It was this that led her to attending on Monck, as a laundry woman and seamstress, during his imprisonment. There, her intelligence and sharp wit caught the bored soldier's attention, and they fell in love. And once Monck had been released by Parliament to serve again in Ireland, the relationship continued.

The only problem was, Anne was still married. While the illicit couple had no children this wasn't an issue. Granted, the Adultery Act of 1650 imposed the death penalty for such crimes, but try to find a judge to enforce it. When Anne fell pregnant in 1652, however, things became tricky: Monck fathering a bastard would not only bring his reputation into serious question, but also that of his unborn child. By now, Monck had worked his way up the chain of command, gained particular favour with Oliver Cromwell, and been appointed commander-in-chief of Scotland. It was not especially difficult, then, to find the ready cash – and the military might to back it up – to convince Anne's husband to disappear. He had already faded into obscurity during the later 1640s, so it took only a few steps more to convince any casual observer that he was dead. Add to that an easy-going minister, who didn't insist on surnames for the register or ceremony, at a church where they weren't known, and the wedding went off smoothly. In the words of one historian, 'It was an astonishing business.'[28] Not only did the couple avoid the much more likely death sentence for bigamy, they escaped notice altogether. Even when Anne's first husband re-emerged in the 1660s in Derbyshire, very little was thought about it. The most that Samuel Pepys could discover was that 'some of [Monck's] family' said that the couple's son was a bastard.[29] The even greater gossip, John Aubrey, writing shortly after the couple had died, went a bit further: 'her brother ... came a ship-board to G. M. and told him his sister was brought to bed. "Of what?" said he. "Of a son." "Why then," said he, "she is my wife."'[30]

Perhaps because of their dirty little secret, or perhaps because of the frugality in which both Anne and George were raised, they kept to themselves in Scotland and ever after were known for keeping a mean table, even when he was nominated to the 'Barebones' Parliament in 1653.* But Monck was no wallflower. A hardened man with a tough past, he was pragmatic and determined in military matters, no matter the cost to human life. In Ireland he was only typically brutal, but his suppression of Scotland was another matter entirely.

In 1650, Charles Stuart, son of Charles I, had travelled to Scotland seeking his birthright. The Scots had been prepared to help, on a few conditions. The barely twenty-year-old king had endured a deeply unpleasant time spent on his knees in supplication, with lectures filling his ears and denunciations of his parents forced from his unwilling lips. Too much for the still-pampered youth, Charles attempted a coup and escaped the Scottish government's clutches, only to falter and be found curled, foetal-style, 'on an

---

* After the delightfully, puritanically named Praise-God Barebone, London's nominee. Praise-God's son, Nicholas If-Christ-Had-Not-Died-for-Thee-Thou-Hadst-Been-Damned Barebone (or Barbon), became an economist and was a central figure in rebuilding London after the Great Fire.

old mattress, still in his thin riding suit, inside a stinking cabin, exhausted and terrified.'[31] After that, an accord was found. Scotland declared for the king, invaded England, and was roundly defeated. But resistance thereafter simmered resentfully beneath the surface.

It was of the upmost importance to the English government, then, to suppress Scotland, so Monck 'made himself as terrible as man could be'.[32] As an example to other towns, when Dundee was taken he 'put five or six hundred to the sword, and commanded the governor, with divers others, to be killed in cold blood'.[33] It is little wonder that 'upon which all other places rendered'.[34] Unwilling to face the same treatment as Dundee, town after town came to heel, capitulating without a hint of resistance.

As the urban areas calmed, Monck next tamed 'these wild people' of the countryside.[35] With the rebels unwilling to meet in pitched battle, Monck turned to scorched earth. Cattle were killed or driven, crops and houses burned, the people pursued relentlessly. Thousands of Scots, civilians as well as combatants, were slaughtered, with many more dying the agonisingly slow death of starvation and exposure. A tenth of the total adult male population was killed – a higher proportion than that suffered by any Western European nation in either world war.[36] But nothing seemed to sate Monck. As his slash and burn tactics began to pay off and rebels surrendered, Monck suggested he 'hang twenty of those in prison here' to 'conduce much to the peace of the country'.[37] Luckily for the selected examples, his plan was too extreme even for Cromwell.

Order, then, was what Monck sought, and the situation in London in 1659 was too chaotic to be borne. With protests rising, members of the now defunct Rump seizing Portsmouth, and troops switching sides, it looked as if the country would once again slide into civil war. Something had to be done, and a return to some semblance of parliamentary legitimacy was the obvious solution. Writing to expelled Rumpers, Monck entreated them to 'let me know whether you will join with me in this just cause . . . I expect your answer, and resolve with my army, which is very unanimous for the parliament, to prosecute this business against ambition and tyranny to the last drops of my blood till they be restored'.[38]

But no matter how much he boasted about the commitment of 'his' army – those soldiers under his command who had decimated Scotland in the preceding years – they were by no means as united, or fearsome, as Monck made out. Time, therefore, needed to be spent on preparations before he could march south. Loyal deputies were sent out, removing officers from commands, while Monck ensured the common soldiers were well fed and well paid. Even so, many deserted. It was not until the new year, 1660, that Monck finally crossed the Tweed, and 3 February that he reached Westminster. By that point, the English army had already relented and the Rump had resumed business. Nevertheless, MPs hailed Monck as a saviour, granting him £1,000 per annum and extending his powers over the English military.

All was not yet well, though. The English populace still remembered the extremism of the Rump who were, after all, the fanatical remnants of the Long Parliament left after Pride's Purge in the dying days of 1648. Throughout his march south, Monck had been presented with an unending stream of petitions requesting free and full parliaments. People wanted a voice. The Rump, with so few members representing too few constituencies and preoccupied with godly ideas alien to the everyday concerns of the people, did not provide it. The City of London in particular was not happy: apprentice riots spread, demands of the aldermen increased, disobedience to government grew. The Rump, once again with more passion than sense, commanded Monck to quiet the capital, and slight its defences in the process. As a soldier he was obliged to obey – after all, he had just brought his army to London because he believed civilian authority paramount. But it set the wheels of the Restoration in motion. It proved, beyond doubt, that the Rump could not control the country, and it certainly couldn't keep the peace. New elections absolutely had to be called, a mandate from the people had to be given.

But while the Rump argued over exactly who should be allowed to vote – not anyone who had fought for the king, obviously, and perhaps only the godly, who truly understood what was good for the country – Monck was meeting with the expelled members of the Long Parliament.

On 21 February 1660, in a wonderfully ironic twist, the army that had prevented members from entering Parliament in December 1648 now enabled seventy-three of their number to return.

With the members who had objected to the execution of Charles I now back in Parliament, full and free elections were declared. That done, after nineteen years and four months – with a few hiatuses – the Long Parliament finally dissolved itself. The next month, on 25 April 1660, a new 'parliament' – the Convention – assembled. Exactly a month later, Charles II landed at Dover, and Monck was there on bended knee to greet him. On 29 May 1660, Charles's thirtieth birthday, the new king was welcomed in triumph to London. Monck also had something to celebrate: he was set for life with a dukedom, estates and a pension worth £7,700 per annum, his value increased as he handily discovered private correspondence that would condemn former friends to death. George and Anne Monck, the Duke and Duchess of Albemarle, would live, in declining importance and health, for another ten years, George dying of dropsy at the dawning of the new decade, surrounded by loyal officers. Anne, committed to her second husband to the end, followed George to the grave less than a month later.

Not everyone was as thrilled at the prospect of the Restoration as Monck. After a brief joyous moment when Rump and army had once again co-operated, Daniel Axtell had suffered more disappointment. Joining with other disgruntled officers, he had ridden out against the forces of the Long Parliament in one last desperate bid to keep the Good Old Cause alive. It had failed. Although Axtell escaped the battlefield, just a few miles south of Daventry, he was soon captured and transported to the Tower. If he had hoped the Act of Indemnity and Oblivion – passed by the Convention to keep the nasty business of the last two decades in the past – would spare him the traitor's death of hanging, drawing and quartering, he was quickly disabused. Axtell's role in the late king's trial was too great to be overlooked.

On 19 October 1660, unrepentant and 'with a cheerful countenance', Axtell was 'drawn to Tyburn, the place of execution, where a cart was set ready'. Clambering onto it, his 'countenance not at all changed though now the king of terrors stared [him] in the face', a rope was placed around his neck and a burning fire kindled before his eyes. Turning to address the crowd, his final speech was standard fare: 'You see a dead man living and yet I hope I shall live to all eternity, through the mediation of Jesus Christ.'[39] It was not as stirring a scaffold speech as the one he'd guarded eleven years before, and nor did it have the same impact. The prophecy of a dying man in 1649 had come to pass. Axtell's prophecy, that the 'surplice and Common Prayer Book shall not stand long in England', came to nought.[40] His head, placed on the roof of Westminster Hall after the whole grisly business was over, was his longest-lasting legacy. Years later it would still be there, hollowly staring down from its seat on high, judging the debauched multitudes below.

Chapter Three

A House of Ill-Repute
1660–85

Dramatis Personae

11. Samuel Pepys (1633–1703)

    Castle Rising (Norfolk) … … … … … … … … … … 1673–79
    Harwich (Essex) … … … … … … … … … … … … 1679 (I)
    Harwich (Essex) … … … … … … … … … … … … 1685–87

12. Charles Sackville, Lord Buckhurst (1643–1706)

    East Grinstead (Sussex) … … … … … … … … … … 1661–75

13. Sir Charles Sedley (1639–1701)

    New Romney (Cinque Ports) … … … … … … … … 1668–78
    New Romney (Cinque Ports) … … … … … … … … 1679 (I)
    New Romney (Cinque Ports) … … … … … … … … 1679–81
    New Romney (Cinque Ports) … … … … … … … … 1681
    New Romney (Cinque Ports) … … … … … … … … 1690–96
    New Romney (Cinque Ports) … … … … … … … … 1696–98
    New Romney (Cinque Ports) … … … … … … … … 1698–1700
    New Romney (Cinque Ports) … … … … … … … … 1701

14. Sir Henry Belasyse (c.1639–67)

    Great Grimsby (Lincolnshire)… … … … … … … … … … 1666–67

15. Henry Savile (c.1642–87)

    Newark (Nottinghamshire)   … … … … … … … … … 1677–78
    Newark (Nottinghamshire)   … … … … … … … … … 1685

Samuel Pepys had come a long way from the gangly schoolboy who'd pushed his way to the front at the late king's execution. Of course, now working for the two sons of Charles I, he liked to keep that nugget of information carefully concealed. There were other areas of his life equally well hidden – at least, he liked to think so. But no time for that now, as he pushed his way through a different crowd, on a different day, for different reasons. Yet, there was nonetheless an uneasy undercurrent of fear swirling around those he passed.

It had been a stormy few days, with an unseasonable wind blowing the petals from the remaining spring flowers and spreading the dandelion seeds far and wide. It battered the fresh leaves from the trees and threatened havoc with petticoats and periwigs. But on that particular day, 10 June 1667, the weather was not the source of the tempest.

As Samuel Pepys, Clerk of the Acts at the Navy Board, Fellow of the Royal Society, diarist and not-yet MP, hurried to reach Deptford, he contemplated his diary entry from just a few days earlier: 'for aught we see, the kingdom is likely to be lost, as well as the reputation of it is, for ever'.[1] Was it melodrama, or was it prophecy? For the moment, the latter seemed to be true: reports had been circulating that a Dutch fleet of eighty ships had set sail and was aiming directly at London. Now they had made it as far as the Nore, a sandbank at the mouth of the Thames Estuary – less than fifty miles from the capital. What they planned to do from there was anyone's guess, and whether or not they'd follow through was entirely based on an ill-prepared, underfunded and undermanned navy.

The Second Anglo–Dutch War had been provoked by the new king, Charles II, and his brother James in 1665, just ten years after the hostilities of the first war had ended. It had seemed a good idea at the time, bringing together the state in pursuit of national glory, and winning colonies and trading outposts – and thus profit – for the country. England's navy had seemed strong, its sailors confident, and it was through this bastion of pride and power that the war would primarily be pursued. Yet within months of its outset, disaster had struck. The country had been laid low with plague, reaching levels of devastation unseen for centuries. And then came fire, sweeping through London, destroying much of the old city including its beautiful, if somewhat decrepit, cathedral. If anyone were prone to question – and many were – it would seem that God was not very happy with the return of the king.

What was needed was a sweeping victory in the war, but the Navy was no longer capable of delivering it. Some superb gains had been made, and then lost, as the war swung one way and then another. And all the while the country suffered. Cash leaked out of the government's coffers at the same alarming rate as water seeped into the rapidly decaying battleships. The money that had bought all the firepower was gone, with not enough left even to pay the contractors and sailors. Of necessity, the Navy had to be scaled back and peace terms sought. But before anything was signed, the Dutch were intent on one more gamble.

It was this knowledge then, rather than the blustery weather, that sped Pepys towards the royal dockyard. Joining him were his fellow officers, the MPs Sir William Penn and Sir William Batten, for all the good they might do. To their faces, Pepys hid his dislike well, but he spewed forth his vitriol in his diary, his contempt for their corruption and incompetence boundless. Penn, father of the founder of Pennsylvania, was merely pitiful to the grasping, green-tinted Pepys, but Batten was something more. He was an ugly man, but this wasn't Pepys's only complaint. Batten would lie to worm his way out of trouble, often blaming Pepys instead; friends and his own business interests were favoured over those of others; he wouldn't do anything without additional payment for the trouble, and 'hardly anybody goes to sea or hath anything done by Sir W[illiam] Batten but it comes with a bribe'.[2] These faults were common enough, but another was more egregious, and awfully important now: Batten had withheld considerable sums of money, totalling more than £1,000 (£200,000 today), from funds reserved for sailors' welfare.

It was a significant failure. With the Dutch making their way upriver, causing destruction at every stop, the royal dockyards – and London – were almost undefended, limited to 'a great many idle lords and gentlemen, with their pistols and fooleries', a six-inch-thick chain across the Medway, and some ships scuttled in useless places. Men who had not been paid for months, or who had been issued with IOUs instead of cash, simply refused to fight. The distrust was so great that even when additional funding was secured, 'people that have been used to be deceived by us as to money, won't believe us; and we know not, though we have it, how almost to promise it'.[3] A dejected Pepys, writing a few days later, recorded that there were 'many Englishmen on board the Dutch ships, speaking to one another in English, and they did cry and say, "We did heretofore fight for tickets; now we fight for dollars!"'[4] Nor was he the only one to notice. As the poet and MP Andrew Marvell wrote:

> Our Seamen, whom no danger's shape could fright,
> Unpaid, refuse to mount our ships for spite:
> Or to their fellows swim on board the Dutch,
> Which show the tempting metal in their clutch.[5]

The damage done by that Dutch raid was immense. The defensive chain across the Medway was broken, the enemy easily sailed their way around the hastily made barricades, straight into the royal dockyard at Chatham virtually unopposed. Three of the four largest English warships were destroyed, going up in flames with a heat almost as intense as the flush on the Navy Board's collective faces. To add insult to injury, HMS *Royal*

Charles, the ship that had brought the returning Charles II to England at the Restoration, was captured, taken to Holland and put on display at Hellevoetsluis as a tourist attraction.*

Pepys, despite his position, emerged unscathed from the subsequent inquisition into the Navy Board. He would, in fact, go on to improve the Navy's practices, the thing for which he was best remembered – until his diary came to light, along with its cipher (cunningly hidden in the same collection of books donated to Magdalene College, Cambridge). And that's where things really became interesting. For it was discovered that, despite all the excellent things he did and supported, he was also a lying and occasionally vindictive toerag who used coercion and blackmail to bed a number of women who weren't his wife.

Pepys was what one might call a sex addict. Between 1660 and 1669, the years Pepys kept his diary, he gleefully recorded over twenty extra-marital conquests – or attempts at conquest. In what would be a psychiatrist's field day, his particular fancy was caught by women he deemed his social inferiors – servants, wives of clients, daughters of so-called friends. Perhaps he believed it would be more likely to go undetected; perhaps he considered himself unworthy of peers or social superiors. Or perhaps he realised how much easier it was to cajole, bully and exploit those of a lesser standing. Mrs Bagwell, for example, was the wife of a ship's carpenter who worked on naval contracts. Over the course of several meetings, where Pepys's behaviour became increasingly obscene, she was slowly convinced that submitting to her husband's boss would help further her husband's career. Eventually, as Pepys gleefully recorded in his diary, 'with many hard looks and sighs' and 'after many protestings, by degrees I did arrive at what I would, with great pleasure'.[6] Thereafter she had sex with Pepys regularly, although she once injured his hand in her efforts to resist. Pepys did at least keep his side of the bargain: he was still helping Mr Bagwell fifteen years later.

---

* More insulting still, the *Royal Charles* was sold by the Dutch government for scrap in 1673. The counter, however, can still be seen on display at the Rijksmuseum.

Nor was Mrs Bagwell the only woman Pepys supported financially. Betty Lane was considerably more 'available' than some ladies – as, it seems, was her sister. She didn't mind, for example, when her paramour took her to a pub on King Street and, as he recorded in the odd mixture of languages reserved for intimate diary jottings, 'je l'ay foutee sous de la chaise deux times'.*[7] Even when she married a chap who worked at the Ordnance Office, Pepys continued to court her. And when Betty's husband died in a debtor's prison, a pension for £100 per year under a Privy Seal warrant was awarded, probably at Pepys's instigation. Considering the number of mistresses Pepys was asking the government to help, it is little wonder that the military was short on funds.

Not all of Pepys's pursuits were as successful. Sometimes all he achieved was a quick grope; other times, he was fended off entirely. During one church sermon he was distracted by 'a pretty, modest maid, whom I did labour to take by the hand and body'. She was having none of it, sliding further and further away along the pew. When this didn't deter him, she took 'pins out of her pocket to prick me if I should touch her again'. With this he was discouraged enough to give up and let his attention stray to 'another pretty maid', who let him hold her hand for a while, before withdrawing it. 'So the sermon ended and the church broke up, and my amours ended also.'[8]

Pepys was by no means alone in his amorous pursuits. After years of austerity and war, when adultery theoretically carried a death sentence, it now seemed that everyone was at it. Licentiousness was the order of the day, and restraint was taking a well-earned break. The Court led the way: James Duke of York played havoc with his brother's plans for an international alliance when he married his pregnant, English mistress; and Charles II himself was famed for his many paramours, some of whom were shared around his close circle of drinking partners.

Letters and journals are full of the exploits of these 'Court wits' – some gentlemen of leisure, some aspiring younger sons on the make, some politicians and some poets, but all rebels against anything tainted with the

---

* 'I f***ed her twice under the chair.'

vaguest whiff of 'decency'. Pepys was delighted to record the 'debauchery' of these men, including members of Parliament such as Charles Sackville, Lord Buckhurst, and Sir Charles Sedley, 'running up and down all the night with their arses bare through the streets, and at last fighting and being beat by the watch and clapped up all night', only for the king to come to their rescue – and lock up the arresting constable for good measure.[9] Or when, with the whole group gathered at Thetford, His Royal Highness grew bored of the clean, upright entertainment laid on for them and commanded the fiddlers 'to sing them all the bawdy songs they could think of'.[10]

There were also the escapades of the fat, jolly Henry Savile, over-indulged younger brother of the Earl of Halifax, who fled to France every other month to escape the consequences of his actions: for engaging in a bout of fisticuffs and, when that didn't satisfy, for fighting a duel; for carrying a challenge for someone else; for insulting the Duke of York's naval abilities; even for becoming romantically involved with the Duke of York's wife. This was nothing, however, to the debacle of 1671.

'Twas a night in September, and through Althorp House, not a creature was stirring – except future MP and current rake Henry Savile. Creeping along, as quiet as a mouse and half dressed in his shirt and nightgown, he had meticulously planned for this moment. Earlier, he had asked his friend and owner of the house, Lord Sunderland, for a master key on pretence of wanting to play billiards. Now, gripping the same key, he quietly inserted it in the lock and turned. The latch slid silently, as well oiled as Savile himself, who had imbibed even more than usual in an attempt to steady his nerves. Pushing the door open, he spied the object of his desires: the widowed Lady Northumberland, soundly asleep. Padding over to her, he kneeled by her bedside and touched her gently to rouse her. Slowly she stirred, blearily opening her eyes. Now was the time.

'Madam, I am come with great confusion of face to tell you that now, which I durst not trust the light with, the passion with which I serve and adore you.'[11]

Barely had he managed to get this first sentence out before the good lady shrieked in alarm, scrambled backwards and leapt out of bed, reaching to ring the bell 'with that violence as if not only a poor lover's heart but the whole house had been on fire'.[12]

This was not going as expected. Unable to gather his thoughts well enough to stop her ladyship darting past, he watched in increasing anguish as she made her escape down the gallery and into a friend's bedroom. The thud of the door closing, firmly, was akin to a coffin lid, forever separating him from the recipient of this most 'unseasonable declaration'.[13]

Alone in Lady Northumberland's bedroom, Savile felt as shocked as its former occupant. And reality, hazy at first but becoming clearer, was starting to set in. The incident was bound to be told, so to be caught here, *sans culottes*, would make matters decidedly worse. An immediate exit was the first step towards clemency. Retracing his path, Savile retired to his own room to ponder his next move. A letter: that would do the trick. But what to say? To repeat his declaration at this point was folly. So instead he turned joker: it was a prank; I was the spectre in a haunted house; are you not diverted?

Lady Northumberland was not diverted. For she had another version, and as soon as she recovered, she recounted it with relish. It was the more to be believed, because Savile's ways – his affairs and his paying for sex (including, according to rumour, with adolescent boys) – did little to allay doubt. To the listening Savile, shuffling his feet and sinking under searing shame, it was obvious that 'the place would quickly grow too hot for him'. Stealing down to the stables, he grabbed a horse and rode away posthaste, leaving the family to 'breathe nothing but battle, murder and sudden death'.[14] They pursued him to London, but he hadn't stopped there. Reports had him riding until he hit the Channel, not stopping until he reached safe haven in France.

Despite that scandal sweeping the Court, no excess could beat the Wits' escapades at the aptly named Cock Tavern a few years earlier. The fun had started when three Court gallants – Sackville, Sedley and a friend – sat down in a private room for dinner. Served food and enough booze to sink a ship by six naked wenches, the company decided that, to be polite, they too should strip. It was a warm June day, and stuffy in the tavern. To cool off further, Sedley, unsteadily followed by his companions, emerged to take the air on the balcony. With cue and cullions on full display, the friends – lovers of the theatre all – put on a show for the crowd forming below. Starting with a recital of their own poetry, they acted 'all the postures of lust and buggery that could be imagined'.[15] Next, 'with eloquence [they] preached blasphemy to the people', proposing a toast to 'the salvation of Judas and another to the Babe of Bethlehem'.[16] The sermon done, the pulpit transformed to an auctioneer's rostrum, with Sedley selling 'such a powder as should make all the cunts in town run after him'. Finally, thankfully, running out of words, Sedley 'took a glass of wine and washed his prick in it and then drank it off; and then took another and drank the king's health'.[17]

The 'unholy trinity' had some final gifts with which to grace their audience, showering the increasingly infuriated crowd with more than words, slobber and wine.[18] The mob, finding it worse to be pissed off *and* pissed on, started hammering at the tavern's doors, hurling rocks at the performers and shattering the windows. The gentlemen responded as much in kind as possible: presenting their rears to the seething mass, 'they excrementiz'd in the street'.[19]

Within two weeks, the company had been indicted at the Court of Justice, where a very angry judge, amid a cacophony of harrumphing and 'Sirrahs', lectured the three lads on their responsibility for the entirety of 'God's anger and judgements [that] hung over us'. Perhaps there was some truth in this – on the same day as the performance, the mausoleum of the Sackvilles, down in Sussex, had been struck by lightning and nigh on burned to the ground. But, unlike the crowd beneath the balcony, very little could be found to stick to the Wits. Sedley alone was bound to good behaviour and fined £500 – to which 'he made answer, that he thought he was the first man that paid for shitting'.[20] The other two escaped without punishment.

Maybe the judge thought he already understood something of Sedley's character, having perhaps even read some of his work. After all, a man who could write openly about threesomes, anal sex and a whole lascivious feast more, was certainly no gentleman:

Members Behaving Badly

In the Fields of Lincoln's Inn
Underneath a tattered blanket,
On a flock-bed, God be thanked,
Feats of active love were seen.

Phyllis, who you know loves swiving
As the Gods love pious prayers,
Lay most pensively contriving
How to fuck with pricks by pairs.

Coridon's aspiring tarse
Which to cunt had ne'er submitted,
Wet with amorous kiss she fitted
To her less-frequented arse.

Strephon's was a handful longer,
Stiffly propped with eager lust;
None for champion was more stronger;
This into her cunt he thrust.

Now for Civil Wars prepare,
Raised by fierce intestine bustle,
When these heroes meeting jostle,
In the bowels of the fair.

They tilt, and thrust with horrid pudder,
Blood and slaughter is decreed;
Hurling souls at one another,
Wrapped in flaky clots of seed.

Nature had 'twixt cunt and arse
Wisely placed firm separation;
God knows else what desolation
Had ensured from warring tarse.

> Though Fate a dismal end did threaten,
> It proved no worse than was desired:
> The nymph was sorely bollock-beaten,
> Both the shepherds soundly tired.[21]

Then there were Sedley's other exploits. During one drinking game, in which the players each had to throw a named piece of apparel on the fire, Sedley was wearing a favourite, and valuable, cravat, 'which ... he was obliged to sacrifice to the flames'. Wincing as he watched it burn, he plotted his revenge. A few weeks later, when memories of the incident had blurred, he suggested a replay. But he had come prepared. Having for some weeks been suffering from a rotten tooth, he had a secret weapon. When his turn to nominate came round, he called in his concealed tooth-puller. Quickly, and without much ado, the rotten source of his discomfort was removed and thrown on the fire. But everyone else was in sparkling dental health. It was thus with 'tears from their eyes and oaths enough from their mouths' that the rest of the company, blood gushing, noses dribbling and jaws aching, had perfectly healthy teeth extracted, while a cloth-wodged Sedley advised 'Patience, gentlemen, patience, you know you promised I should have my frolic too.'[22]

Sometimes, Sedley's desire for revenge could take an even darker turn. Edward Kynaston was a young actor, with the flair and looks to make him a star – indeed, so lovely was he that even with women now gracing the stage, he was still known for playing female parts. But his repertoire stretched beyond that. For Kynaston bore a striking resemblance to Sedley, a fact particularly useful when, in 1669, he performed an unflattering portrait of the MP on stage. Honour abused was honour owed, so when the actor was strolling in St James's Park one evening, still wearing his Sedley-esque costume, the original paid to have him 'exceedingly dry-beaten with sticks'.[23] Sedley, of course, denied all knowledge of the incident, suggesting that the ruffians had meant to thrash him rather than the actor. Kynaston, although bed-bound for a week, survived. And he never dressed up like Sedley again.

Still, it was the more surprising that Sackville avoided any penalty for the balcony affair, for it was not the first time he'd appeared in court. In February 1662, Sackville had been travelling with fellow MP Sir Henry Belasyse north of London. Hearing report of highwaymen in the area, 'They spurred on their horses and overtook a couple of men.'[24] Supposing these rustics to be thieves, they bid them stand. The men, however, were in no mood to be ordered around by a couple of out-of-town toffs, and so resisted – perhaps a little too roughly. In the one-sided battle that followed, one man was wounded, the other escaping to alert the town. It was only then that the MPs realised they had just attacked two innocents who had been trying, unsuccessfully, to mind their own business.

With the hue and cry raised, it took no time at all for the two assailants to be apprehended and incarcerated in Newgate prison. Four agonising hours later, the injured victim died. Charges of assault turned to manslaughter, then to murder, and the two were unanimously convicted. With their recourse to the 'neck verse' removed – a get-out-of-gaol-free card originally used to determine whether a criminal was a member of the clergy and therefore entitled to be tried under Church law, which applied to manslaughter and duelling but not to murder – they were forced to appeal to the king's mercy. A pardon was duly granted, and both continued in much the same vein as before – for a short while only in Belasyse's case.

※

It was the silliest start to a quarrel, but 'a kind of emblem of the general complexion of this whole kingdom at present'. On 28 July 1667, a normal day like any other, a group of Wits – the usual crowd of playwrights and poets, players and politicos – had gathered for dinner at the house of Robert Carr, a politician famous for never letting guests leave sober. As usual, drink was flowing, chaps were guffawing, toasts were quaffed to the king, to love, to the Muses. But tucked into a corner, appearing far too serious for the company, Belasyse was attempting to offer some advice to his bosom friend, the actor Tom Porter. Raising his voice a tad too loudly, simply to be heard above the uproar, Belasyse made the mistake of attracting the attention of the rest of the room.

'What! are they quarrelling, that they talk so high?'

Belasyse, swigging from his cup, responded with a laugh, 'I never quarrel but I strike.'

Porter, not to be outdone, bragged, 'I would I could see the man in England that durst give me a blow!'

It was too much temptation for Belasyse. Immediately turning to his 'most extraordinary' friend, he 'did give him a box of the ear'.

Perhaps it was a bit too hard. With reflexes blurred on the one hand, and judgement departed on the other, the blow landed solidly, the slap of fist on skin heard by a room that was suddenly silent. Shaking off the ringing in his head, Porter rose to his feet. No matter the person, no matter how well loved, an insult such as this could not be ignored. Reaching for his sword, he offered challenge then and there. Belasyse had no choice: to decline was to admit cowardice, and so he laid his hand on his pommel, ready to draw and fight.

The rapidly sobering audience at last gathered their wits. Stepping between the two friends, they talked them down as best they could, offering more booze, drinking games and raucous entertainments as a better way to heal the breach. After a moment to reflect, Belasyse sat down and resumed his drinking; he was happy to forget.

Porter excused himself, going outside for fresh air and a clearer head. Pacing up and down, pondering the ignominy of the affront, he bumped into the poet John Dryden. When asked why he was out of sorts, Porter 'told him of the business and that he was resolved to fight Sir H. Belasyse presently, for he knew if he did not, they should be made friends tomorrow, and then the blow would rest upon him'.

Like a fool, Dryden agreed to help Porter, allowing the use of his servant to spot when Belasyse left the party, Porter heading to a coffee shop and a restorative shot of caffeine in the meantime. By and by, the lad came trotting up: Belasyse was getting into his coach now; if Porter hurried, he should be able to stop him.

The coach was just pulling away as Porter approached, but he somehow managed to halt it, ordering Belasyse out. Belasyse initially refused to emerge, thinking that Porter meant to run him through undefended. But the purpose was not to attack an unprepared and unarmed man, as his opponent had done; it was to uphold a point of honour.

Assured of his friend's intentions, Belasyse descended into the street. Facing each other, the one wary and weaving, the other still angry, they drew and 'fell to fight'. They circled and parried and struck. Blood was drawn on both sides, but Porter's coffee had refreshed him, while Belasyse had carried on drinking. It was inevitable who would win. Belasyse, at last pulling back and 'finding himself sorely wounded, he called to Tom Porter . . . "Tom, thou hast hurt me, but I will make shift to stand upon my legs till thou mayest withdraw, and the world not take notice of you, for I would not have thee troubled for what thou hast done."'[25]

Needing no more encouragement, Porter fled to France. Having already pleaded benefit of clergy for killing someone in a duel in 1655, with the brand on his hand marking his second and final chance, he would not be spared the gallows again. His opponent and best friend died two weeks later. Porter's time in exile was not long, however: at the inquest, the coroner's jury was directed to find that Belasyse had died from causes unknown.[26]

❊

Belasyse had lived through the best of the Restoration. By the beginning of the 1670s, the peaks of debauchery had already been scaled; from that point on, decline was inevitable and the wine seemed to turn sour in the Wits' mouths. There were still hints of summer but the days were drawing in, a chill could be felt in the air, autumn was approaching. They would all, in various ways, fight against the dying of the light, but even for these immortals there were some battles that couldn't be won – as Belasyse had proven. No matter how they railed against it, they were growing up, they had responsibilities, and they reformed.

With Sedley, conversion started around the time he met his second wife – hampered only slightly by the awkward fact that his original, insane, wife was still alive. To get around the issue, he packed the first off to a nunnery in Ghent – after removing her jewellery – where she lived a strange half-life, sometimes believing herself to be a queen and sometimes the wronged and discarded wife of a rake. Reformation was completed after a royal tennis court collapsed on Sedley in 1681, injuring him to the point that rumours quickly circulated of his death. Glad to be given a second chance, he made the most of it and thereafter 'lived happily and decently in his bigamous relationship'.[27]

Sackville, created Earl of Middlesex in 1675 and then succeeding his father as Earl of Dorset in 1677, was another reformed by marriage. Having remained a player – although not a bachelor – throughout the 1670s, in 1685, aged forty-two, he married a seventeen-year-old who absolutely captivated him, with friends complaining that 'my Lord Dorset has given over variety and shuts himself within my Lady's arms'.[28] Taking his new-found responsibilities seriously, he lined his pocket and furnished his house – where the loot can still be seen, under National Trust management at Knole – from the perquisites of his role as lord chamberlain, which ironically was a post supposed to oversee etiquette at Court. Inherent professional laziness caught up with him, however, and he was pushed from his position, accompanied by a golden parachute of £10,000 and 1,126 ounces of undeclared silver – which he refused to return. Rumour later had it that, with another new wife (the second having died after just six years of marriage) who had literally captured him, keeping him cooped up in a house in Bath, his mind going, his body failing and almost £35,000 in debt, Sackville tried to take his own life while drunk. Nature eventually took pity on him, and he died of natural causes in 1706. As his descendant wrote, 'He could not hope to enjoy his life at both ends.'[29]

Even the larger-than-life and now almost larger-than-an-elephant Henry Savile was struggling to hold his drink. By 1677 he was writing to his brother, in his usual delightfully witty manner, to complain of the exertions of the Newark election campaign:

> I came hither on Thursday morning last; since which time I have been so continually drunk ... I have been all this day sick to

agonies with four days' swallowing more good ale and ill sack than one would have thought a country town could have held; and this worthy employment must be begun again tomorrow though I burst for it. Therefore pray for me and pity me, for I would gladly change my next three days with any slave at Algiers.[30]

Happily for Savile, he carried the day at the election, helped by threats of the withdrawal of his brother's patronage. But it did not end so well for one of Savile's opponents, who had obstinately refused to stand down: already perilously close to bankruptcy, he was sent to debtor's prison where he languished, dying in 1693. By then, Savile had already shuffled off his mortal coil. Hoping to cure his string of health conditions, he had gone to Paris for an operation in 1687 with 'his viscera gangrened and his liver parched'.[31] He never recovered.

No wonder, however, that Savile and his opponents had fought tooth and nail in the 1677 elections, because politics was becoming nasty. And once again, religion was partly to blame. Charles II's permissive attitude to life extended even to matters of faith. When meeting the son of Pepys's colleague, the Quaker and founder of Pennsylvania, William Penn the Younger, who for religious reasons refused – against custom and basic civility – to remove his hat, Charles instead removed his own. 'Friend Charles,' said Penn, 'why dost thou not keep on thy hat?' ''Tis the custom of this place,' replied the monarch, 'that only one person should be covered at a time'.[32] And the king, having been saved by the Catholic underground after the failed Scottish invasion in 1651, would eventually convert to Catholicism on his deathbed, the rite being conducted by the same priest who had sheltered him years earlier. So Charles held no qualms on his restoration of promising freedom of conscience, or later of issuing a declaration of indulgence for religious practice. But others did have a problem with it. And as the 1670s continued, those people would raise their voices louder and louder.

The king's brother, James, Duke of York – never the sharpest tool in the box – had converted to Catholicism in the late 1660s or early 70s.

Perhaps, if the king had produced a legitimate heir, it wouldn't have been too troublesome. The problem was, as fertile as her husband was – proven by the humiliating spectacle of the royal nursery filled with illegitimate offspring – the queen was unable to conceive. The Catholic Duke of York was therefore next in line to the throne. And the English Parliament *really* didn't like Catholic monarchs, resorting to suggesting increasingly desperate alternatives for the succession, including Charles's first-born natural son, the Duke of Monmouth.

Then, to lob a grenade into an already hot situation, a foul, opportunistic criminal by the name of Titus Oates came forward in 1678 announcing that he had discovered evidence of a Jesuit-sponsored 'Popish Plot' to assassinate Charles, which stopped only at the very top. The king laughed the notion literally out of Court but had still been obliged to refer it onwards. The twitchy and gullible Privy Council was less inclined to dismiss the allegations, and then the mysterious murder of a London justice to whom Oates had sworn the veracity of his statement put all to chaos. Parliament – particularly those virulently anti-Catholic MPs who had already pushed for a change to the succession – became involved and, in a rabid frenzy not dissimilar from the earlier years of the century, it found 'that there hath been, and still is, a damnable and hellish plot contrived and carried on by the popish recusants for the assassinating and murdering the king, and for subverting the government and rooting out and destroying the Protestant religion'.[33]

Anyone vaguely associated with Catholicism was hauled to the bar to explain themselves – and often hauled away in chains, either to imprisonment or the gallows. Five lords, including the late Belasyse's own father, were imprisoned and one – the doddery, mild Lord Stafford – was executed. As another politician, Charles James Fox, wrote a century later, the Plot 'must always be considered as an indelible disgrace upon the English nation'.[34]

After the deaths of at least thirty other innocents, sense began to return, not least because eyes started to be turned on the likes of Pepys – who both worked for the Duke of York and expressed admiration for the beauty of the Catholic service – and the respected and admired queen. Eventually, Oates was sentenced to a £100,000 fine, and 'to be whipt by the common hangman from Aldgate to Newgate one day, and the next from Newgate to Tyburn; which was executed with so much rigour, that his back seemed to be all over flayed'.[35] Further, he would suffer perpetual imprisonment, only emerging from his gaol for the pillory on the anniversaries of every occasion he had perjured himself. Or that was the idea: released from prison in 1688 when the political tide turned once again, he took a rich wife, ran through her money, became a Baptist preacher and died in obscurity in 1705.

By that point, the damage had already been done. The most immediate consequence was the Exclusion Crisis, fed by a run of three successive parliaments determined to deny the Duke of York's right to the throne. But, more importantly, the English political nation had been torn asunder: Catholics (and other religious dissidents) would be excluded from political life for over a century; and the two-party political system had put down such strong roots that it broadly remains today, with Tory supporters of the soon-to-be new King James VII and II – their name taken from slang for dispossessed Irish Catholics ('tóraidhe', meaning 'outlaw' or 'bandit') – clashing with the Whigs (from Scottish Gaelic, implying horse thief and rebel). As Parliament began to meet more frequently, party machines organised, structures and strategies developed, political clubs coalesced around groups meeting in coffee houses and taverns, and party whips emerged, born to force reluctant MPs to see issues the 'correct' way. With vitriol and violence the order of the day, the next decades would witness upheaval as great as – and more permanent than – anything that had gone before. The 'rage of party' had begun.

Chapter Four

House Party
1685–1715

Dramatis Personae

16. Thomas Wharton (1648–1715)

    Wendover (Buckinghamshire) 1673–79
    Buckinghamshire .... 1679 (I)
    Buckinghamshire 1679–81
    Buckinghamshire 1681
    Buckinghamshire 1685
    Buckinghamshire 1689
    Buckinghamshire 1690–95
    Buckinghamshire 1695–96

17. Henry Wharton (1657–89)

    Westmorland 1689

18. Sir Robert Rich (1648–99)

    Dunwich (Suffolk) 1689
    Dunwich (Suffolk) 1690–95
    Dunwich (Suffolk) 1695–98
    Dunwich (Suffolk) 1698–99

19. Richard Coote, Earl of Bellomont (c.1655–1701)

Droitwich (Worcestershire) 1690–95

20. John Sinclair (1683–1750)

Dysart Burghs (Fife) 1708

It was as sparkling an occasion as it could possibly be: the new Catholic king, James VII and II, dressed in 'his royal robes of crimson velvet, furred with ermine and bordered with gold lace ... under a canopy of cloth of gold'. At his side, his Catholic consort, Mary of Modena, clad in purple velvet and 'a circle of gold' resting on her dainty dark curls.[1] Arrayed about them in the sanctified halls of Westminster Abbey were officials and government ministers, the lords temporal and spiritual, great ladies and gentlemen of the realm and beyond, representatives of the City and the universities, musicians and splendidly garbed guards. At precisely three o'clock on the afternoon of 23 April 1685, as James sat on his throne surrounded by the objects of state, the Archbishop of Canterbury placed the crown on the king's head. 'Trumpets sounded a point of war, the drums ... beat a charge, and the people with loud and repeated shouts cried, "God save the king."'[2] The coronation was a statement of unity, of royal power.

But it was also a wary compromise. For days, a close check had been kept on the abbey and its surrounds, and the traditional entry through the City quietly pushed aside, allegedly because James, 'being very frugal and cautious ... thought it best to save a charge of at least threescore thousand pounds', but in reality because he would rather not be attacked by a mob. The Protestant archbishop presided, but the traditional Anglican communion service was axed, ironically bringing the ceremony more in line with European counterparts. And it 'wanted much of the grandeur and magnificence' of previous coronations.[3] Nevertheless, the celebratory feast was sumptuous, with 144 dishes served as a first course, and the fireworks dazzling. Despite the odd bad omen – like the king's inability to keep the crown on his head – it wasn't the worst of beginnings.

From across the country optimistic loyal addresses flooded in, and with good cause: James had promised to 'make it my endeavour to preserve this government, both in church and state, as it is now by law established'.[4] So when the Earl of Argyll invaded from the north, and the Duke of Monmouth from the south, the people rallied to the king's defence – and looked away as 'Hanging' Judge Jeffreys, spurred on by James, wreaked furious vengeance upon the defeated rebels. Yet with all this, the new king still felt he needed to manipulate the elections to his first – and only – Parliament in 1685.

✽

'Honest Tom' Wharton, later Baron Wharton (and later still, Earl and then Marquess of Wharton), had grown up in a strict household. With fervent political principles and 'fanatical' religious beliefs set by a father who was 'easy to honour and impossible to follow', the family had produced some very odd children.[5] One, a regular member of Parliament from 1679 to 1704, had become a treasure-hunting, deep-sea-diving communicator with angels; another, Henry, a warrior and well-known scrapper. Tom himself had turned into 'one of the greatest rakes in England', with a string of mistresses, a love of wine and an obsession with horse racing.[6] And when not more pleasantly engaged, he would turn his hand to drunken pranks, midnight raids on houses and a spot of vandalism. But despite some shared pastimes, Tom was not a favourite of James II. So, when the time came for the Buckinghamshire election, the new king did everything he could to destroy Tom's chances of success.

The crowd had already gathered for the election in Aylesbury, Buckinghamshire, on that April morning in 1685. There was a buzz in the air as voters milled around, on the surface with a carnival spirit, but with something darker lurking in the shadows. The 1,800 supporters of Tom Wharton suspected they would have a fight on their hands, and they were right: one among the crowd was determined to see Tom lose. Previously handsome, now squidgy around the edges from heavy drinking to dull the pain of kidney stones, it was his style and bearing, an aura of command, that set Judge Jeffreys apart. For as lord chief justice, Jeffreys really did have power, including the ability to interfere in elections.

Calling the crowd's attention, his large, heavily lidded eyes daring any to object, Jeffreys adjourned 'the poll from Aylesbury to Newport Pagnell at a minute's warning by his own authority'.[7] The voters were dismayed. The Herculean task of transporting the throng to the furthest end of the county meant the fight was over before it had even begun. Tom Wharton, however, was an old hand at this, almost the exact same trick having been played on him in 1679. Then as now, he kept a calm head and ordered his supporters thence. The ones who had access to transport immediately set off on the twenty-odd-mile journey – that today will take forty minutes and at the time would have taken no less than three hours under perfect conditions. The others loitered, but Tom dug deep into his pockets, hiring all manner of horses, carriages, carts and wagons for additional transport. It was a blessing, on this very limited occasion, that England was in the midst of a drought that wouldn't see any relief until June. So although this was early April, there were no April showers; no water at all, really. Yet although the roads were not covered in puddles or oozing with mud so thick that carts could sink to the tops of their wheels, they were rock solid and laced with cracks so deep it seemed the pits of Hell itself were visible. The journey was bumpy and dusty and hard-going and long.

The relief was palpable when the weary, jostled travellers finally reached Newport Pagnell, comforted by thoughts of a pitcher or two of beer or sack, a warm meal and a soft bed. But that relief quickly turned to bitter disappointment as they realised there was no room at the inn – or anywhere. Door after closed door was tried in ever-increasing circles, but everywhere – all the inns, taverns, boarding houses, random spare rooms, barns – was full, packed with the forewarned supporters of Tom's opponent. With no other option, 'the far greater part of them were forced to tie their horses to trees, gates and hedges, and themselves to lie on banks and in ditches'.⁸ They couldn't even source any decent beer. At least it didn't rain. It was a tired, crumpled and £3,000-poorer Tom who triumphed over the following days.

This fighting spirit had served, and would continue to serve, Tom well for years. In 1673, having 'gone only to meet the cold air' in a vain attempt to combat a raging fever, he had bumped into the rival for his fourteen-year-old fiancée's hand. Courageous rather than wise, the woozy Wharton met the challenger 'with his sword in his hand' – and lost.⁹ The rival, however, was so impressed that he granted Tom both his life and his future wife. Suitably humbled, 'he made a vow to himself never [thereafter] to give or refuse a challenge'. And thanks, according to one of his disciples, to his 'great agility of body and constant presence of mind', he never again lost – once even besting a man more than thirty years his junior. Yet he never killed anyone, instead using a 'particularly dexterous way of disarming them, flinging up their swords and closing in with them, which never failed of giving him an opportunity to show his forgiving, as well as his heroic, temper'.¹⁰

If only Tom could have taught his younger brother something of this temper. Banned from Court in 1680, just months after being dangerously wounded in a duel, for 'running through one of Madam [Nell] Gwyn's horses' that 'drove too near him', Henry Wharton failed again and again to apply the lesson.¹¹ Five years later, another bout of road rage raised eyebrows further. Cockily riding along a road, proudly clearing the way for the commander of his regiment, he was stopped by a coach blocking the lane, the driver hastily fixing a broken harness. The impatient Henry dismounted, but he was no Good Samaritan. Instead of assisting, he threatened and bullied, beating the man to the ground, creating such a ruckus that he roused the coach's occupant. Irate, Henry turned on the passenger, bidding him emerge so he too could be knocked down. Only then did he realise it was the none-too-pleased brother of Judge Jeffreys. Henry had little choice but to take a breath, count to ten, cool his temper and rely on his commander to smooth things over.

His superior officer, however, wasn't always willing to help. Just a year later, the drunken Henry was offended by a fellow officer at a tavern.

Hot words turned into fisticuffs; fisticuffs into what barely passed for a duel. But there was no honour in this fight, and when Henry slew his comrade, he was charged with murder. With no sponsor this time, it took a sympathetic jury to turn him free, excusing his behaviour as 'self-defence'.

More dishonourably still, both Wharton brothers took the fight to the Anglican Church. Drunkenly breaking into the church at Great Barrington, Gloucestershire, they spent a pleasant hour, ringing the bells 'backward' and cutting the ropes, tearing up the Bible, trashing the pulpit and befouling the communion table. But the bells raised the villagers, who, fearful of some calamity, raced to the church. Pushing past the door, they found it wasn't the Catholics who had risen, but two trolleyed politicians. Caught in the act, arses bare, the Whartons hastily pulled up their breeches and legged it to a different form of sanctuary – a friend's house. As word spread, and the wincing light of sobriety dawned on the brothers, the renegades were forced to throw themselves on the mercy of the bishop. Given their standing in society, it made little sense to antagonise them: there would be no ritualised humiliation for the sons of a lord, no grovelling apology to the community that found itself scrubbing the mess the Whartons' red-faced servants had missed. Instead, they were fined a mere fifty guineas (ten of which were returned) and forced to pay for the many necessary repairs.

Tom Wharton's true fight, however, was against the king. In just three years since his accession, James VII and II had broken every initial promise. Hoping to bring England back to the Catholic fold by a combination of encouragement and coercion, he had replaced Protestant army officers and government officials with his co-religionists, ousted any who questioned the legality of his actions, put seven Anglican bishops on trial for seditious libel, and dismissed Parliament without even trying to work with it. The Tories sighed and shrugged; the Whigs shouted.* Yet there was still one small glimmer of hope for the adamantly anti-Catholic party: James

---

* And, bizarrely for a former puritan, Samuel Pepys quietly got on with his job, still loyally serving the increasingly unpopular James.

remained without a Catholic heir. As it stood, the Crown would pass to James's Protestant daughter, Mary.

But then the king made a joyous announcement: on 10 June 1688, the queen had been delivered of a boy. Despite the 'spirit of incredulity gone out among men in this matter' – a cynicism that went so far as to suggest a male infant had been smuggled into the queen's bed in a warming pan – this was a heavy blow to the Whig political establishment: the nation was surely under threat; something must be done.*

Honest Tom, once and future MP, was well prepared. Along with squirrelling away weapons, he had created a web of contacts throughout the English military, whispering dissension and treason into the ears of any who strayed close. Sitting in the Rose Tavern in Covent Garden, surrounded by wine and women, the subtly named 'Treason Club' plotted and planned and waited. And then came the opportune moment. After years of clandestine correspondence, William of Orange, military leader of the Dutch republican state, expressed an interest. Why would he not? Not only was he the leader of a coalition against the expansionist aggression of France, but his wife was the just-displaced Princess Mary, the former heir to the throne, and he himself was a grandson of the executed Charles I, and nephew of both Charles II and James II. So when William intimated that he would happily 'rescue' Britain from James, and a group of Whig malcontents – the 'Immortal Seven' – invited him to intervene, William invaded.

All the plotting, all the scheming, all the conspiring worked. Tom's supplies of men and arms, his outward show of support for the usurper once William had landed, and his central role in allowing all conspirators to communicate – along with his penning 'the first song hit in recorded history' that 'sung a deluded prince out of three kingdoms' – were essential in establishing the subsequent regime.[12] James, not even bothering to put up a fight and disheartened by desertions, fled for France – twice. The first time, much to the chagrin of William who was hoping to avoid a confrontation

---

* DNA testing has since proven the child to be legitimate. Clark, *Whig's Progress*, p. 222.

with his father-in-law, he was recognised and returned to London. With laxity commanded in his Dutch guards, his second attempt bore fruit.

Safely in exile, James tried to regroup, but once again was outmanoeuvred. A Whig-dominated parliament – technically a convention – decided that 'King James the Second, having endeavoured to subvert the constitution of the kingdom ... and ... having violated the fundamental laws, and having withdrawn himself out of this kingdom, has abdicated the government, and that the throne is thereby become vacant.'[13] Acknowledging Mary and William as monarchs thereafter was one small step for the gathered members, but one giant leap for Parliament, allegedly. Only by acceding to certain conditions were the new king and queen accepted, and this agreement – covering regular parliaments, free elections, members' freedom of speech and freedom from government interference, among others – has gone down in history as the Bill of Rights. But despite its position as a cornerstone of Britain's, and later America's, constitution, it would be many years before it came to be more honoured in the fact than in the breach.

So regardless of the optimistic attitudes of Whig members, regardless of Parliament's rights being enshrined in law, the imagined utopia never materialised. If anything, the change in monarchs charged the political atmosphere further. Tories who had defected to, or been bullied into supporting, William of Orange had worked alongside their enemies for the 'greater good'. There had even been a coalition of sorts, with representatives of both sides of the divide working together, causing new factions to form between 'Court' and 'Country'. But once William and Mary were firmly established, Tom and his cronies, 'the five tyrannizing lords' of the directing 'Whig Junto', made every possible use of assassination plots and rumours of corruption – combined with their own judicious use of bribery – to upset the careful balance.[14] As party politics again came to the fore, camps were established, tents were pitched with venom for guy ropes, and pegs knocked in with hammers of bitterness and intrigue, as each side fought tooth and nail for power and position.

✻

Dunwich today is a pretty Suffolk village pressed right against the coast. In summer it is thronged with day-trippers, enjoying the National Trust-owned shingle beach and heathland or hoping to find a table in one of the tea rooms; at night it is allegedly haunted by a fright of ghosts, mourning the loss of their once-glorious town. For in the Middle Ages Dunwich was a thriving port, challenging the likes of Norwich in wealth and importance, boasting at least one hospital, two friaries, six churches and a Templar preceptory, as well as a magnificent harbour at the point where the River Dunwich met the North Sea. Here, merchantmen and warships converged, disgorging soldiers and sailors, traders and travellers, bringing news, wares, money and interest to this bustling hub.

And then the storms came. For almost a century, surge after surge lashed the town, washing away houses and churches, literally sweeping the ground from under them. Further encroachments ensued, with author Daniel Defoe lamenting that 'fame reports that once they had fifty churches in the town; I saw but one left, and that not half full of people . . . this town is, as it were, eaten up by the sea'.[15] By the turn of the century, it was a much reduced Dunwich, with the waters lapping at the foot of the market cross, that presented two members to Parliament.

With the town literally crumbling into the sea, one might have assumed that its residents would work together rather than inflict further damage on the community, yet there were bitter divisions. The root cause was the 1691 by-election, in which the loser, the Tory John Bence, overturned the result on the basis that the winner's patron and current sitting MP, Sir Robert Rich, had conspired to pack the electorate with 500 new voters, 'Two whereof were Scotchmen, and others lived very remote; and particularly he made 42 free[men] at an alehouse; whereas there are not above 40 freemen resident.'[16] In other words, from an original voting base of roughly forty, Rich had octupled the franchise using his own clients – regardless of where they lived. The House of Commons duly flipped the result, and Rich went to war with his neighbours.

It was fitting that Sir Robert engaged in battle with his local opponents, as he had just been made Lord of the Admiralty by William III, a position he used to full advantage. The first port of call – pardon the pun – was the illegal impressment into the Navy of his political enemies in the council, achievable only through his new high office. One poor alderman, sent to sea as a lowly common seaman, would enjoy none of the comforts or pleasantries that had marked his life to that point. Bunking uncomfortably in common quarters, the few personal items allowed pervaded by the stench of life below deck, surrounded by dirt and disease and surviving on rations of increasingly rank ship's biscuit, salt pork or beef and cheese, it represented a swift and steep slide down the social scale.

But this wasn't Rich's only strategy. While his enemies scrubbed decks and endured bouts of seasickness, Rich campaigned for a new charter to give him and his cronies more control of local politics. Signatures were required, and found – through more threats of impressment, outright lies and the use of '3 or 400 foreigners' to force the point – and eventually a new charter was granted.[17] Not that this bit of paper mattered one jot to those still on the council, who continued working from the old framework, determinedly ignoring the steadily increasing numbers of freemen admitted to the borough. By the next election, in 1695, there were effectively two administrations operating, at odds but in the same space. And both were engaged in foul play.

It is, perhaps, surprising that Bence stood for re-election; after all, he hadn't bothered – even after all the fuss he'd created – to turn up to the House of Commons much. His absence was so bad that in 1693 the House ordered him into custody for non-attendance. He bucked up his ideas a bit after being held in confinement for a fortnight, at his own charge, but he was still more conspicuous for his silence than his diligence for the remainder of the Parliament. Maybe by 1695 the machinations of Rich had irritated him into action; maybe he simply felt it would be a dishonour not to contest the seat. But given his history of 'serving' his constituency, he had much to make up for. Charm was turned on, excuses were made and cash was left behind a local tavern's bar for any who cared to support him and his running mate.

Whatever Bence could do, Rich could do better. Bence might have paid for beer, but Rich offered one voter a house for the tiny sum of £3, to be paid in lobsters. Other voters were offered anywhere between 10s. and £20 (between £100 and £3,000 today) or, in one case, a scarlet waistcoat, to support Rich. Debts were written off and commissions in the Navy purchased. When this didn't produce results, other tactics were used. Local men such as James Farro were visited by Sir Robert's agents. Bribery was the first course: 'Archer told him he would give him £14 or £15 to vote for Sir Robert Rich and Mr Heveningham [Rich's partner], but he answered he would not for £100 go against his conscience.' The carrot having failed, the only thing left to use was the stick, with which they 'afterwards beat him, and said that if he would not vote for them, he should not go out of his house alive'.[18]

But the *coup de grâce* was the perfectly timed arrival of three men-o'-war just before the election. The display of might, and the threat of what might be, could be no better illustrated than with these magnificent vessels, bristling with weaponry and teeming with men, all loyal to Sir Robert. Just their looming presence was enough to make one voter hot-foot it out of town, and the fear of impressment of either themselves or their employees swung many more. And all those sailors, ungainly lurching forth from the battleships, were nevertheless poised to raise their voices – regardless of their permanent addresses – for their admiral. Despite the obvious corruption, on petition the Commons found in favour of Rich and Heveningham. Enough doubt had been placed on the veracity of some complaints that the decision was based more on the technicalities of the franchise – which reversed the Commons' decision of just a few years previously – than on extenuating factors.

Rich couldn't evade censure forever. Across the subsequent 1698 session, the Commons busied themselves debating the 'miscarriages of the Navy': the 'many new and unnecessary charges by the Admiralty'; of officers refusing to have their accounts verified; of untraceable sums of money spent on untraceable goods.[19] Despite the dots not connecting Rich's abuse of the Navy to his election, he was found culpable in other ways: 'The house Sir Robert Rich lives in cost the king £3,000 or thereabouts, and was purchased on pretence of keeping the Admiralty Court there; but Rich has got it now for his own use, and let his house in Soho Square, and he puts the king to £500 a year expense for alterations, furniture, firing, candles, etc., which are all placed to the account of incident charges of the Admiralty Office.'[20]

The state of the Navy was all the more important because William's focus rested squarely on his ongoing wars with France. Britain's potential might and money, combined with its strategic position on the Channel, were essential components in his grand plan, and he thus remodelled the military and the economy – with the establishment of the fractional-reserve Bank of England, national debt (which had risen from nothing to £17.3 million by the end of the century), paper money and a growing range of insurances – into something approaching its modern form.[21] But by claiming the British thrones, William gave his French adversaries a legitimate *casus belli*, that justifiable provocation, in the person of the deposed James VII and II.

On James's 'abdication', Lowland Scotland had obediently followed England in accepting the usurper as king. The Highland clans were another matter – until an exemplary massacre at Glencoe quietened them – but it was in the rugged hills and green valleys of Ireland that the main battles of the not-so-'Glorious Revolution' were fought. In February 1689, just days after William and Mary were proclaimed, James VII and II set out for Ireland at the head of an army. By March he was in Dublin, hailed as a hero by both sides of the sectarian divide, his procession from Christ Church Cathedral to Dublin Castle preceded by virgins scattering rose petals – or, at least, by 'ladies of purchasable affection' doubling as such. But the good mood didn't last. James, with his eye on the English prize, turned his Irish hosts into second-class citizens, while the Protestant contingent suffered from James's continuing Catholic crusade. With 'their estates being taken away', they 'were in a manner necessitated to espouse' the Williamite invasion.[22]

Nevertheless, James garnered enough support to force a reluctant William – whose attention, as ever, was focused on the Continent – to make a sally across the Irish Sea. In the van went Honest Tom's brother,

Henry Wharton, fighting bravely at the siege of Carrickfergus despite 'much bad company, and debauchery and drinking'.[23] But the enemy wasn't the only danger awaiting Henry in Ireland. A 'raging sickness, occasioned by the unwholesomeness of the place, wet weather and ill food' swept the Williamite camp, carrying Henry with it.[24] Two months after setting foot in Ireland, he died with the world dropping out of his bottom.

To the elder Wharton, news of his brother's death felt like the bottom dropping out of his world. But he had distractions. Despite William III's wariness of the scheming Tom, position and power followed the Revolution, with promotion to the Privy Council and in the localities. And within the Whigs, Honest Tom rose to pre-eminence, guiding the party as a leader until his death in 1715.

Tom's old adversary from the Buckinghamshire election did not do so well. Staying in position longer than the king he had so well represented, the unpopular Judge Jeffreys was discovered, with eyebrows shaved in a hopeless disguise, attempting to board a ship bound for Hamburg. Sent to the Tower, he succumbed to ill health and perished. He was initially buried – according to rumour – next to the body of his other enemy, the Duke of Monmouth.

James II fared only marginally better than Jeffreys. Choosing poorly situated ground by the River Boyne, ignoring passes 'which are so straight for some miles, that it had been easy to have disputed every inch of ground', he made his stand against William.[25] Or, at least, his army did – for a while.

> The Irish horse made some resistance, but the foot threw down their arms, and ran away. The most amazing circumstance was, that King James stayed all the while with his guards, at a safe distance, and never came into the places of danger or of action. But, when he saw his army was everywhere giving ground, was the first that ran for it, and reached Dublin before the action was quite over.[26]

By the following morning James was aboard a ship, making his way – once again – to France. His pretence to the throne was over.

※

With Ireland subdued, William was free to turn his attention back to the Continent, but in reality he had more than just Europe to consider. Across the Atlantic, and around the tip of Africa were brave new – and old – worlds to exploit. Since before the Middle Ages, intrepid travellers had been forging connections with the East, bringing back spices, silks and riches. But it was dangerous and, by the end of the seventeenth century, somewhat crowded. England had, like the ugly duckling, been a late bloomer, its more forward relatives – the Portuguese, French and Dutch in particular – already firmly establishing factories and outposts in these far-flung places. In the other direction was a wild west. 'Claimed' in the fifteenth century by the Spanish and Portuguese, the vast Americas promised wealth unimagined, the precious metals alone funding Spain's century-long dominance in Europe. Snot-nosed and scabby-kneed England had likewise started to muscle in here, desperate to find similar caches of treasure to fund her expansion and her wars. By and large, she had been unsuccessful in this aim, but there were other benefits to be had: not least, the sugar and tobacco trades that fed the insatiable British addiction.

Nowhere was the expansion of horizons better represented than in the person of Captain William Kidd, the political pawn turned by propaganda into a dread pirate. Leaving his humble Scottish Presbyterian roots behind, Kidd had spent his early life swashbuckling around the Caribbean gaining riches and reputation, before clawing his way up through 'honest' New York society to become Someone.* Granted, the rag-tag men recruited to his 1689 privateering adventure against the French had done what thieves usually do – mutinied and sailed off with his ship – but this hadn't set him back much. Proving his worth to city leaders by crushing a 'rebellion' and

---

* A recent book suggests that he was, instead, born in Cambridgeshire. As the commonly accepted date of birth is out by almost a decade, however, this seems unlikely. (Samuel Marquis, *Captain Kidd: A True Story of Treasure and Betrayal* (New York: Diversion Books, 2025), p. 22.)

allowing a new set of politicians to rise to prominence, he found friends in high places. By 1695 he was sitting pretty with a rich wife, daughters to cherish and the ears of the powerful to pander to his ego. Life was sweet. Only, Kidd didn't really like sitting still; give him long enough and his feet would begin to itch.

That's why he'd loaded his small cargo ship with goods and journeyed across the Atlantic, speeding along the Gulf Stream to London. That's why he'd used his connections to search out the cash-strapped MP and soon-to-be governor of New York and Massachusetts, Richard Coote – Lord Bellomont – and his Whig Junto cronies. And that's why they'd come up with a sure-fire plan to line their own pockets and smash the gangs terrorising the trade networks spreading like ivy around the globe. In what has been described as 'one of the greatest political blunders made by the Whig Party', the king himself granted letters of marque, allowing Kidd to attack the 'wicked and ill-disposed persons' committing 'many and great piracies, robberies and depredations upon the seas, in the parts of America, and in other parts and places'.[27] No one need know the group intended to split the spoils between themselves rather than submit them through official channels or return them to their rightful owners.

Despite cold feet – warmed when Bellomont threatened to impound Kidd's boat and impress his men – Kidd had sailed out of London with his motley crew puffed up like peacocks, the whole lot of them mooning the Royal Navy ships they passed. In retrospect, antagonising the Navy probably hadn't been the wisest move. They'd crossed the Atlantic, taking a little French boat in the process, and spent a pleasant two months provisioning and partying in New York, determinedly ignoring the pirates there. The problem was, the gangs needing to be smashed in America were Kidd's friends and neighbours, as well as the local politicos who held favour in their grasp. The mother country put too many restrictions on trade for anyone in the colonies not to welcome 'free-traders' with open arms. Who were these pirates hurting, really, aside from the super-rich corporations that charged an arm and a leg for staple goods, becoming fabulously wealthy as a result? Pirates were the new Robin Hood.

On the other side of the globe, the East India Company saw things differently, and it had been struggling of late. Its profits, once averaging £416,828 per annum had, by the 1690s, slumped to a measly £134,893 each year, with its share price – 'stock-jobbing', dabbling in the stock market, being another infatuation of the financial revolution – falling similarly.[28] Partially this was down to some particularly stupid decisions that provoked the ire of the Moghul emperor; partially to the 'interlopers' and the Whig-friendly New East India Company, which the old one had unsuccessfully spent £200,000 bribing members of the Commons – including the Tory Speaker of the House – to destroy. But the East India Company had also suffered from the depravations of the pirate Henry Avery, who had attacked the pilgrim convoy returning from Mecca, laden not only with many pious ladies – including a Moghul princess – to ravish, but also an estimated £325,000 (£60 million today) of treasure.[29] The emperor, accurately enough but unfortunately for the Company, decided that all pirates were English and put the blame – and expense – firmly on the struggling organisation. A manhunt for Avery and his treasure quickly followed, but to no avail, spawning three centuries of treasure hunters willing to try their luck. And so, following the Company's desperate pleas for aid, by the end of 1696 Kidd had weighed anchor and followed in Avery's wake towards the Indian Ocean, there to catch his prey.

That's where things began to go wrong. Kidd really had tried to do the right thing. He'd sailed away from treasure-laden Company and pilgrim ships. He'd sailed away from vessels of countries neutral in King William's wars. But his crew became restless – he'd even had to kill one mutineer. And you can always trust a dishonest man to be dishonest, and a desperate man even more so. Beneath all the refinement, all the patronage and official recognition, Kidd was still an adventurer. In the end, the draw was too great. So, he'd done what he could to cover his tracks, employing the old privateering tactic of flying false colours – French, of course – to trick his targets into showing the wrong papers from their own varied collection of flags and 'official' passes, and thus becoming legitimate objects of prey for a privateer tasked with destroying the enemies of England in whatever guise they might take. The ruse had worked: French commissions were shown, and the prize became lawful bounty. But he'd kept the ships' papers as evidence of his good behaviour, just in case.

Then they'd sighted the Indian-owned *Quedah Merchant*, riding low in the water, too richly laden with gold and silver and cloth and spices and slaves and opium to be ignored. At last his crew – paid only out of the proceeds of prizes – had won a proper haul.

Retreating to Saint Marie, a pirate enclave off the coast of Madagascar, to reprovision and relax, the men had greedily counted their shares before blowing their load on gambling and women. And Kidd had contemplated his next move. There was no way the story of the *Quedah Merchant* wouldn't get out – its lease for the voyage had been arranged by the East India Company, and its former captain was English. Even if, somehow, word didn't reach England and her colonies, it would be a stretch for Kidd to sail back to Lord Bellomont, now ensconced as governor of New York and Massachusetts, in his new prize vessel. Nothing said 'pirate' like an Indian merchantman far from home crewed by men wearing fancy fabric and throwing gold around as if it were nothing but sand.

Yet events conspired to set his course. Crew members, having binged their winnings, began looking greedily at the share of spoils saved for their political sponsors. Drink fuelled the ill-feeling until mutiny erupted, the rampaging men ransacking and then stealing the little flotilla of boats they'd collected, forcing their former captain to barricade himself in the cabin of his one remaining vessel, the *Quedah Merchant*. As Kidd watched his ships sail off into the sunset, he knew any chance of further buccaneering – licensed or unlicensed – had sunk without a trace. Only a handful of loyal men remained, and he couldn't return to an Indian port in the merchantman he had so recently appropriated. The only way forward was to sail to America after all and hope his sponsor would protect him.

As luck would have it, barely had Kidd made the decision before he received correspondence confirming Bellomont's continuing loyalty: 'Some flying reports about this town that his excellency should have conceived an ill opinion of you and that it was not safe for you to return here. Upon which his lordship did assure me that there was no such thing, but on the contrary, he ever has a good opinion of Captain Kidd.'[30]

So Kidd had returned to North America, minus the majority of his crew. He'd been careful, moving the goods aboard a less conspicuous locally obtained craft; offloading as much as he could through his network of contacts; skulking in the channels until his solicitor confirmed Bellomont's intentions. Those assurances were still ringing in his ears as he'd entered Bellomont's Massachusetts mansion on Thursday, 6 July 1699, and the guards arrived to drag him away.

Looking back, he'd been a fool to trust the word of such an avaricious man. Of course, Bellomont's share of the loot would increase five-fold if Kidd were treated as a pirate rather than a business partner. Yet Kidd had still played his part, sheltering his Junto sponsors as he was held in custody, first clapped in irons in solitary confinement in Boston gaol, then in the freezing hold of a transport ship, then in the foetid close quarters of Newgate prison back in London. He'd still believed he would be rescued by his patrons as he was hauled in front of the Admiralty, and a year later questioned by the House of Commons, resolutely keeping schtum and protecting those who had no interest in protecting him. Even when individual Tory MPs, desperate to find mud to sling at their opponents, entreated Kidd to 'say anything in relation to the Earl of Bellomont . . . or any other of the owners, touching any private directions, articles, or instructions', he refused to alter his story.[31]

It was only when his trial date was set and he was given just two weeks to prepare his own defence – being denied counsel on anything but strictly legal points – that the horrid realisation set in. Only when the papers he'd so carefully stored as proof of his innocence mysteriously disappeared did he know he'd outlived his usefulness to both political parties.

At last understanding his place, that he was just a lowly pawn in a political game that would last centuries, Kidd wrote a letter:

> my Lord Bellomont, having sold his share in my ship and in the adventure, thought it his interest to make me a pirate, whereby he

could claim a share of my cargo ... The more effectually to work my ruin, he has sent over all papers that would either do me little service or, as he thought, would make against me, but has detained the French passes and some other papers which he knew would acquit me and baffle his design of making me a pirate and my cargo forfeited.

If the design I was sent upon be illegal, or of ill-consequence to the trade of the nation, my owners who knew the laws ought to suffer for it, and not I, whom they made the tool of covetousness. Some great men would have me die for salving their honour, and others to pacify the Moghul for injuries done by other men and not myself, and to secure their trade.*

The trial was just as expected – apart from a surprise tacked-on charge of murder. Kidd had been bullied and badgered and hectored until he'd submitted a plea of 'not guilty', and then ripped apart by judge and jury. The first day he had fought valiantly; by the second, he knew his battle was lost, only stating, 'I have nothing to say, but that I have been sworn against by perjured and wicked people.'[32]

And so that is what brought him here, on a fine May afternoon in 1701. It would have been nice to say that the late spring heat warmed the face and made him think of happier times spent in sunnier climes. In reality, it only accentuated the stale air of Newgate prison, turning the stench into a chewy, tangible beast that would grip the throat and rip its jaws through the airways of those foolish enough to keep breathing. It was almost a relief when the cart that would transport him to his final destination trundled into view.

What was a definite relief, amid the jeering crowds that lined the three-mile journey, was the Dutch courage offered by sympathetic souls en route. By the time Kidd reached Execution Dock at Wapping, he was 'inflamed

---

* The paperwork eventually turned up in the Public Record Office in the twentieth century. Cited in Ritchie, *Captain Kidd*, pp. 209–10.

with drink'. He was unfazed as he gazed on the gallows, swatting away the well-meaning clergy as they fussed around him. Swaying up to the platform, he managed to gather his wits somewhat for his last speech, but it wasn't the contrition demanded by the authorities. '[U]nwilling to own the justice of his condemnation', he instead became 'more reflective upon others than upon himself . . . going about to excuse and justify himself, much about the same manner as he did upon his trial.'[33]

His speech finished, and still ruminating on the palpable injustice of it all, the noose was tightened around his neck. A shove in the back; a short fall forward into gaping empty space. The rope strained, then a sudden jolt as he slammed into the ground. Dazedly, Kidd realised the rope had snapped. He lay crumpled on the mudflats, attempting to catch his breath, but the brief, beautiful moment of respite was not to last. Hauled to his feet, bruised and with the adrenalin of near-death throbbing through his veins, he was offered a second chance. Not for a reprieve – the Powers That Be would never allow that – but for redemption. The divines on hand rushed forward, and this time Kidd was more ready to accept absolution, 'declaring openly that he repented with all his heart'. Another climb, another push, and this time the perfidious rope held true. As he swung, and jerked, and twitched, and choked, Kidd 'died in Christian love and charity with all the world'.[34]

Respite for the captain's Whig sponsors was likewise only temporary. Bellomont had already died, painfully, in March 1701 of gout in the stomach, leaving destitute his wife and children. Then, two months after Kidd's execution, impeachment proceedings were started by the Tories against three Junto members who'd hoped to profit from the privateer. The charges should have been damning: 'always preferring [their] private interest to the good of the public', converting to personal use 'great sums of the public money' and, last but not least, allying with 'Kidd, who was known to be a person of ill fame and reputation . . . in violation of the law of nations, and the interruption and discouragement of the trade of England'.[35] Unlike Kidd, the Junto's own friends did what the Junto refused to do for the privateer, protecting them from a guilty verdict.

House Party (1685–1715)

※

The English weren't the only Brits making adventurous reaches around the globe. For decades, the Scots had been chafing under the superior economic power of their southern neighbour, and dislike mounted as William refused to have anything to do with his northern kingdom – even visiting it was, apparently, beyond him. So, when opportunity arose in 1695 to escape English hegemony, Scotland took it, investing somewhere between 17 and 51 per cent of its entire cash supply in the Company of Scotland.[36] The Company's plan, 'an early example of corporate cock-up on a grand scale', was unduly optimistic: to steal the strategically important area of Darien in Panama from the Spanish Empire, establish a colony and exploit an overland route to carry goods from the Pacific to the Atlantic.[37]

Given its goals, the project was doomed to failure from the beginning. But disaster was compounded by a run of bad luck, with harvest failures, bullion shortages and rocketing food prices; financial mismanagement and astronomical levels of embezzlement; and the resolute machinations of the English East India Company – and government – that stymied the Scottish company before it was even launched. After two abortive expeditions to the isthmus, and the deaths of somewhere between half and three-quarters of the colonists, the company and the nation were broke.[38]

The upshot was formal political union with England, sweetened with a one-off bail-out of just under £400,000 for Scottish Company shareholders and government officials. Those not on the favoured list were less impressed, 'left in that disgraceful degenerate state, groaning under a load of taxes which accumulated on us every day; while our nobles and great men, the happy instruments of so good a work, went to Court to reap the fruits of their perfidy'.[39] The benefits to the English were simple: acquiescence in the English plan for the succession, and the removal of a potential French ally, with whom, by 1707, England was once again at war. But if any hoped the Scottish MPs joining the Commons would soothe the raging political divisions, or raise the general standard of the collective parliamentarians, they were to be disappointed.

Among those elected in 1708 was John Sinclair, not that he was allowed to take his seat. The primary reason was that he was the eldest son of a Scottish lord and so technically disqualified by a clause in the Act of Union from sitting. There was a lesser reason though: since his election, he had been found guilty of, and was facing a death sentence for, the murder of two men. That year, during action in Flanders, an ensign in Sinclair's own regiment, Hugh Schaw – whose brother would also win a seat in the Commons – had the temerity to accuse Sinclair of cowardice. It was not to be borne. As convention and honour dictated, a challenge was offered and accepted. But the manner of the meeting was anything but conventional: there were no seconds to witness the duel. So when Schaw's blade bent on Sinclair's chest, and Sinclair ran his opponent through with a mortal wound, there was no one who could say, beyond doubt, there had been no gross duplicity on the victor's part. It was enough to make another Schaw brother step forward, claiming Sinclair had padded his clothes with paper to act as armour. This time barely a challenge was offered. Sinclair simply shot his accuser. Imprisoned, awaiting confirmation of the death sentence by the Privy Council, the felon escaped to serve time instead with the Prussian army. Vengeance, however, was reserved for the dead men's politician brother, Sir John Schaw. And it was a dish best served cold.

※

The daughters of James II were not particularly long-lived. The childless Queen Mary had died in 1694 of smallpox, with her wheezy, asthmatic husband gasping his last eight years later. On William's demise, his sister-in-law Anne had become queen. Anne was definitely fertile: across twenty-five years of married life, she had fallen pregnant at least seventeen times – or on average once every eighteen months.* But only five pregnancies had resulted in live births, just one of which surviving beyond infancy. He, however, was a sickly child, dying a week after his eleventh birthday, and

---

* Although these pregnancies all occurred within seventeen years, making it one a year.

leaving a distraught and childless mother behind him. Thinking perhaps it was divine retribution for supporting her sister during the Revolution, Anne was rumoured to have 'turned Tory', even improbably supporting the claims of her half-brother, the 'warming-pan baby' and darling of discontented Tories, to the succession.

It was not to be. In a 1701 Act, the English Parliament determined that no Catholic – nor even the spouse of a Catholic – could accede to the throne. In doing so, Parliament leap-frogged over several people closer in line to settle on a new dynasty via the only descendants of James VI and I who didn't follow the old religion: the Hanoverians.* So when a bloated and depressed Queen Anne was finally released from life by a stroke in 1714, Georg Ludwig of Guelph – a man with limited English, but who was a Protestant – became King George I. Some, in both Scotland and England, were deeply and publicly unimpressed; many more were 'Hanoverian when sober, Jacobite when drunk', grudgingly bowing to the new monarch when dry but loudly toasting the deposed monarch's son, nominally James VIII and III, when in their cups.[40] In 1715, they rose in the name of James for the Stuart cause with more passion than prudence, having tested their mettle 'recruiting with wine, and fighting with bottles and glasses', and dragging a doubting, recently pardoned, Sinclair with them.[41]

'The 'Fifteen', as this rising would later become known, was an omnishambles. While the British government was forewarned, well organised and prepared, the rebels were a hodgepodge of competing and sometimes outwardly hostile interests, capable of attacking undefended towns – or each other – but not skilled in the arts of grand warfare. Jacobite resources were lacking, the dearth of money encouraging unpaid soldiers to loot; training was haphazard, with command and control worse; and desertions were constant. Stuck on the other side of the Channel, James couldn't reach his supporters in time to make any difference, either in morale or materiel. As Sinclair complained, 'Certainly we are the first

---

* The story of 'about fifty' people being closer in line to the throne is an utter fallacy, however.

who ever made war out of no other view but ruining ourselves and posterity, without knowing how or what we were doing.'[42] 'While everyone was building castles in the air and making themselves great men, most of our arms were good for nothing', and when battle was eventually met against a smaller Hanoverian force at Sheriffmuir on 13 November 1715, the Jacobites were so desultory in their attack on the government troops that they turned a promising victory into nothing more than an uninspiring draw.[43]

By the time the 'King across the Water' was able to land in Scotland in December, the rebellion was, to all intents and purposes, already dead. After a few hopeless months, James returned to France and then Italy, there to await a better opportunity. The Jacobite cause still had miles to go, and it would take another great clash of armies before it would finally run its course. But the idea of the Tories as a party capable of government had been discredited. Tainted by association with the 'Fifteen, it would take them half a century to regain reputable status. In the meantime, the Whigs would reign supreme. Political oligarchy, supported by George I and then George II, would replace the rage of party, and for the next fifty years it would be different factions within the same wing vying for power.

Sinclair, like the Tories, was also done. One of the first officers to call it quits in 1715 – a treacherous crime for which he was never forgiven – and with George I stubbornly refusing to grant clemency to former rebel leaders, he once again fled to the Continent to save his skin. There he would remain for over a decade, with the vengeful Schaw – who had fought for the Hanoverians – still smarting over the murder of his brothers and stymying every attempt at a pardon.

Chapter Five

Capital Offence
1716–46

Dramatis Personae

21. John Aislabie (1670–1742)

    Ripon (Yorkshire)... 1695–1702
    Northallerton (Yorkshire) 1702–05
    Ripon (Yorkshire)... 1705–21

22. Charles Stanhope (1673–1760)

    Milborne Port (Somerset) 1717–22
    Aldeburgh (Suffolk) 1722–34
    Harwich (Essex) 1734–41

23. James Craggs (1657–1721)

    Grampound (Cornwall)................................... 1702–13

24. James Erskine, Lord Grange (*c.*1678–1754)

    Clackmannanshire 1734–41
    Stirling Burghs 1741–47

25. Norman Macleod (1706–72)

Inverness-shire 1741–54

The Pretender mistimed his attempt on the Crown. Had he waited just a few short years, he might well have received a different welcome. For by 1721 there were many – and not just Jacobites – questioning George I and his government's worthiness to rule.

It wasn't just that George was deeply unappealing as a person, with one popular verse complaining:

> Hither he brought the dear illustrious house;
> That is, himself, his pipe, close stool and louse;
> Two Turks, three whores, and half a dozen nurses,
> Five hundred Germans, all with empty purses.[1]

Nor was it his clear favouritism towards Whigs, or his patent preference to spend his time in his ancestral lands around Hanover rather than in Britain, or the cruelty directed towards his son. Instead, what nearly toppled him was a much more mercenary affair.

In the first quarter of the eighteenth century the industrial and agricultural economies, along with overseas trade, flourished. The population, on the other hand, expanded far less rapidly. That meant, quite simply, individuals had more cash to spend. And spend it they did. On exotic treats and fine clothes; on stunning art to grace their new Palladian mansions; on theatres and lavish entertainment; and on drinking and gambling.

However that might be, the country itself was in trouble. The state had started to sweat in 1710, as the latest war with France dragged on. Anne, in her opening speech to Parliament, begged that because 'the Navy, and other offices, are burdened with heavy debts, which so far affect the public service . . . I most earnestly desire you to find some way to answer those demands, and to prevent the like for the time to come'.² Yet the state purse remained empty. By George I's accession, national debt was spiralling out of control, having risen from £17.3 million at the turn of the century to £36.2 million by 1714, and the country's credit rating was suffering.³

So ministers, like everybody else, decided to play their hand at the stock market. Although the ability to purchase shares in joint-stock companies had been around for over a century, the stock market as it emerged in the early eighteenth was as a shark to a goldfish, 'a trade founded in fraud, born of deceit, and nourished by trick, cheat, wheedle, forgeries, falsehoods and all sorts of delusions'.⁴ Yet in the first half of 1720 business was booming, with one particular company – the South Sea Company – tipped to make everybody, whether the government, individual members or the public, rich.

A 'chimerical project', the Company launched in 1711 as a public-private partnership attempting to make money through slaving and trade with the Spanish Americas.⁵ But thanks to wars and bad treaties, this aspect never really got off the ground. Instead, in 1719–20 they concentrated on making paper money through promissory notes and stocks, and by offering to take on, consolidate, service and reduce Britain's national debt, converting it into newly created South Sea stock offered to the original creditors on the promise of immense returns. In exchange, government would give the Company regular payments and special privileges. It was, effectively, a debt-for-equity swap, 'allowing the proprietors of those debts and deficiencies an interest of 6 per cent per annum redeemable by Parliament; and incorporating them to carry on the trade of the South Seas, which, if once settled, will yearly bring vast riches from Peru and Mexico into Great Britain'.⁶

It was no easy proposal for policy-makers to swallow. After all, MPs and ministers like the chancellor of the Exchequer John Aislabie had other vested interests – particularly in the East India Company and the Bank of England – that could suffer from the South Sea's success. So, they would need to be convinced, and the South Sea Company had just the ticket: £574,500 of low-priced fictitious stock, which recipients could trade in for real money whenever they fancied. The Company was so slippery that only about 60 per cent of that stock is traceable now: £216,000 (£38.3 million in today's money) went to government ministers and courtiers; £81,000 (£14.4 million) to twenty-seven MPs; £38,100 (£6.8 million) to six lords.[7] The bribes did their job: not only did they bolster the share price, but the South Sea Bill passed through Parliament unimpeded, concerned proposals for an inquiry were blocked, and finally another bill was passed by avaricious politicians banning the establishment of new competition.

So the madness started. With brains befuddled by thoughts of immediate wealth, no consideration was given to long-term dividends or Company viability. It was all about capital gains, and share prices rocketed. Even before they went public, from a par value of £100, by 1 January 1720, individual shares were at £126 and on Valentine's Day reached £138. Gaining 12 per cent in the next twenty-four hours to hit £155, they steadily climbed to £350 by 4 April, only to wobble and hover around the £320-mark.[8] Then, on the 14th, they went on general sale.

It was rumoured that £1 million – approaching £200 million today – was sold within an hour of the Company opening their books that morning. As quickly as the Company released shares at £300, they were sold for profit – at £317 – in the coffee shops down the trading epicentre of Exchange Alley. Two weeks later, shares were selling at £339; another fortnight and they had almost reached £400. By the end of May, they were at £595.[9] At its height, of £1,050 per share on 24 June, the company's value equalled 'all the fixed property – all the real estate, every acre of useful land and all the buildings on it – in the whole of Great Britain'.[10] To those not caught up in the hysteria, it looked 'as if all the lunatics had escaped out of the madhouse at once'.[11]

> All ranks and orders of men were almost confounded . . . The sudden increase of imaginary riches by the artificial rise of the public stocks and everything else that could bear but the name of a stock, so intoxicated the minds of the gainers . . . that all other considerations were laid aside. The people thought of nothing but their immense estates, all acquired in a few months, some in a few weeks, nay some in a few days, and this in many from not being worth a shilling before.[12]

A tiny minority kept their heads. The 'notoriously disputative' MP Archibald Hutcheson insisted on asking the Commons, over and over, one simple question: how much would the Company have to earn through the government's regular payments towards the national debt, plus its other revenue streams, for it actually to be worth its share price?[13] The answers were bleak: at £300 – the price at which shares were first floated – the Company needed to make an annual profit through trade of £5.3 million; at £500, £9.2 million per annum was necessary; at £1,000, additional annual profit would need to be over £22 million – at a time when the British government's total annual receipts were around £6 million.[14]

Hutcheson might as well have been urinating in a hurricane, but one or two tried to heed his advice. Thomas Guy, former MP for Tamworth and renowned miser, had accumulated £54,000 worth of South Sea stock before it began to simmer. When he saw the bubbles break the surface, he started slowly selling – but never enough to scare the market. Within six weeks, he had £234,000 of real money at his disposal. Unlike his former colleagues in the Commons, he didn't splash it around on trinkets or mansions. Instead, he established a hospital in London, which still bears his name today. It was, as one historian has written, 'the best memorial the Bubble has left behind'.* Others did less well. The greatest mathematician of the age, warden of the mint and MP Sir Isaac Newton, had owned his South Sea shares for years, and likewise sold out at a profit at the beginning of the year. Then he sat back and watched his former shares' worth escalate further and further, his friends becoming apparently richer and richer. Within two months, he had bought them back – at double the price.†

Of course the bubble burst, as they always must. By the start of September that same year, shares had lost 25 per cent of their 'value'; a month after that, they were once again back below £300. By November, they

---

* Carswell, *The South Sea Bubble*, p. 113. However, Guy wasn't all good, having initially increased his fortune trading in pirated Bibles and making a tidy profit trading in sailors' tickets – or IOUs – that were issued in lieu of actual payment by the Navy.
† In the end, he lost £20,000.

were approaching par.¹⁵ The speculators themselves, the landed classes and those with cash to burn, were the obvious victims. Banks, insurance firms and other companies felt the shock, both in terms of their own worth and in their holdings in the South Sea. But pain was also caused by trickle-down economics. Money stopped circulating; payments couldn't be met for works commissioned and completed; tradesmen and staff weren't paid; and necessities became luxuries. The devastation seemed absolute, the whole nation suffering from 'the universal poverty, which is the consequence of universal avarice'.¹⁶ Fortunes and lives were lost; dark tales abounded. Everyone sank in the South Sea – everyone, that is, except those at the helm.

Drowning in petitions, Parliament established an inquiry, in which Hutcheson was naturally included. The results were damning. Not only was the Company 'managed with the utmost negligence', making use of all manner of schemes 'for the raising and keeping up the price of stock at an extravagant height', but 'several members of this House, and of the House of Peers' had been complicit in it. Beyond that, even,

> it doth not appear to your committee, that any of the persons who had the honour to serve his majesty in the Treasury, or in any other part of the administration, used any endeavour to prevent the directors of the South Sea Company from taking in subscriptions at the aforesaid extravagant prices; but on the contrary, it doth appear, that some of them . . . did not only encourage and promote the said subscriptions, but did greatly enlarge the same.¹⁷

Politicians had forgotten, it seemed, that 'in all public bargains, it is a duty incumbent on them who are entrusted with the administration, to take care that the same be more advantageous to the state than to private persons'.¹⁸ As Defoe had so presciently written the year before, 'when statesmen turn jobbers, the state may be jobb'd' – not that Defoe himself had remained sane.¹⁹

Heads naturally rolled. The chancellor of the Exchequer and MP for Ripon, John Aislabie, was an easy target. Known to be 'dark, and of a cunning that rendered him suspected and low in all men's opinion ... He was much set upon increasing his fortune', to the tune of £27,000 in initial Company stock.[20] Absolutely demolished at both committee and the subsequent parliamentary debate, his actions were condemned as 'a most notorious, dangerous and infamous corruption'.[21] '[S]o little respected that he fell almost unpitied by anybody', he was expelled from Parliament, fined £45,000 and committed to the Tower.[22] Yet despite having his estates sequestered to compensate his many victims, he in fact lost only a quarter of them. Soon released from the Tower, he retired to his not-too-reduced estate at Studley Royal, near his former parliamentary seat in Yorkshire, turning his gardens into some of the most admired in Britain.

A cushty, well-funded retirement was harsh compared to the punishment of others in government. Charles Stanhope, secretary to the Treasury, for example, was charged with accepting substantial payouts to bribe other members of Parliament and of gaining a cool £50,000 (about £9 million today) for himself. But when his inquiry began, the government ministers, who 'sat mute as fishes' during Aislabie's trial, swung into action.[23] Despite five witnesses called against the defendant, MP Robert Walpole, only just emerging from the political wilderness, baffled the House with lawyer's logic, suggesting first one extenuating factor and then another, despite them being entirely mutually exclusive.* George I himself lobbied members on Stanhope's behalf. Then a relative stood up and offered a moving appeal on compassionate grounds, inspiring fifty abstentions when the time came to deliver a verdict. Stanhope scraped an acquittal, by just three votes. London was in uproar, 'the whole kingdom ... enraged against the South Sea scheme, and not less so, against those who support their abettors'.[24] Not that public opinion mattered: as soon as Parliament was dissolved, Stanhope received another government post. He would continue to sit in Parliament for twenty more years, although not always as a favourite of the

---

* Walpole himself was only accidentally clean in the whole South Sea debacle, but he was no Boy Scout. Aside from being a philanderer and spendthrift, he also sat at the centre of an international smuggling ring, despite some of the harshest measures against smuggling being enacted during his 'reign'.

Crown: when the new monarch, George II, came to the throne in 1727, he discovered a letter in Stanhope's hand among the late king's papers, recommending that he, then Prince of Wales and now the man holding the letter, be kidnapped and removed from the kingdom.

James Craggs, however, fared less well. Up until that point, Craggs had been remarkably fortunate. Coming from an impoverished country family that was one step up from the yeomanry, he had fudged his ancestors' pasts and instead of cultivating the land had cultivated an air of gentility. This, combined with 'an understanding superior to most men, [and] an undaunted spirit', gave him a foot in the door.[25] From there, he had worked his way up the proverbial ladder, becoming an MP in 1702 and then an intimate of the Whig Junto, until he reached the position of joint postmaster-general. Admittedly, he had a few hiccoughs along the way, being committed to the Tower not only for obstructing parliamentary enquiries into the 'world's first corporate lobbying scandal', which found the Old East India Company guilty of bribery and insider trading, but also for accepting the single largest 'gift' – of £4,540 (about £1 million today) – from the Company.[26] It was not such a leap of faith, then, to assume he had been involved in the dodgy dealings of the other company, particularly when he had so enthusiastically trumpeted its advantages, and more especially when it was discovered he had received a whopping £30,000 of South Sea stock for which he never paid a penny.

Incarcerated in the Tower, Craggs' luck finally ran out. The day before he was due to appear before the Commons, he died. The official reason was a stroke, though rumour insisted that 'the fear of appearing before the House tempted him to dispatch himself with a large dose of opium'.[27] Either way, stress was almost certainly the ultimate cause, not helped by news that his only son, also involved in the Bubble, had just died of smallpox.*

With useful scapegoats silenced by Death's convenient scythe, and a few more MPs expelled and imprisoned as sacrificial lambs, the vengeful

---

* Most of Craggs' estate – worth about £1.5 million – was preserved, to be inherited by his three daughters and his late son's natural daughter.

Capital Offence (1716–46)

bloodlust of the public was abated, if not sated. It no longer served Walpole's interests to pursue other offenders too closely: it wouldn't do to bring the entire edifice down. So while diplomatic moves ensured that the star witness, the scheming and unscrupulous former cashier of the Company who had absconded with damning evidence earlier in the year, stayed in exile, Walpole concentrated his considerable force on both an economic rescue package for the country and fortifications for his own power base. It worked on both counts. Britain did not crumble into bankruptcy: the Company was, after all, too big to fail. A bail-out designed in conjunction with the Bank of England (for which Walpole took the credit) saved the Company, but did little for individual investors. And Walpole made sure that those who got off lightly – or completely – owed him favours. By 1722, Walpole had emerged as the most powerful man in politics – the first British 'prime minister' – and would reign as such until the 'Robinocracy', as his reign became known, collapsed under the strains of war and its own weight in 1742.

*

Not everyone liked Walpole. James Erskine, raised to the Bench as Lord Grange, certainly had no love for the prime minister – and the feeling was mutual. It didn't help that the first time Grange rose to speak as an MP in the Commons, 'he made a long canting speech that set the House in a titter of laughter'.[28] It didn't help that his brother, the Earl of Mar, had led the Jacobite rebellion of 1715. It didn't help that, in an effort to regain the forfeited family lands, Grange put any hint of principle firmly behind self-interest. And it didn't help that Grange's righteous piety was nothing more than duplicitous dissembling, passing his time 'in alternate scenes of the exercises of religion and debauchery, spending the day in meetings for prayer and pious conversation, and [his] nights in lewdness and revelling'.[29]

Grange's married life bore all the marks of scandal as well. In 1707 he had 'courted' Rachel Chiesley, the deserted daughter of a murderer. In a lifetime of questionable decisions, this ranked among Erskine's most stupid, for something of the father's temperament had passed to the daughter who, known for 'her violent temper and ungovernable rages', dragged her lover down the aisle under pain of death.[30]

Despite such 'auspicious' beginnings and a whole clutch of offspring, the marriage was not a success. Erskine, obviously, was not a man without fault. A secret door to his specially built occult library in his country house near Prestonpans, Scotland – a library that would apparently aid him in his pursuit of witches and demons – 'according to local gossip admitted by night shapes more tangible than those of the spirit world'.[31] He was a soak and a philanderer, and no kind husband. Lady Grange – as she insisted she be known regardless of the fact that, as it was a professional title, she had no right to share it – had no temperament to take it quietly, however, and was prone to outbursts, harangues and threats against her husband. By 1730 Grange had had enough of his wife's lectures and tantrums. She was packed off to live in the countryside, on an allowance of £100 per annum.

Lady Grange had other ideas. Returning to the family home in Edinburgh, she attempted to re-enter her house. Finding the doors barred, she stood in the street and hollered at her husband through a window, accusing him of any number of crimes, against both her and the state. The husband, possibly deaf to every word she now uttered, chose not to respond. But his lady was not to grow bored so quickly. Day after day she returned and 'attacked my house and . . . cried and raged against me and mine, and watched for me in the streets and chased me from place to place in the most indecent and shameless manner, and threatened to attack me on the Bench'. For a change, she would seek out her sister-in-law or daughter, railing at them 'with violent scolding and curses'.[32]

If it had been nothing more than complaints about her treatment, or scandalous tales about his personal life, it would have been merely embarrassing, perhaps not easier to ignore but certainly less dangerous. But it didn't stop there. For Lady Rachel Grange had something much more incriminating to divulge. Her husband, pillar of society, was guilty of a capital crime: secretly plotting in the Jacobite cause against Hanoverian rule. She had the documents to prove it and, as she tired of shouting day in day out at a closed window, she began to consider blackmail. The documents would go to London. For Grange and his fellow Jacobites, it was essential that something be done to silence her.

✻

The clock echoed through the strangely silent house as it struck eleven on that Saturday evening, 22 January 1732. For some unbeknown reason, Mrs Maclean, the rough Highland owner of the boarding house, had insisted that all her guests retire early – an hour and a half before the usual time. Rachel supposed she didn't mind too much, because in two days she would have quite a journey on her hands – Edinburgh to London, and in winter too. So a good night's sleep would do her no harm. Making the best of it and settling down, Rachel cast her mind over all she had planned. The preparations had all been made, possessions packed, documents in order, the coachman already paid the advance. Sending her imagination further forward, she quailed just a tad over the task in front of her, but she was resolute, she was determined and she was made of sterner stuff than that good-for-nothing husband of hers allowed. Yes, it would be difficult; yes, it could be construed as petty treason. But he really had left her no choice. She had begged, and reasoned, and cajoled, and pleaded. She had gone unheeded. Instead, he had recommitted himself to his treacherous ways, plotting sedition if not outright rebellion, while carrying on with every floozy who passed his way. He had turned her out of her house, he had prevented access to her children – those ungrateful wretches, born of her body, born of her love, who had not lifted a finger to help her, even to see her. Rachel's resolve stiffened further: she knew what she had to do. She owed it to herself; she owed it to her king; she owed it to God.

A sound at the street door roused Rachel from her musings. Footsteps approaching, most heavy, one light, accompanied by the low murmur of voices through wood. Nevertheless, Rachel recognised the dulcet tones of the house mistress, talking quietly with gruff male voices. A knock at her own door; what could it be?

'A letter for My Lady.'

A letter? It must be an urgent matter to be delivered at this time. Unless it was dear James reconsidering. Perhaps he had, at last, seen the error of his ways. Surely this was a letter of apology, begging her to return, so they could start again with renewed love and renewed happiness.

Rushing forward, barely taking the time to attire herself in half-decent fashion, she fumbled with the lock for a second before swinging the door open.

She didn't even have time to blink. Men in Highland garb, armed and threatening, rushed her. Unbalanced, she was thrown to the floor. But if they'd hoped to wind her, they were disappointed. Taking a breath, she screamed and she kicked, she clawed and she flailed, biting and wrestling her attackers as she tried to stand.

A fist came down hard. And again. Once more. Hands grabbed her face, rough, reeking of dirt and horse. Another fist, baring a cloth, plunged towards her. Her shouts were cut off. She choked and gagged as her mouth was filled with filthy fabric, but she was not done. Straining, twisting, wriggling, she freed a hand and pulled the rag from her mouth, screaming again, banging her heels on the floor hoping to raise the house.

The moment of clean, fresh air was just that. However feisty, she was but a woman, already downed, and they were many, and men. The gag was once again stuffed into her mouth, so forcefully this time that a tooth was knocked out. Again she fought back, pulling out the rag once more, spitting blood at her assailants, not giving up. A third time cost more teeth; a fourth turned her gums into a bleeding, bruised, mangled mess. Her lips swelled and split, but still she resisted as the men's 'hard, rude hands' tore at her face.[33]

And then – thank Heaven – a face looked in at the door. Finally, a rescuer, and a kinsman no less! Rachel's pleading, puffing eyes turned towards him, framing the appeal that her mouth could no longer form.

His gaze drifted over her, never deigning to connect. 'For God's sake, tie her hands, and cover her head.'

If Rachel had harboured doubts about who had directed this attack, those were over now. Only one man could command this; could make a cousin override every better sentiment, every claim of honour, honesty, duty: James Erskine, Lord Grange, judge, man of God, aspiring politician – her husband.

It would take more than this crushing realisation to squeeze the fighting spirit from her body. She writhed and she squirmed, she did everything in her power not to be overcome, not to have that foul cloth forced in her again. But her arms were pinned now, bent unnaturally upwards, agonisingly, popping her shoulders out of their sockets. She could barely catch her breath, her chest tightening, the world rushing, going dim. Suddenly, everything was dark, muffled, close, suffocating. They had covered her head. They had tied her hands. She was caught.

A strange sensation: the floor dropping away. Lifted. Not gently, as a parent might carry a child. Roughly, like a corpse, like meat. Downstairs, the muted clomp of boot on wood. Outside into the cold night. Frost in the air. Then upright, forced to sit. On what? Slightly soft, but not comfortable. Then held fast, restraints from behind clamped around her chest. Hard, determined. The smell of man-sweat. Hot, rank breath on her neck. Lord! Sitting on a person? More movement. Fast. Rocking. But no horses' hooves. A sedan chair. Swaying. Nausea. Panic.

An abrupt halt; sudden, sweet stillness. Stumbling forwards, more cool night air. And then blessed relief as the covering was removed from her head. Everything hurt: Rachel's face had swollen beyond the point of recognition, fresh red trickles of blood muddling with the browning smears from earlier. Her eyes could barely open, her scalp stinging where clumps of hair had been ripped out in the tussle. Still, for that one moment, under the brilliant light of the quarter moon, it felt like Heaven. She could breathe clean air, the chill on her face soothed her skin and calmed her mind.

The man on whose knee she had sat stood up and stretched, and made his way to six or seven horses, mostly mounted with riders. In a farce of societal norms, he presented himself as Alexander Foster of Carssbonny, and then introduced his servants – an obvious falsehood as Lady Grange knew at least three to be no retainers of Foster.

What she really wanted, apart from the numbness of sleep, was to sit down on the whitened, icy grass and collect herself. But there was no time for that. Once again unceremoniously dragged from the ground, she was slung on a horse behind Foster and tied close to his body, trussed in a most uncomfortable position, a blindfold again blocking her sight. It was a small solace to think that the blood oozing from her face would seep into his clothes, though given his current odour, he probably wouldn't even notice.

And then they were off. Bumping along, the horse's rhythm – the clip-clop, the sway as the animal's muscles bunched in turn to carry them onwards – kept the disorientation at bay. It did nothing, however, to dull the pain of being held in an awkward stance, the nagging ache of a stitch peaking as if a knifepoint were piercing her side. Once again she was gasping. Despite herself, she whimpered, and then moaned.

'Please,' she begged her captor, 'please let me alight a while. It hurts so much. Please let me down, only for a moment, to ease my pains.'

'Be silent, you damned bitch. I'm venturing my life, so hold your peace unless you want me to break your neck.'[34]

It wouldn't take much for him to kill her. So she submitted. With back breaking and side splitting, she rode on as silently as possible, ignoring the pain, holding her tongue and trying, once again, to cast her mind into the future. Here, at least, she was helped. With her head pressed tightly against her abductor, the rocking motion of the horse slowly loosened her blindfold. At last, she could see. She knew this road well, she knew they were travelling west, she knew where they were going. The hours crept by, the moon arced across the sky, its reflection glittering in the waters of the Forth, and eventually set. The first hints of morning appeared, a few lonely robins attempting a feeble dawn chorus, and yet they still journeyed on.

※

It was a grey half-light when they eventually arrived at the house of a respected lawyer just past Linlithgow. Met with candles, Lady Grange was shown 'into a very good room', with a much welcome fire burning brightly. Steered upstairs, her temporary prison was 'a very good bedroom, which had a fire, and good linings in the bed'. After a night – and such a night – without sleep, the siren's call of the bed was almost too much. But then one of Foster's men entered and stood silently inside the door – her guard – 'for which reason I would not throw off my clothes, for as wearied and cold as I was, [he] was so barbarous and cruel'.[35]

The day passed in silence and confinement, the bed never losing its appeal. Then, as night approached and the desire to sleep became almost unbearable, the posse made to move. Forced downstairs, tied as before behind Foster, they rode with her through the night. The destination this time near Stirling, Rachel's cell – 'a room of the vault, the windows of the room being nailed with thick boards, and no light in the room' – locked constantly for the next three months.[36] Her health deteriorated with no light or fresh air, until the gardener charged with her upkeep took pity and insisted she be allowed – under strict supervision – outside. Then up and away again, always the same way, trussed and gagged, from place to lonely place, west across the Highlands, riding at night, sleeping outdoors during the day, manhandled and hurt and miserable.

When the land ran out, they boarded a sloop, sailing across the choppy waters to Haskeir, a remote, exposed island on the edge of the Outer Hebrides. Two years in this desolate place, half starved, with no meat, and no fresh clothes to protect against the blowing gales and freezing cold; her keeper 'bidden treat me harshly . . . and to cross me in everything'.[37] But if Lady Grange believed it could get no worse, she was in for a shock. In June 1734, men arrived to bundle her into yet another galley, taking her a further seventy miles across the grey, fathomless Atlantic Ocean to St Kilda. Here she was abandoned to the care of the few locals, with 'nobody to wait of me that understood me, but one ill-natured man who understood a little English, and explained to others what I wanted; and he was not only ill-natured, but half-witted, and one day drew out his dirk to kill me'.[38] For years she was left in this miserable condition, with 'no provisions sent me but two pecks [28 oz] of flour, and what the place can afford, such as milk and a little barley knocked, and that forced from them by threatenings, for the people is very poor and much oppressed'.[39]

For a brief time, it seemed that the blessings of God were just around the corner. Visiting the island came a minister and his wife, who did what little they could for what was left of Lady Grange. In 1738 the minister promised to deliver a letter from her, detailing 'all the misery and sorrow and hunger and cold and hardships of all kinds that I have suffer'd since I was stolen', to her kinsman.[40] '[B]ut his life being threatened, he left this island, and he was after hindered either to go to Edinburgh, or to write to anybody about me.' Resourceful as ever, Lady Grange still managed to smuggle out an account of her life in a ball of wool carried by the minister's daughter, with the epilogue: 'I am not sure who of my kin and friends is dead, or who is alive; but I beg whosoever hands this comes first to, to cause write it over in a fair hand, and to shew it to all my friends.'[41]

It did her no good. Alerted by the well-meaning cousin, Lord Grange pre-emptively had his wife moved, first to a cave on Skye and then to the slightly more upmarket accommodation of a shack on the same island. Rachel died, still a prisoner, in 1745. Never, in her own time, would her awful fate be well known beyond the clans who had conspired to kidnap her.

※

Those clans were good at conspiring, and by the start of the 1740s they had grand plans afoot. Norman Macleod, chief of the clan of that name and MP for Inverness-shire, was not dissimilar to Lord Grange. Like Grange, he had contracted an unhappy marriage with a woman of unequal status; like Grange, it was rumoured he had imprisoned her on Skye; and like Grange, he had a particular set of skills for kidnapping.

In 1739, while Lady Grange was still residing at her husband's pleasure on lands owned by Macleod, the laird developed a plan that would see him rich and see off the noisome tenants on his estate. For by this point the slave trade had been booming for half a century, and many of Macleod's contemporaries were making a fortune. Between 1672 and 1752, sixty-five MPs were directors of the Royal African Company that had monopolised the triangular trade from Britain to Africa to the Americas, while twenty-four were independent slavers.[42] With so much money to be made, the debt-ridden Macleod decided to try his luck in the most unusual way. In conjunction with a neighbour, he chartered a ship mastered by a particularly nasty rogue, that landed first on Skye and then Harris. In the dead of night, with the aid of clansmen and favoured locals, houses were raided. Victims were 'taken by force out of their beds' or lured away from safety by requests for help, then dragged to the ship and bundled on board.[43] When they set sail, bound first for Ireland to reprovision and then to the slave markets in America, there were upwards of one hundred people – about forty men, thirty women and the remainder children – on board. Just as with any slaver, the men were separated and stored in the hold; the women and children cramped between decks. Fresh air, space, food was limited, the conditions rapidly growing foul in the filth and fear.

Not all the captives made it even to Ireland. About ten children, considered too young for the eager purchasers across the Pond, were put ashore on a small Inner Hebridean island – but were not too young, apparently, to be abandoned without their parents in an alien landscape. An old man, too ill to be a good investment, was likewise dumped, as were 'two big-bellied women'.[44] One young woman who hadn't survived the initial capture was also unceremoniously discarded on the shoreline, her body left to rise and fall, in uncanny imitation of life, as the waves lapped around her.

When they arrived at Donaghadee, Ireland, on the night of 20 October 1739, there were ninety-six people left, herded into two barns as if there were no distinction between them and cattle. There they 'were confined, imprisoned, watched and guarded', but not well enough.[45] After just over two weeks, the guards had grown complacent, their patrols too routine, their habits obvious. The prisoners, taking the chance offered, escaped.

They weren't free long. Reports among the locals circulated of foreign felons roaming. Constables and villagers were put on alert, the strangers found, bound, beaten and dragged back to confinement. Yet something was wrong: these seemed like no ordinary criminals, opting for transportation rather than the noose. They were children, women, elderly. And all were scared, cowed. Translators were found, the captives interviewed.

Their stories all tallied: they had committed no crimes, they had been to no court, they had been sleeping innocents dragged from their slumber.

New arrest warrants were issued, but this time not for the victims of the crime. Instead, the perpetrators would feel the full weight of the law. Or at least that was the idea. The men in charge of the slaver, including a kinsman of Macleod, sought the protection of their chief. Their chief sought the protection of friend, fellow MP and most senior judge in Scotland, Duncan Forbes, protesting 'that we are entirely innocent of the crimes laid to our charge'; so innocent, indeed, that he would be happy to go to trial, but 'a prosecution would be attended with a multitude of inconveniences'.[46] Macleod walked away scot-free. But at some point, Forbes would expect a favour in return.

❋

The Jacobite cause may have been defeated in 1715, but it hadn't been crushed. Simmering beneath the surface was a current of resentment – in Scotland about the Union, and in general about the Whig ascendancy that showed no sign of diminishing despite the fall of Walpole – sweetened with a rose-tinted sprinkling of romanticism. So when Britain once again went to war with France and the treaties restraining it from helping the Jacobite cause were thus rendered obsolete, the moment seemed propitious for another attempt on the Hanoverian throne.

It wasn't. France initially was willing to provide military support for a fresh Jacobite uprising across Britain, until another waft of the 'Protestant wind' wrecked half its fleet. Thereafter, it proved more reticent: there would be no timely French invasion force, no bottomless purse, no limitless armoury to maintain the Stuart cause. Not that this was enough to stop the exiled Bonnie Prince Charlie, son of the titular James VIII and III, from keeping in touch with optimistic Scottish clan chiefs, who promised 'that if the prince landed in the present circumstances with ten battalions, or even with a smaller body of troops, there will be no opposition, but, on the contrary, that his royal highness will be received with blessings and acclamation'.[47] The bored and impatient twenty-four-year-old prince heard what suited him. On 15 July 1745, having waited for the French for more than a year, he decided to risk it all and set sail from Brittany to the Western Isles of Scotland.

Duncan Forbes had not forgotten that Macleod owed him a favour, and when rumours started flying of a Stuart attempt in the summer of 1745, it was the perfect time to call it in. Macleod was, indeed, the perfect person to sow discord and indecision in the Jacobite ranks. For years he had given multiple assurances – both in his cups and sober – 'that tho' it was a rash design, he would join the Pretender if he came over'.[48] But when the prince landed at Eriskay on 23 July 1745, Macleod did not honour his promise. Instead, he worked with Forbes, employing 'every art' to delay correspondence, to delay much-needed support and to keep a steady flow of intelligence to the Hanoverian forces, while still giving the outward appearance of loyalty to the Stuarts.[49] The subterfuge worked so well that he was still considered trustworthy for months; indeed, many believed rumours that the hold-up was caused by nothing more than the slow mustering of his men.

Whether the prince's rash scheme could ever have succeeded, at least in the limited goal of securing a Stuart Scotland, should be a discussion reserved for table nights, those wine-fuelled nights around a table. Certainly, the Jacobites met with some early victories, taking Edinburgh without a shot being fired, trouncing ill-prepared government forces at Prestonpans in September and marching as far south as Derby by December. Nonetheless, they faced some fundamental issues. The absence of foreign aid was enough to make better men than Lord Grange forget every former promise and retreat to the safety of London with tails between legs. And there was a strategic vacuum, with no agreed war aims: the prince had his heart set on winning all of Britain; his Scottish friends more concerned with their own corner.

Having marched their army almost four hundred miles south, at Derby – just 130 miles away from London – the prince's council voted to turn back. There were good reasons. The pledged risings of English Jacobites had failed to materialise; a promised French landing on English soil had morphed into a small force deposited in Scotland; and the Jacobite army was looking increasingly bedraggled and fatigued. To top it all, reports were reaching the council that Hanoverian forces were looking to cut them off. Strategically, it was the only sensible move.

Strategy didn't come easily to Prince Charles. Disappointed and frustrated, despite some victories once back in Scotland, his impetuosity was exacerbated. Eventually, on 15 April 1746, he chose to risk it all on an improvised night-time attack on the enemy camp sleeping eight miles away at Nairn. In theory a good idea, but his already much smaller force was missing a significant contingent, having taken the order to 'return home' a wee bit literally. And then, neglecting to tell the remaining force the plan, even more went missing as they dispersed to forage. Down by about 2,000 men – over a quarter of their strength, depleted anyway after supply issues – they nevertheless set off on time for their trek across dark marsh and moorland.

They didn't arrive on time. In fact, they didn't arrive at all. Surprised by the difficulty of crossing uneven, boggy ground at night, 'Many were so fatigued that they slept on their march; others to a great number wandered.'[50] As day broke, some in the van – without awaiting orders – turned back. Others followed. Full retreat thereafter was the only possible option. Arriving back at their original encampment, 'Everybody seemed to think of nothing but sleep.' Even the officers 'were so much tired that they never thought of calling a council what was to be done, but everyone laid himself down where he could, some on beds, others on tables, chairs, and on the floors'.[51]

A mere two hours later, and still 'half dead with fatigue', they were shaken awake.[52] The Redcoats were just four miles off and advancing quickly. On the 'dark, misty, rainy' morning of Wednesday, 16 April 1746, the army of the half-dead attempted to form battle lines in a field outside Culloden.[53] Pipes were playing and drums were banging but were barely audible above the roar of the wind. At about half-past eleven in the morning, the Hanoverians came into view, the prince's army unable to do anything but watch and wait as the enemy moved into position, then stand steady as the Redcoats advanced under 'a continued fire both of cannon and musketry, which kill'd a vast number of the prince's people'.[54] Eventually, it was too much for some, and the 'whole left wing of the prince's army gave way, and run [sic] away without firing their muskets'.[55] The prince, in an act reminiscent of his grandfather at the Boyne, saw the panicked flight and didn't wait to see anything else. He 'turn'd about his horse and went off as soon as the left wing gave way, and never offer'd to rally any of the broken corps'.[56] He made it back to France alive. Many of those who had followed him had no such escape route. About two thousand Jacobites died on or fleeing the field, a further five hundred were taken prisoner, executed, transported to the Americas or died in captivity.

After Culloden, Macleod's true colours emerged, as he exacted vicious retribution for the crime of treason on the Scots people and land, burning farmsteads and homes, driving the populace to starvation. His name was forever blackened among his former friends. Allowing his love of gambling, drink and, more endearingly, marmalade, to take hold, Macleod's funds dwindled. Increasing the rents of his tenants did little to alleviate the situation, particularly when famine hit hard in the early 1770s. Eventually forced to abandon his estates and move to a modest house near St Andrews, he died, £40,000 in debt, from excruciating gout and stomach pains on 21 February 1772. The Stuart cause – and the Highland culture – had already died at Culloden, never to be revived.

Chapter Six

Liberty and Libertines 1746–75

Dramatis Personae

26. John Wilkes (1725–97)

 Aylesbury (Buckinghamshire) … … … … … … … 1757–64
 Middlesex … … … … … … … … … … … … 1768–69
 Middlesex … … … … … … … … … … 1769
 Middlesex … … … … … … … … … … 1774–90

27. Sir Francis Dashwood (1708–81)

 New Romney (Cinque Ports) … … … … … … 1741–61
 Weymouth and Melcombe Regis (Dorset) … … … 1761–63

28. Thomas Potter (*c.*1718–59)

 St Germans (Cornwall) … … … … … … … … 1747–54
 Aylesbury (Buckinghamshire) … … … … … … 1754–57
 Okehampton (Devon) … … … … … … … … 1757–59

29. Samuel Martin (1714–88)

    Camelford (Cornwall) 1747–68
    Hastings (Cinque Ports) 1768–74

30. John Huske (1724–73)

    Maldon (Essex) 1763–73

31. Charles Townshend (1725–67)

    Great Yarmouth (Norfolk) 1747–56
    Saltash (Cornwall) 1756–61
    Harwich (Essex) 1761–67

The crowd was too great; there was no way the hackney carriage could be driven across the recently opened Westminster Bridge, from the beating heart of political London to King's Bench prison, over the river in Southwark. It simply had to stop, and no amount of whipping or clicking could make the horses move through the surging throng. So, like the cornered 'criminal' it carried, the coach was caught. The horses snorted, shifting uneasily as the mob pressed forward, their distress quieting only after they were unhooked from their harnesses and turned free. The coachman, guards and marshal watched on in amazement, unsure what to do, surrounded by the heaving mass of the metropolis that seemed touched by madness, unruly and unpredictable.

    For a brief moment the coach stood still, an island of calm in a swirling hurricane. But not for long. Amid cheers of 'Wilkes and Liberty', burly members of the public took the place of the horses and, with a heave, the coach was once again mobile.

Liberty and Libertines (1746–75)

It was a strange turn of events, John Wilkes, MP for Middlesex and occupant of the coach, reflected as manpower pulled him along, not to gaol but to an unknown destination. Yet it was not wholly unexpected. This particular kerfuffle had begun five years ago, in 1763, but its roots went much deeper. As Wilkes watched London pass slowly before his eyes, he cast his mind back along the extraordinary trajectory of his career.

Everyone knew that Wilkes was something of a libertine; indeed, he positively revelled in it. He boasted of his days at Leyden University where 'My father gave me as much money as I pleased. Three or four whores; drunk every night. Sore head morning, then read.'[1] Nor was that just youthful exuberance. Almost twenty years later fellow MP and future famed historian Edward Gibbon described him as 'infamous, his life stained with every vice, and his conversation full of blasphemy and bawdy'.[2] Wilkes himself admitted that he was so ugly that even polite society gawked, with one commentator stating, 'You are a most shocking dog to look at, and ought not to be exposed to pregnant women's view.'* His eyes were permanently crossed, and his lower jaw protruded so far that his teeth would have been visible when he lispingly spoke – if, that is, they hadn't started falling out by the time he was thirty. Yet 'he loved all women except his wife' and had the libido to sustain it – at least until his seventies when, it was reported, a friend attempted to grab a chat as Wilkes scurried to his mistress's house: 'Don't stop me. I have got an erection now. Did it go down I don't know when I shall have another.'[3] But despite all this, he was known as 'one of the most . . . agreeable rakes about town. He was a man of taste, reading and engaging manners. His sprightly conversation was the delight of greenrooms and taverns, and pleased even grave hearers when he was sufficiently under restraint to abstain from detailing the particulars of his amours, and from breaking jests on the New Testament.'[4]

---

* At the time it was believed that the looks and behaviour to which pregnant women were exposed could affect their unborn babies. *A Letter from Scots Sawney the Barber to Mr. Wilkes an English Parliamenter*, cited in Shearer West, 'Wilkes's Squint: Synecdochic Physiognomy and Political Identity in Eighteenth-Century Print Culture', 65–84, *Eighteenth-Century Studies* 33 (1999), p. 65.

He even managed to charm the determinedly dour compiler of the dictionary, Dr Samuel Johnson.

Of course, Wilkes thought wryly as Whitehall disappeared behind him, he wasn't the only reprobate out there. There were many like him, fitting snuggly into the libertine lifestyle of the fashionable, choosing rebellion over the restrictive reformation of manners, and frittering away time in the 'hell fire' clubs modelled on Philip Wharton's 1719 example.

Philip, son of the Whig grandee, in many ways had been a chip off Honest Tom's block. Like his Junto father, Philip enjoyed drinking and gambling and women. Also like his father, he had no problem in sticking it to the established Church. Yet in terms of religion and politics (although never becoming an MP, inheriting the Wharton dukedom as a minor), he was from an entirely different planet. Where Tom – when not excrementalising in parish churches – leaned towards dissenting Calvinism, his son questioned the very existence of a supreme being. And nowhere were Philip's predilections more apparent than when the 'infernal spirits' of his club congregated not only, so it was alleged, for 'the advancement of that branch of happiness which the vulgar call whoring', but also 'in the most impious and blasphemous manner, [to] insult the most sacred principles of holy religion, affront Almighty God himself, and corrupt the minds and morals of one another' through blasphemous and 'Satanic' ritual.*[5]

Wine, women and Satan could not hold Philip's attention for ever, though, and by 1722 he had drifted instead towards Freemasonry. Switching clubs wasn't his only transformation. In a move that would have set his father spinning in the grave, Philip converted to Catholicism, becoming an ardent supporter of the Jacobite cause. Participating in unsuccessful traitorous projects that couldn't thereafter be sanitised as a 'glorious revolution', he spent his remaining years deeply in debt – to the tune of £70,000 – on the Continent. Broke and starving, subsisting almost entirely on brandy, he died in a Spanish monastery in 1731. What was left of the

---

* The second of these quotations is actually about a different club, but deemed by all contemporaries to be similar.

Wharton estates and titles died with him. The Hellfire Club, however, was to find an afterlife.

A quarter of a century after the demise of the first club, a new one – that very quickly became known as the Knights of Saint Francis of Wycombe, or the Medmenham Monks – was created by MP and gadabout Sir Francis Dashwood. Allegedly 'the worst chancellor of the Exchequer that ever appeared', 'the most confused, most incapable, and most ignorant of all, who ever accepted the seals of that high office', he made some very unpopular decisions about taxing cider.[6] Underqualified and outmanned, Dashwood perhaps should never have held any high office, but his failure as a minister is not the only reason he is remembered.

As with Wilkes, Dashwood had established his reputation when barely more than an adolescent. Young, dumb and full of fun, 'He roamed from court to court in search of notoriety', acquiring 'a European reputation for his pranks and adventures'.[7] In one escapade, as remembered by Horace Walpole – politician, diarist and son of prime minister Sir Robert – 'accoutred like Charles XII [of Sweden], he had travelled to Russia in hopes of captivating the Czarina – but neither the character nor dress of Charles were well imagined to catch a *woman's* heart'.[8] And when in Rome, 'Dressed as a watchman, he secreted himself in the Sistine chapel before the penitential scourging ceremonies of holy week.' Hiding away, waiting for the moment where the celebrants would participate in their ritualised punishment, he suddenly 'emerged from the darkness at the most sacred part of the ceremony, lashing out severely with an English horsewhip'.[9] The pope was not happy, and Dashwood was lucky merely to face banishment from all the dominions of the Catholic Church.

Returning to England, Dashwood wanted to bring some of the glamour, some of the freedom, culture and spirit back with him. So in 1734 he became one of the founding members of the Society of Dilettanti, 'a club, for which the nominal qualification is having been to Italy, and the real one, being drunk'.[10] But the Dilettanti rapidly became too respectable to satisfy all his impulses, morphing instead into the culture-changing centre for the study of classical antiquities. Happily, the Medmenham Monks were just around the corner and, unlike their more respectable cousins, would never shake off their notorious reputation.

Having rented a ruined Cistercian abbey in Buckinghamshire in Dashwood's name, 'Thither at stated seasons they adjourned', entering through pleasure gardens decorated with imaginative topiary, past statues of gods of silence and passion, and under the sign instructing all visitors to '*fay çe que vouldras*', or 'Do What Thou Wilt'.* They 'had each their cell, a proper habit, a monastic name, and a refectory in common'.[11] The walls of the inner sanctum, denied to all but members, were said to be adorned with pornographic and sacrilegious images. The secrets of their ceremonies were likewise guarded from all but initiates, but not well enough to stop the rumour mill. 'Among other amusements, they had sometimes a mock celebration of the more ridiculous rites of the foreign religious orders', shamelessly declaring '*Peni tento non penitenti*' (roughly, 'With a stiff prick, not with penitence').[12] But when not mocking Christian ceremonial, 'their practice was rigorously pagan. Bacchus and Venus were the deities to whom they almost publicly sacrificed; and the nymphs and the hogsheads that were laid in against the festivals of this new church, sufficiently informed the neighbourhood of the complexion of those hermits.'[13]

As with all great clubs, the Monks attracted some of society's most impressive and influential. The vows of secrecy even now make knowledge of the full membership difficult, but attendees allegedly included Founding Father of the United States of America, Benjamin Franklin, as well as at least eight of Dashwood's fellow members of Parliament. Thomas Potter, when not 'accidentally' miscounting votes as a teller in the Commons was one such. Ironically the second son and heir of the Archbishop of Canterbury (the eldest having been disinherited for an unapproved marriage), he

---

* This, of course, is a familiar refrain, in this instance taken from the French philosopher Rabelais. Although the saying can often be taken as a licence for doing pretty much anything, that would be missing the point. As a more recent 'philosopher' known for using the phrase said: 'Do what thou wilt shall be the whole of the law . . . Love [i.e., higher consciousness] is the law, love under will.' Aleister Crowley, *The Book of the Law* (1904), Laws 41 and 57.

sought solace and release at the abbey, away from his terrible father and – to his mind – even worse wife. Ultimately obedient to his overbearing father's wishes, and happy to get his hands on the £100,000 inheritance, the 'unhappy, miserable beyond remedy' son had married where instructed, despite his heart belonging elsewhere. Again overruled when he swore of his wife that 'I never can nor will live with her; I shall settle her somewhere at a distance', Medmenham was a sanctuary from his torment.*

The most notorious member, however, was the man in the coach now being pulled through the city of London: John Wilkes, whose political campaigns against the government had dragged the Monks into the limelight. By 1762, not only had Wilkes failed to achieve any sort of success in obtaining a ministerial role, but he had also realised that his route to fame and popularity lay not in his oratory – according to one fellow MP, 'He spoke coldly and insipidly, though with impertinence; his manner was poor, and his countenance horrid' – but through his pen.[14] So in June of that year Wilkes had launched his satirical weekly, the *North Briton*, and the enemies started lining up. Some, such as William Hogarth (another possible Monk) – whom he slammed not only for being 'perfectly ridiculous' in his writing and serious works, but also for his skills as a husband and his alleged plagiarism – had their revenge by immortalising Wilkes in cartoon; others preferred more direct means.[15] Lord Talbot, for example, challenged Wilkes to a duel after the latter lampooned the former for his horsemanship – or lack thereof – during the coronation of George III. As part of the ceremony, Talbot as lord steward had to ride into Westminster Hall to declare the monarch's champion, but it quickly turned into a farce as the horse pranced around, backed up and farted against the new king's table. Luckily for Wilkes, the duel with Talbot was bloodless. Even better, Wilkes's charm worked to such an extent that after the contest Talbot 'said

---

* Luckily for him, the time in purgatory was mercifully short: his wife died in 1744, after four foul years of the facade of marriage. Maud Wyndham, *Chronicles of the Eighteenth Century, Founded on the Correspondence of Sir Thomas Lyttelton and His Family* (Boston: Houghton Mifflin Company, 1924) vol. 1, p. 101.

he would declare everywhere that I was the noblest fellow God had ever made. He then desired, that we might now be good friends, and retire to the inn to drink a bottle of claret together, which we did with great good humour, and much laugh.'[16]

Government was more implacable. The first hint that something was seriously wrong came after the furore caused by the forty-fifth edition of *North Briton*, which dared to mock the king's closing speech to Parliament. Libel charges were levelled under an open-ended general warrant. As officers turned up at Wilkes's house, word had spread at the speed of light across the city, drawing supporters in to defend their hero and secure a writ of habeas corpus from a well-inclined judge. All to no avail: within a few hours Wilkes was in close confinement in the Tower while ministers ransacked his house for incriminating evidence.

Still, if the government thought it had finally silenced Wilkes, it was quickly disabused. The friendly judge issued a new writ of habeas corpus and ruled that Wilkes was protected by parliamentary privilege: he should, therefore, never have been detained in the first place. On 6 May 1763, a week after his initial arrest, Wilkes was released and escorted home by a crowd of ten thousand Londoners, all chanting the now-familiar refrain of 'Wilkes and Liberty'. Unwilling to let the matter lie, Wilkes published a letter to the responsible ministers: 'I find that my house has been robbed, and am informed that the stolen goods are in the possession of one or both of your lordships. I therefore insist that you do forthwith return them.'[17] This was followed up by another letter: 'I fear neither your prosecution, nor your persecution; and I will assert the security of my own house, the liberty of my person, and every right of the people, not so much for my own sake, as for the sake of every one of my English fellow-subjects.'[18] He even requested a warrant to search the ministers' properties for his 'stolen' goods.

It was all for nought. When Parliament reconvened that autumn, in the face of custom the ministry pushed its agenda in the Commons before Wilkes could assert his traditional right as an MP and stake his privilege claim. In a simultaneous attack in the Lords, segments of *Essay on Woman*, a parody of Alexander Pope's famous *Essay on Man* that had been intended purely for circulation among friends, were read out to a howling House. Penned by Wilkes, with some help from Potter, it began:

> Awake, my Fanny, leave all meaner things,
> This morn shall prove what raptures swiving brings.
> Let us (since life can little more supply
> Than just a few good fucks and then we die)
> Expatiate free o'er that lov'd scene of man;
> A mighty maze! for mighty pricks to scan.[19]

It continued by comparing Fanny, a well-known courtesan, favourably with the Virgin Mary, and declaring that 'the ass, that had been a noble animal, was . . . disgraced for having carried the Messiah into Jerusalem'. The bench of bishops bayed for blood. One in particular, who had been cuckolded by Potter, foamed at the mouth, his anger almost preventing him from declaring that 'the blackest fiends in Hell would not keep company with Wilkes – and then begged Satan's pardon for comparing them together'.[20]

Having ignored the basic grounds of libel – that a publication must, by definition, be public – the attack on *Essay on Woman* was absolutely without foundation, but by hooking it onto the *North Briton* bandwagon, few seemed to notice. And to add insult to injury, the chief protagonist of the attack was another associate of the Monks – and thus no choirboy himself – Lord Sandwich of the Lunch.

Just to top it off, because *North Briton* was technically anonymous, Wilkes was called 'a cowardly, scandalous and malignant scoundrel' – twice – by the 'trembling with rage' MP Samuel Martin.[21] Needing to prove that his *cajones* were indeed *grandes*, Wilkes privately admitted his authorship and provoked a duel. Meeting at Hyde Park on the morning of 16 November 1763, after a late night debating Wilkes's case in the Commons:

> They brought each a pair of pistols . . . the first fire was from Mr Martin's pistol, which missed Mr Wilkes. The pistol in

Mr Wilkes's hand only flashed in the pan. The gentlemen then each took one of Mr Wilkes's pair of pistols. Mr Wilkes missed; and the ball of Mr Martin's pistol lodged in Mr Wilkes's belly. He bled immediately very much. Mr Martin came up, and desired to give him all the assistance in his power. Mr Wilkes replied that Mr Martin had behaved like a man of honour; that he was killed; and insisted on Mr Martin's making his immediate escape, adding that no person should know from him (Mr Wilkes) how the affair happened . . .

Unable to walk, the bloodied Wilkes was carried home in a chair. Doctors and surgeons were summoned and the ball, which had 'first struck Mr Wilkes's coat button, then his waistcoat button, entered his belly about half an inch below the navel, and sunk obliquely, on the right side, towards the groin', was removed.[22] Wilkes would live to fight another day.

Despite the invalid taking Martin's behaviour at face value, rumour thought otherwise. Martin came from a line of Antiguan plantation owners – whose grandfather had been such a dreadful master that he was killed by the family's slaves – and was not known for his winning personality. Even his biographer wrote that Martin was 'A joyless man, solitary and self-centred, he could not stand anyone permanently near him; he remained unmarried. There was little warmth, sympathy, or loyalty in him.'[23] So it was no surprise that Martin had turned Wilkes's squint, which made him a notoriously poor shot, to his advantage. Nor that Martin had been practising with pistols all summer, after being offended by an edition of *North Briton*, in the hopes of provoking just such an incident. Indeed, it was considered by some contemporaries 'a plot against the life of Wilkes'.[24]

But Wilkes refused to look a gift horse in the mouth. Healthy enough to travel to Paris on 29 December to visit his daughter – and to receive Martin, who had fled there initially to avoid prosecution and who remained to avoid giving evidence against Wilkes – his injuries were too severe, apparently, to undertake the return journey. Consequently, Wilkes could not appear at any of his upcoming trials.

For things hadn't stopped during his convalescence. The Commons had already condemned the *North Briton* as seditious libel and ordered copies to be burned publicly by the city hangman, provoking an entirely foreseeable riot. While Wilkes was away, they had also found against his privilege claim, opening him up to pursuit through the courts. In a debate lasting until half-past three on the morning of 20 January 1764, the House next voted to expel their member, resolving:

> that the said John Wilkes, Esquire, is guilty of writing and publishing the paper intituled the *North Briton* No. 45, which this House has voted to be a false, scandalous, and seditious libel, containing expressions of the most unexampled insolence and contumely towards His Majesty, the grossest aspersions upon both Houses of Parliament, and the most audacious defiance of the authority of the whole legislature; and most manifestly tending to alienate the affections of the people from His Majesty, to withdraw them from their obedience to the laws of the realm, and to excite them to traitorous insurrections against His Majesty's government.[25]

The next month, Wilkes was tried *in absentia* for publishing – rather than writing – *North Briton* and *Essay on Woman*, and outlawed the following November after failing to answer five court summonses. To keep his property, and some income, Wilkes had placed his finances in the hands of a trusted friend, who decided that the best way to look after it was to squander it. The 'friend' was subsequently declared bankrupt – but Wilkes forgave him. On the bright side, he did win his own case against the misuse of general warrants, but couldn't collect the damages because of his outlawry. No wonder he chose to remain on the Continent, primarily in France but also touring Italy, for the next four years.

Profligacy and promiscuity – for Wilkes would insist on finding expensive mistresses – eventually forced his hand. As he apocryphally said, 'What the devil have I to do with prudence? I owe money in France, am an outlaw in England, hated by the king, the parliament, and the bench of bishops . . .

I must raise a dust or starve in a gaol.'[26] So raising a dust is exactly what he did. In February 1768, he returned to Britain and the following month requested a pardon. With no pardon forthcoming, but equally no attempt at an arrest made, he announced his intention to submit himself to the justice of the law courts. And to ensure he couldn't be ignored, he also declared his potential candidacy in the next election. Whether or not 'an outlaw backed by an infatuated multitude' could, in fact, do so was open to debate, but Wilkes was never one for due process.[27]

The Middlesex electorate certainly thought he could. And on 28 March 1768, he was declared one of the two MPs for the county that included the great metropolis of London, winning over 50 per cent more votes than his next closest competitor. Jubilant scenes met his success. Bonfires and candles were lit, and notables stopped in their passing coaches were forced to swallow their pride – or a fist – and toast 'Wilkes and Liberty'. Less enthusiastic Londoners developed a siege mentality, very aware that by not showing due fervour they were asking to have their houses and coaches attacked. The people had shown 'the administration that though they may buy Lords and Commons and carry on their measures smoothly in parliament, yet they are not so much approved of by the nation'.[28]

A pantomime ensued. Before the new Parliament convened, Wilkes, as promised, presented himself to the courts. The government expected to lock him up and throw away the key; Wilkes expected the reversal of all decisions against him. The judge found a middle ground: as he had freely walked into court, he could freely leave it, with no decision being made. But something still needed to be done. A new warrant for his arrest was therefore issued, but it only covered Middlesex, while Wilkes chose to visit a friend in Surrey. Once again Wilkes saved the day by presenting himself to court. This time, the judge refused to grant bail and, on 27 April 1768, Wilkes was remanded in the custody of the King's Bench prison in Southwark.

And that was where Wilkes should have been going in his horseless hackney carriage. Instead, he was being dragged up the Strand, then down Fleet Street, until at last he reached his destination: the Three Tuns Tavern in Spitalfields, apparently. Many times throughout the journey, he had tried to make himself heard above the din; many times he had attempted to tell them that 'I am the king's prisoner and must obey the law'.[29] Each time his 'rescuers' had drowned him out with cheers and chants. Even now, having seemingly secured their goal, they refused to listen. Instead, they turned their attention to the guards, who, deciding it better to escape and live to deal with the consequences, abandoned their charge and disappeared into the multitude amid howls of derision.

Meanwhile, Wilkes took the opportunity of the mob's distraction to seek haven in the tavern. Head down, darting through the door, then wending his way up to the second floor, he opened the window to address the crowd. Even in the fading light of this April evening, he could see it was immense, jamming the streets, jostling and joking, a giant beast with many heads and limbs. But as it noticed its waiting hero, the animal calmed, at last ready to pay attention to its master.

Wilkes took a breath and spoke. He thanked the crowd for their care but begged to be allowed to go to gaol. 'No!' the mob returned: Wilkes was free; they were free; Wilkes and Liberty!

Again and again he pleaded for reason, but the mob was beyond that point. In a bizarre reversal of circumstance, they would stand guard all night; they would keep watch over him; no one would be able to enter. Wilkes would not be able to leave.

So the mob drank and celebrated until late. But by ten in the evening, they were sozzled enough to lose their focus. Making the most of what little chance he had, Wilkes swapped clothes with a fellow drinker, grabbed a different hat, and in disguise sneaked out through a back door. Later still, he recrossed the Thames and handed himself into the custody of the King's Bench. He would remain there for two years.

Not that it hurt his cause. Every day for two weeks crowds flocked to the prison. And then, on 10 May, as rumours swirled that either the government or the mob would release Wilkes for the opening of Parliament, somewhere between fifteen and forty thousand people congregated in St George's Fields, crushed up against the prison walls. The twitchy government responded in the only way it knew how, despatching troops from a Scottish regiment to throw menacing looks at the protesters. The Riot Act was read, ordering the crowd to disperse. It did not have the desired effect: instead of moving the mob on, it enflamed the situation. Words became sticks and stones – and started to hurt. A justice of the peace shouting threats was felled, and itchy trigger fingers flexed. Seven people were killed in the Massacre of St George's Fields, including two innocent bystanders; scores more were injured. The men who had directed the suppression of the protest received a vote of thanks from the now-assembled Parliament.

Wilkes was not summoned to Parliament, but nor was he expelled from the House, even after he was sentenced to twenty-two months (plus two for time served). The hope was that by ignoring him, his fame would fade until he was no more than a half-remembered name. But that was a fate too terrifying for Wilkes. Needing to do something to keep his popularity high, in December 1768 he submitted a petition about the treatment he had received in 1763–4, together with a follow-up newspaper article in which he declared that 'the horrid massacre in St George's Fields had been planned and determined upon before it was carried into execution' by the government itself.[30]

It did the trick. When Parliament reassembled after the Christmas break, Wilkes was expelled from the Commons and a writ for a new Middlesex election was issued. Thirteen days later, the electors of Middlesex gathered at Brentford and let their will be known. The still-imprisoned Wilkes was returned unopposed. The House hated the challenge to its authority. Rather than humbly bowing to the public will, it instead allowed itself to buckle under government pressure, declaring Wilkes incapable of standing at the by-election, rejecting the popular vote, and calling yet another election. There are no prizes for guessing the victor. Nor was the government lucky on the third attempt, with Wilkes polling 1,143 against its own candidate's 296.[31] This time, the ministry simply chose to ignore the wishes of 'the lowest scum' of the electorate and announced the loser as the elected 'representative'.[32] Until there was a new Parliament, heralded by a general election, there would be no further seats for Wilkes to win.

It did not stop the reverberations, however, echoing like thunder through the hallowed halls of Westminster and rolling along the streets of the capital, spreading across the country and bouncing off the hills and vales from places as far distant as Cumberland and Cornwall. The following year the prime minister, the Duke of Grafton, was forced to resign, and government – of whatever ilk – was compelled to confirm the inalienable right thenceforth of electors to choose their representatives.

Despite his significant moral victory, Wilkes was not done yet. Released from prison in April 1770, with his considerable debts paid off by subscription, he instead turned his attention to the City of London, that privileged area of ancient London contained within the old walls. While still in gaol, in 1769 he was elected alderman, and then became sheriff in 1771. All the while he continued to poke Parliament, and in the year of his shrievalty he found the perfect stick.

Parliament had long been precious over the reporting of its debates; indeed, it was strictly *verboten* and so, as with most things parliamentary, the rule was honoured more in the breach. Even so, political reporting had ballooned in response to the Middlesex elections farce, as the wider populus began to flex its political muscles. And Parliament was not happy. Heavy handed as always, it used a thirty-two-pounder to kill this particular fly, issuing warrants against printers and a £50 reward for their capture. It was an exquisite opportunity.

At the heart of the tussle was overlapping privilege: Parliament could question and arrest people for breach of privacy; the City owned the exclusive right of arrest within its boundaries. So when the arrests started, Alderman Wilkes and friends overruled them, releasing prisoners as there was 'no legal cause of complaint'.[33] There was, however, legal cause of complaint to be made against the arresting officers – stamping on the City's time-honoured rights – who were therefore locked up instead. True to form, Parliament responded in the predicted manner: by imprisoning some of Wilkes's brothers-in-arms, including the gout-ridden lord mayor. But no politician was stupid enough to risk yet another riot by arresting the ringleader, and the government instead vowed to have 'nothing more to do with that devil Wilkes'.³⁴ The City thereafter became a haven for journalists and printers, now protected from the jealous House. What had started as a slap in the face of the Commons, in one historian's words, 'proved to be the most conspicuous incident in the history of the freedom of the press'.³⁵ Wilkes's heroic status within the City was confirmed with him becoming lord mayor in 1774 – the same year he won his old seat of Middlesex in the general election. Each year, from then on in, he made the same motion in the Commons: that the ruling over his incapacity to stand as an MP in 1769 be overturned. In 1782 he eventually won his point.

Wilkes once wrote an explanatory letter to his constituents:

> While I live, I shall enjoy the satisfaction of thinking that I have not lived in vain ... and that my name will pass with honour to posterity, for the upright and disinterested part I have acted, and for my unwearied endeavours to protect and secure the persons, houses, and papers of my fellow-subjects from arbitrary visits and seizures.³⁶

He had done a lot more than that: standing up for press freedom, pressing for the rights of the electorate, and fighting for protection from general warrants in most cases. The libertine had fought, and achieved considerable concessions, for liberty. But once Wilkes had won his political game, the radical became conservative. Time and the man had moved on. At last with some financial security, accompanied by more wisdom and experience – and a dislike of some aspects of the younger politicians' new radical agenda – Wilkes was becoming respectable. Throughout the 1780s, he voted more with the government than against it; made use of his old foe, the general warrant, to suppress riots; and was allowed into the royal presence, even joking to George III, when the king asked about the health of a friend, '[H]e was no friend; he loves sedition and licentiousness, which I never delighted in. In fact, Sir, he was a Wilkite, which I never was.'³⁷ By 1790 the mob that had gone against king and Parliament to ensure *their* Wilkes was elected wanted nothing more to do with him: he was forced to stand down without a contest. The second part of the famous demand – 'Liberty' – was, meanwhile, growing louder.

※

Wilkes had been a terrible distraction to successive government ministries. More than that, in his claims in defence of liberty and in his toppling the generally level-headed Grafton, he laid the groundwork for events of even greater consequence. While ministers were busily chasing their tails, and Wilkes, around London, they had been neglecting the storm gathering in the west. For America was not happy. The first rumbles of thunder had sounded across the ocean as the ministry was raising its blood pressure over the *North Briton* case, and the booms had become successively louder thereafter, but it seemed that no one – not even Americans within the Commons – had taken time to consider the flood defences before the surge hit.

John Huske, 'a wild absurd man' who was nevertheless considered to be 'very conversant with America', was one such MP.[38] A Boston merchant who travelled to England in 1748, he had fallen in with the politically active Townshend family before trying his hand as an electoral agent. Yet his tactics of raising the mob, coupled with his veiled and public threats, were so unscrupulous that they embarrassed his friends as much as they angered his opponents. Unsuccessful in this line of work, and hoping, futilely, for a respite from creditors chasing him for fraudulent dealings, Huske next attempted to apply his techniques to his own 1763 election. Perhaps to the surprise of everyone, he won – no doubt helped by his campaign of 'great violence and open bribery'.[39] With Huske now embarking on a parliamentary career, his prospects looked good: his patrons were eager to advance him and when Charles Townshend became treasurer of the chamber, he made Huske his chief clerk and deputy. The political paths of the two men – and of America – would be entangled for the rest of their lives.

Charles Townshend had experienced a difficult childhood. Born into the family of the legendary 'Turnip Townshend', who had forever changed British agriculture through his promotion of turnips in crop rotation, life was nevertheless no bucolic dream. Charles's father, who was as promiscuous as his mother, was cold and overbearing, even banning Charles from playing cricket, believing it a waste of time and money. This strict upbringing, compounded by being forced to choose between divorced parents, made Charles eager to please and consequently a great entertainer, but also fickle and shallow, as he attempted to be something to everyone while prioritising his own interests.

He was not, therefore, known for his probity or sense, instead flip-flopping and performing more about-turns in the Commons than a guard on parade. Indeed, 'he seemed to think duplicity the simplest conduct' and 'neither caring whether himself or others were in the right, only spoke to show how well he could adorn a bad cause, or demolish a good one. It was frequent with him, as soon as he had done speaking, to run to the opposite side of the House, and laugh with those he had attacked at those he had defended.'[40] Nonetheless, this lack of fidelity did not hold him back, with his orations entering the annals as some of the greatest ever heard in the House. His famed 'champagne speech', for example, was a feast for the senses, 'a descant on the times, a picture of parties, of their leaders, of their hopes and defects'.[41]

> Townshend rose, half drunk, and made the most extravagantly fine speech that ever was heard. It lasted an hour, with torrents of wit, ridicule, vanity, lies, and beautiful language ... His variety of tones and gesticulation surpassed the best actor in comedy, yet the faltering of his pronunciation from liquor, and the buffoonery of his humour and mimicry, would not have been suffered in high comedy. Nothing had given occasion to his speech, and there was no occasion on which it would not have been as proper, or, to say truth, as improper; for if anything could exceed his parts, it was his indiscretion ... The whole of his speech was diverting to every man that hated any set of men; it was impertinent and offensive to all it described or seemed to compliment ... Nobody but he could have made that speech; and nobody but he would have made [it], if they could. It was at once a proof that his abilities were superior

to those of all men, and his judgement below that of any man . . . The House was in a roar of rapture, and some clapped their hands with ecstasy, like audience in a theatre.[42]

With skills as great as Townshend's, the ministry made every effort to keep him in the Cabinet, all the while knowing he would cause more problems than he solved. By 1766 he was elevated to chancellor of the Exchequer, tasked with sorting out the East India Company, which was refusing to give the huge tracts of land – the whole of Bengal – it had acquired through 'regime change' to the British government. As negotiations ran on, all sorts of rumours swept the City and Whitehall and, as they did, Townshend jobbed in Company stocks – in other people's names and with government cash. When, in the early part of 1767, his dealings came to light, an irate Horace Walpole wrote to a friend:

> He had dealt largely in India stock, cried up the company's right to raise that stock, has sold out most advantageously and now cries it down . . . In truth, it is a very South-Sea year – at least one third of the House of Commons is dipped in this traffic . . . From the [Exchange] Alley to the House [of Commons], it is like a path of ants.[43]

Townshend had made over £7,000, the equivalent of £16 million today.[44]

Yet neither Townshend's dodgy dealing nor his champagne speech is the cause of his greatest infamy. Rather, it is the duties that took his name – and that provided one of the sparks that set off the tinderbox of American independence.

❋

There were perfectly good reasons to tax the American colonies: after the last excruciatingly expensive war with France, ignited in the colonies by a combined French/Indigenous attack on Ohio, British influence over the land, and thus the areas requiring defence, continued to expand. To Britons groaning under the burden of additional taxes to pay for the war, a glance across the Atlantic suggested that their American brethren were not pulling their weight – even for their own defence. Furthermore, in at least some of the thirteen colonies, state officials appeared almost as hostages to the populace that paid their wages. Combining these issues, the only sensible solution was a tax, the proceeds of which could raise revenue and ensure the 'independence' of Crown appointees. The British ministry's first try was a stamp duty – applied to everything, from legal documents to playing cards, using officially stamped paper – and the resultant shout of indignation could be heard across the ocean. Under pressure from the colonies and the merchants whose trade subsequently suffered, a new government eventually repealed the Stamp Duty Act.

Rather than solving problems, the repeal instead raised a whole patch of thorny issues. Parliament never liked a challenge to its authority – Charles I could attest to that – and America had just thrown down the biggest gauntlet in its history. The principle of the matter was at stake. To Parliament, it was obvious that as the colonies were owned by Britain, where Parliament ruled (almost) supreme, it had a fundamental right to tax and legislate across the Atlantic, just as it did in Britain. It was rebellion to suggest otherwise. But America had refused to play. So, in a display of intellectual acrobatics in which members, led on by colonial representatives, tried to turn their wished-for version of truth into fact, Parliament decided that America's problem was, actually, the imposition of *internal* taxation, rather than of *all* taxation, period.

Townshend thus turned to his friend, the American MP with all the answers, allegedly. Together with Huske, he initiated a new plan to levy *external* duties on a range of imports to America: on glass, paint, paper, lead and, importantly, tea. Despite Huske's assurances that, with some concessions, the duties would be 'perfectly agreeable' to America, another outcry was the predictable response.[45] Angered by the disobedience, but 'afraid of provoking the Colonies too far, lest a rupture should become inevitable', the duties were consequently all repealed – all except the only tax that was commercially favourable to Britain: tea.[46] And when Parliament introduced the Tea Act in 1774 to help the East India Company – which had been wobbling on the precipice of bankruptcy following famine and European-wide financial crisis – dispose of its ever-increasing tea mountain by selling directly to the Americas at discount prices, a storm in a teacup turned into a tornado across a continent. Because not only would cheap East India tea be dangerous to others operating – legally and illegally – in the trade, but Townshend's duties would remain. What had started out as a good deal had instead returned American thoughts to the oozing sore: the oppressive subservience of the colonies to Britain's Parliament.

Resistance started in the great smuggling ports of Philadelphia and New York, where those whose trade was threatened raised the spectre of East India monopolies crushing all independent enterprise, supported by a government determined to assert its will regardless of the consequences for liberty. A campaign of intimidation against any working with the Company backed up the propaganda. As the first shipments arrived in port, the stand-offs began.

But it was to be the 'Sons of Liberty's' Boston Tea Party in Massachusetts that was singled out for punishment by the mother country, as by 1774 the colony was considered a nest of vipers. The first hints were complaints about the British government's attempts to pay Massachusetts officials directly. Then came a series of press attacks on parliamentary sovereignty. Next, alarm over leaked letters from the Massachusetts governor to the British government seemingly suggesting 'an abridgment of what are called English liberties', led to his resignation.[47] With East India tea unable to enter the town (because of unpaid duties) nor sail for Britain (thanks to the intransigence of its governor, a Royal Navy blockade and the quagmire of bureaucracy), the Bostonians started dumping the tea into the harbour as a novel solution to the deadlock. And the British whip that had been poised to strike cracked. The 'Intolerable Acts' – that closed the port from trade, amended the colony's charter, threatened to have rebels tried in Britain rather than Boston, and took control of quartering soldiers away from local discretion – seemed to focus entirely on them. The colonies banded together, an 'illegal' Congress was formed and Britain and America went to war. America would emerge in freedom on the other side, in 1783, as its own, independent country.

Townshend never lived to see the world-changing result of his tax policy, his career cut short in 1767 by 'an incurable putrid fever' at the age of forty-two.[48] Nor was Huske to last much longer. By 1770, as word spread that he was a 'complete villain', he had grabbed as much damning evidence of his multiple frauds as he could and bolted to France – his own soon-to-be-independent country unsafe after the Bostonians had burned him in effigy – to escape the growing heat in Britain. Townshend's widow had been contacted by the government, demanding 'between 30 and 40 thousand pounds due from Mr Townshend at the time when Huske was secretary to him'.[49] Huske had repaid Townshend's favour by stealing government money in his patron's name, and using it to open a banker's shop in Paris. By the end of 1773 he too had died, still at liberty.

For three decades cries for freedom had echoed around Britain and her colonies – be it freedom from sexual restraint and the normal social mores, or for the weightier matters of freedom of the press, freedom from arbitrary arrest, freedom from oppressive government. Choruses of 'Wilkes and Liberty' on one side of the Atlantic sang in harmony with a Virginian statesman's insistence: 'Give me liberty or give me death.'[50] Each was a rallying call, and each had powerful, lasting consequences for the world. For, as Wilkes was turning ever more conservative, a new generation took centre stage, and their demands would be even more radical than those that went before.

Chapter Seven

The Revolting Stage
1775–1806

Dramatis Personae

32. Lord George Gordon (1751–93)

    Ludgershall (Wiltshire) 1774–80

33. Richard Barwell (1741–1804)

    Helston (Cornwall) 1781–84
    St Ives (Cornwall) 1784–90
    Winchelsea (Cinque Ports) 1790–96

34. Richard Brinsley Sheridan (1751–1816)

    Stafford (Staffordshire) 1780–1806
    Westminster (Middlesex) 1806–07
    Ilchester (Somerset) 1807–12

35. Charles James Fox (1749–1806)

    Midhurst (Sussex) 1768–74
    Malmesbury (Wiltshire) 1774–80

Westminster (Middlesex) 1780–84
Tain Burghs 1784–85
Westminster (Middlesex) 1785–1806

There was no disputing it: Lord George Gordon was an oddball. One of those men too fond of his own voice, he could empty a packed Commons in seconds. His speeches, performed with a bizarre combination of hyperbole and tedium, 'operated like a dinner bell', sending men scrambling for the exit.[1] Countless times, over seemingly infinite lectures, members had hinted and then heckled, all in a vain attempt to curb his excesses. And more often than not, in the end they would give up and settle down for a snooze while Gordon prattled on. There was one topic in particular, however, that could guarantee a full night's sleep for any MP who so desired it, and that was the compelling – to Gordon – 'Catholic threat'. Get him started, however tangentially, on the subject and he would be off, spewing vitriol and venom for hours. No wonder members refused to pay attention to his anti-Catholic rants during their debate on whether to increase – to a very limited degree – religious tolerance (with the primary, but unspoken, aim of enlisting more people to fight the Americans, since Catholics were barred from the military). No one took Gordon seriously when he warned that the 'Government would find one hundred and twenty thousand men at his back, who would avow and support' his opinions, 'and whose warmth of spirit was still greater than his was'.[2] Even when the batty lord 'openly declared' that he needed 'a noble army of martyrs, not fewer than forty thousand', to accompany a 44,000-signature petition against Catholic relief to the Commons, the response was limited.[3] So, on 2 June 1780, Parliament was utterly unprepared for what was about to befall it.

Just over twelve years after the London masses had gathered in St George's Fields to demand liberty, a vast crowd – reportedly much larger than the numbers on the petition – met in the same spot, this time to campaign for something much darker. In a show worthy of any official procession,

> Between eleven and twelve, the cavalcade set out (six abreast) over London Bridge, through Cornhill, and the City ... with banner, flags, pennants, etc., and the Protestant petition ... of an enormous size, carried in front of the procession on a man's head, in their way to the House of Commons, where they arrived about one o'clock.[4]

The petition, demanding the continuation of religious restrictions, was duly presented to a shocked Commons. That, members hoped, would be an end of it. But the crowd did not disperse. Instead, they waited. Inside the House, for once members were listening as the mob's leader demanded the immediate repeal of toleration. For once, they engaged, debating the principle while Gordon ran 'every minute to the door or windows', bawling to the populace that the prime minister 'would give them no redress, and that now this member, now that, was speaking against them'.[5]

As the running commentary continued in this most literal sense, the crowd outside grew ever more restless, ever more demanding. Finally, it exploded. A late-arriving MP was noticed, captured by the mob and dragged prisoner to the Guildhall. The just-arriving Lords received similar treatment. One was pulled from his carriage, 'thrown down and almost trampled to death'; another was rescued by the Archbishop of York, who 'flew to his rescue, burst through the crowd, and led him off'; a further bishop had to escape over the rooftops.[6] Others had their coaches demolished; many, determinedly fighting their way into the chamber, at last reached safety dishevelled, missing wigs and bags.

While the Lords fought to enter their chamber, the Commons were wondering how they could ever leave theirs. The room assumed the aspect of a besieged fortress, as the doors were barred and swords readied, while members took action against the traitor within. 'Many members who were there present, justly indignant at his conduct, threatened him with instant death, as soon as any of the rioters should burst open the doors'; others blocked Gordon's access to the windows, preventing him from winding up the crowd further. One MP, 'General Murray ... who, when incensed, was capable of executing the most desperate resolution, held his sword ready to pass it through Lord George's body, on the first irruption of the mob.'[7] For four hours the House remained primed for war, the members shooting looks of murder at the instigator.

Eventually, guards arrived to quell the crowd, and 'the pious ragamuffins soon fled'.[8] The rabble might have moved on, but it hadn't finished. As night approached, thoughts of religion turned to thoughts of plunder, thoughts of violence. Already, some politicians were discovering they had been relieved of watches and snuff boxes, but that was just the prelude. The obvious targets were known Catholics, including foreign diplomats. The Bavarian minister's house and private chapel were raided, the gangs carrying away huge quantities of contraband goods. Turning their attention to the Sardinian minister, 'The mob forced his chapel, stole two silver lamps, demolished everything else, threw the benches into the street, set them on fire, carried the brands into the chapel and set fire to that, and when the engines came, would not suffer them to play till the guards arrived, and saved the house and probably all that part of the town.'[9]

As night turned to day, the rabid gangs dispersed, but hours later they were back. And for the following six nights, the mob ran wild. More Catholic chapels, houses and businesses were attacked, financial institutions – the toll houses and the Bank of England – were targeted, the head of the judiciary's house was burned to smoking ruins, the inns of court and prisons set ablaze. Across the city, at least fourteen separate fires could be counted in just one night, and everywhere 'women and children [were] screaming, running out of doors with what they could save, and knocking one another down with their loads in the confusion'.[10] Darting here and there, trying to quench the flames before another Great Fire could take hold, were the Thames watermen employed by the insurance companies, a proto-fire service. Those responsible for the conflagration seemed not to care that they were wrecking their own city. For 'most of the rioters are apprentices, and plunder and drink have been their chief objects, and both women and men are still lying dead drunk about the streets'.[11]

The innocent citizens did what they could to protect themselves and their chattels. As insurance, households lit their windows with candles in feigned support of the cause. Some families merely packed up what they could and left, trusting to chance the rest of their wealth. Others, with too much to lose to abandon ship, called in help. One Privy Councillor was discovered pacing his house with his sons, charging their pistols. Others went fully over the top: 'The situation of [the once and future prime minister] Lord Rockingham's house in Grosvenor Square carries with it every appearance of its being a seat of war. Every front room of the house is full of soldiers, prepared for the reception of the mob, and his Lordship's stables are turned into barracks, in which troops of cavalry are continually in readiness for action.'[12]

At last, at long last, full regiments of horse and foot began to arrive in London. Riding out from their camp in Hyde Park, these 10,000 armed men subdued the capital. 'Shoot at will' orders were implemented. A shocking two hundred-plus were killed on the spot, with many more injured. Others, mainly young apprentices and servants, would have to wait until after their trials to die. And week after week, month after month, the city lived under the watchful, restrictive eye of the military.

On Friday, 9 June, a full seven days after the delivery of the petition, Lord George Gordon was arrested. He would remain in the Tower until his own trial, eight months later. For 'though he had given out most Christian injunctions for peaceable behaviour, he [had done] everything in his power to promote a massacre': he had bated the horde 'to overawe the legislature, disrupt their deliberations, and obtain the alteration of the law, by force and numbers'.[13] He, however, met a more favourable conclusion than many of the mob he'd led: after just fifteen minutes of deliberation, the jury acquitted him. The government paid heed and, as a direct result, instigating riots became a treasonable offence. Catholics, on the other hand, would have to wait several more decades for political emancipation, and until 1871 to be allowed into the universities.

This brush with death did little to curb Gordon. In September 1781, half a year after his release, he ran again for Parliament. The entire political establishment breathed a sigh of relief when he lost. But he still had more to offer. As the decade wore on, his public speeches and bearing became ever more fantastical, his claims and megalomania more outlandish, his thoughts less rational. Rather like the poor wretches suffering in Bedlam, his strange antics could always attract a crowd wondering whatever he would say next. By 1788 he was imprisoned for criticising the British justice system and for libelling the besieged French Queen Marie Antoinette. Ironically for someone so dedicated to defending the Protestant faith, he died five years later at Newgate, after singing the French Revolutionary *Ça ira*, having converted to orthodox Judaism and still preserving 'with great care, the sanguinary proofs of his having undergone ... one of the most painful ceremonies or acts enjoined by the Mosaic law'.[14]

❋

The chattering classes did not have long to wait to be diverted by another scandal, for over in India trouble had been brewing for a while. With the worsening situation in America, Britain had been forced to look elsewhere for its fortunes, and its taxes. Luckily for the British, although not for the majority of the inhabitants of India, the answer was obvious. After its financial meltdown – during which about 40 per cent of MPs lost money as the share price collapsed – the East India Company was front and centre in the British mind. The government had already tried, and failed, to bring it under direct state control, protected as it was by the pesky rights enshrined in its charter. Nevertheless, in return for a bailout and promised access to the American markets, the state expected some involvement in the Company's regulation, achieved through the appointment of a governor-general and a group of overseers reporting to Parliament. It was a good idea, but it was bound to fail. After all, the government had different aims from the directors: while the former saw tax revenue and strategic value, the latter saw raw profit. However, even if the two London-based bodies could have agreed, they had little control over men intent on making their fortunes 5,000 miles away as the crow flies, a journey of seven dangerous months by sea.

For those so minded, India was low-hanging fruit, where 'a moderate share of attention, and your being not quite an idiot are . . . ample qualities for the attainment of riches'.[15] So every year, thousands of intrepid adventurers – younger sons, minor gentry, the debt-ridden – took their chances in this exotic land. The risks were high: in the 1750s, about two-thirds of Brits who went never returned.[16] But the rewards could be worth it, and the Company base of Calcutta, 'one of the most wicked places in the universe . . . Rapacious and luxurious beyond conception', seemed perfect fortune-hunting territory.[17] Parliament was correct in its concern.

Occasionally the British government got lucky in its East India appointees; sometimes decidedly less so. The first governor-general, Warren Hastings, was a kind and genuine Indophile, who admitted that 'In truth I love India a little more than my own country.'[18] Fascinated by the culture, he learned the local languages, improved the infrastructure and worked hard to tame the excesses of avaricious Company employees. But that didn't necessarily make him popular with his staff. In particular, one man, the 'insatiably ambitious', 'oddly malevolent and vindictive' Philip Francis, absolutely loathed him.[19] In any normal situation Hastings would have shrugged and sent Francis home. This time he couldn't: Francis had been appointed by Parliament to keep watch on the Company. Gleefully determined to abuse his position of trust, Francis greedily set his eyes on the prize of the governorship and made it his business to disagree with everything Hastings did. Report after nasty report was sent back to Britain until, at last, Hastings was impeached 'for all the tyranny, robbery, and destruction of mankind practised by the Company'.[20]

Seven years later, in 1795, Hastings was eventually vindicated at trial, but it had been a long, emotionally draining slog against some of the most forceful voices in politics. Armed with powerful oratory that had crowds of ticketed spectators swooning and sobbing, like the great actors of the day the prosecution plucked at every heartstring while playing *pianissimo* around the falsified facts that supported it. In speeches that would have made Cicero weep with envy, and Shakespeare pull out his quill to take notes, every rhetorical device, every dramatic trick, was used to damn the man in the spotlight. Tears, flourishes, cliffhangers: all were employed for the sole purpose of extracting a guilty verdict. And it didn't help Hastings that in this performance some of his supporters were classic examples of villains.

Richard Barwell was a 'nabob', one of the officials who had worked his way up through the Company amassing an obscene £400,000 in India between 1768 and 1780 (enough to give him almost billionaire status today). It was frequently the case that such men operated in the grey area of legality, not necessarily breaking the law but certainly breaking the rules, and Barwell was no exception. After all, costs were high and official Company salaries low, barely enough to scrape a living for six months. So Barwell quite happily profited from the now traditional sidelines of smuggling precious stones, opium and fine cloths, using Company ships as his own transport.

Where he was exceptional was in his pushing beyond this grey area. While the inhabitants of Bengal were struggling under the worst famine in living memory, with perhaps 20 per cent – 1.2 million – dying in just one year, Barwell was busily, and aggressively, making his fortune.[21] 'Heavy charges of oppression' were levelled against him, with locals deprived 'of their employment and means of subsistence . . . by the terror of his threats, by long imprisonment and cruel confinement in the stocks'. Men were starved, 'severely flogged without reason', and forced to stand outside all day in heavy rain or strong sunlight.[22] Barwell's aim was simple: to extort money and deeds to businesses or property. And given that Barwell was one of the judges tasked with overseeing complaints, there were no means of restitution or compensation. If any other members of the board challenged his practices, they were likely to be challenged in turn – to a duel.

And yet for Barwell, so one friend-turned-enemy explained in *The Intrigues of a Nabob: Or, Bengal the Fittest Soil for the Growth of Lust, Injustice and Dishonesty*, 'Money in general, though not in all cases, seems to be viewed by him in a subordinate degree; and to be valued only inasmuch as it may promote his ambitious designs, or secure to him those sensual enjoyments, which can be found in women.'[23] Power, and its perks, was the thing that Barwell lusted after, and nothing – friendship, honour, the law – would hamper his pursuit of it. So, bribing officials in London with £10,000 (£1.6 million) to secure position was a worthwhile expense, as was inviting a Company overseer to a high-stakes card game at one of his notorious parties, 'hoping, that if he should be so fortunate as to win' he could secure his enemy's 'voice at the board, by releasing him from the debt of honour'.[24] Luckily for the target, in this instance Barwell was unsuccessful, reputedly losing £40,000 (approaching £7 million) in the process.

Admittedly, many complaints against Barwell came from men with their own political or personal axes to grind. The author of the above-mentioned pamphlet, for example, lost his mistress (whom he was passing off as his wife) to Barwell and, as a result of the humiliation and scandal – not to mention the breaking of Company rules – his ability to make his fortune. But it wasn't just the shady or biased who had a problem. Almost immediately on his return to England in 1780, Barwell had begun making enemies in the Commons, offending a committee by refusing to respond to a summons until he was dragged from his house by armed guard. Nor were his future parliamentary colleagues the only ones offended. With Barwell having just moved to Sussex, the inhabitants of the local town threw a ball in his honour, which he assured the mayor he would attend. Instead, he stood them up, with no message and no excuse. This antisocial behaviour was soon compounded by a rigorous campaign against the poor of his estates, cutting off access to their water supplies, blocking paths, and 'doing everything that was illiberal, offensive, and ill-natured'.[25] It did not take long for the neighbourhood to be certain of his arrogance, his conceit and his selfish disdain for the feelings of others. In short, it had not known him a month before it felt him the last man in the world whom it would ever elect to Parliament.* No wonder that, when he sought election to protect his Indian money from enquiries, Barwell was not returned by the local borough he theoretically controlled, but by a remote borough in

---

* My apologies go to every fan of Jane Austen: Barwell could never be Mr Darcy!

Cornwall. It did the trick. Speaking only in Parliament to defend himself, he made sure to vote as often as possible with the government, carefully keeping them on side, and he was never investigated for his crimes. By the time he died, in 1804, he had frittered away the majority of his immense wealth on gambling, art and feasting.

*

There had been one huge attraction in the Hastings trial that had bumped ticket sales to a reputed twenty-five guineas – £4,000 today – and that was the prosecution's Richard Brinsley Sheridan. No wonder, for as one spectator recorded, 'It was by many degrees the most excellent and astonishing performance I ever heard, and surpasses all I ever imagined possible in eloquence and ability.' Praise indeed, but there was more: 'It is impossible to describe the feelings he excited. The bone rose repeatedly in my throat, and tears in my eyes – not of grief, but merely of strongly excited sensibility.' He

> worked the House up into such a paroxysm of passionate enthusiasm on the subject, and of admiration for him, that the moment he sat down there was a universal shout, nay, even clapping, for half-a-second; every man was on the floor, and all his friends throwing themselves on his neck in raptures of joy and exultation. This account is not at all exaggerated, and hardly does justice to, I daresay, the most remarkable scene ever exhibited, either there or in any other popular assembly.[26]

Sheridan was used to the applause and adulation of the crowd. Born into an impoverished Irish family of actors, theatre owners and playwrights who had escaped the violent direction of independent Irish politics by moving to the welcoming bosom of Britain, they had based themselves first in London and then in the party town of Bath. With its well-planned streets lined with grand, neo-classical buildings, and its nightly pursuits and healthsome waters attracting society's great, and not-so-great, it was the perfect place for a man like Sheridan. For the budding playwright and actor had no inclination to be the pineapple of politeness, instead becoming easily ensnared by fine wine and good company, and no more so than by the beautiful young soprano Elizabeth Linley.[27]

Eliza was a Georgian superstar, based in Bath but drawing admiring crowds to her nationwide tours. As one contemporary noted, 'The tone of her voice and expressive manner of singing were as enchanting as her countenance and conversation'.[28] She was just sixteen when she met Richard. It was inevitable that the musical Linleys – her brother was a friend of Mozart – would get on well with the showbiz Sheridans. Richard, as well as his elder brother, was captivated – along with everyone else. At a performance in 1773, eagle eyes noted that the king 'ogles her as much as he dares to do in so holy a place as an oratorio', while 'a late bishop used to say that "she seemed to him the connecting link between woman and angel"'.[29] Sadly for Eliza, her admirers also came from further down the social scale, and that is where her problems started.

From the age of twelve, Eliza had been in the spotlight and, likewise from the age of twelve, she had become friends with a married 'captain' (actually the lower rank of ensign) called Mr Mathews. As the young star recalled to a friend, with perhaps more melodrama than truth, 'Mr Mathews, from the first moment he saw me, resolved to make me his prey, and (child as I then was) left no means untried to make himself master of my affections.' After three years, his designs were nearing fruition, and Eliza was inclined to believe herself in love. But, good girl that she was, she knew the impropriety of such an attachment: he could never be hers, her reputation was cherished and people were beginning to talk. There was, therefore, only one way forward and Eliza, having made a solemn promise to her father, broke off all connection between them.

Mathews, however, had invested too much time in this little project to let it fall. Writing to Eliza, he warned, 'If I did not consent to see him sometimes, he would shoot himself that instant.' She was in a quandary: 'To break my word with my father was impossible. If I did not see Mathews, I expected worse to ensue.' Eventually, with all the drama of a Romantic heroine, 'I came to the horrid resolution of destroying my own wretched being, as the only means to prevent my becoming still more guilty, and saving my parents from still more distress.' Visiting the Sheridans, she rifled through Richard's sister's room for some laudanum – used for toothache – and slipped it in her pocket. The following Sunday, she 'sat down, made my will, and wrote a letter to my father, and one to Mathews'.

But Richard Sheridan had noticed something was wrong. Challenging and questioning her, he at last broke down her guard, and she admitted all. Begging her, at least, to wait until the afternoon, he promised he had information to put all her woes into perspective. She agreed, and he left to fetch the needed evidence. 'But the moment he was gone [I] took half the quantity, and after dinner, finding it had no effect, I took the rest.'

Richard returned only just in time. 'When he came, I was on the settee in a state of lethargy. He immediately ran for the doctors, but before they could give me any assistance, I dropped down, as they thought, – dead. I lay for some time in that dreadful state, till by force they opened my teeth, and poured something down my throat.' Much retching and vomiting later, Eliza had recovered enough to be out of danger. Richard at once showed her his proof: a series of letters between himself and Mathews. The latest was the one to catch her eye and break her heart, for Mathews had admitted that Eliza 'had given him so much trouble, that he had the greatest inclination to give me up, but his vanity would not let him do that without having gained his point. He therefore said he was resolved the next time I met him to throw off the mask, and if I would not consent to make myself still more infamous, to force me, and then leave me to repent at leisure.' Whether Richard had befriended Mathews because, as he told Eliza, he'd used 'a little art to endeavour, if he could, to save me from such a villain', or whether he was just more of a cad than he admitted, is, perhaps, a moot point.

A fainting fit later, Richard and Eliza hatched a plan to escape the tangled web: Eliza should retreat to a convent in France, Richard would accompany her and then return to clear her name. Everything went well to begin with but, according to the editor of her account, as soon as they set foot in Europe, this 'chivalrous and disinterested protector degenerated into a mere selfish lover'. Pointing out how dastardly their running away together appeared, Richard suggested they should marry. With what eagerness Eliza consented to the arrangement it is impossible to tell, but at the latter end of March 1772 they were married near Calais, in a (possibly illegal) Catholic ceremony. Remaining true-ish to Richard's word, the newly-weds continued to a convent, where Eliza hired an apartment. She did not remain there long. Mr Linley, at last stirring himself, had followed the couple and – horrified more for the loss of his star performer than the loss of her maidenhead – escorted the couple back home, completely unaware that his daughter was now Mrs Sheridan.[30]

Mathews, however, still needed to be dealt with. Following the elopement, public insults and cowering excuses issued from the ensign, until eventually Sheridan forced a duel. At six o'clock in the evening, 3 May 1772, the two men and their seconds met in Hyde Park. Many craven hours later, Mathews having found an excuse against fighting at every suggested location, Sheridan followed his opponent to a tavern. There, as Sheridan recorded, 'almost immediately on our entering the room, we engaged'.[31] It was a short battle. Swiping Mathews' sword aside, Richard in one swift move stepped in, caught his opponent's wrist, and rested his blade against Mathews' breast. It was a textbook move, expertly executed. With both swords now in hand and Mathews whimpering like a child and begging for his life, Sheridan – the clear winner – disengaged. But as soon as the immediate danger was over Mathews rediscovered his courage. Provoked, Sheridan broke his opponent's sword and insisted on a public apology.

The worthless man did not keep his word, instead misrepresenting the affair, piling insinuation upon insinuation. Another duel was the only possible outcome. Meeting this time near Bath, the two came together quickly. According to one witness, 'Both their swords breaking upon the first lunge, they threw each other down and with the broken pieces hacked at each other rolling upon the ground, the seconds standing by, quiet spectators.'[32] Mathews was but slightly injured and left the scene in a hurry. Sheridan, however, was badly wounded, although not enough to keep him down for long.

For Sheridan was dauntless and had a dazzling career ahead of him. Finally allowed to marry Eliza properly in 1773, the couple set up home in a little cottage in Buckinghamshire, until the pull of London became too much. Soon writing for the stage, within three years he had bought the renowned David Garrick's share in the Drury Lane Theatre. Fame and applause followed him everywhere, with classics such as *The Rivals* and *School for Scandal* skipping from his pen. By 1794 he had bought the entire theatre and replaced it with a new, modern building – the biggest in Europe at the time. And to add gravitas to his popularity, he sought a seat in the House of Commons.

Or, at least, gravitas was the idea. For no matter how much literary and political success Sheridan had, he never grew up. Throughout his life, he was known for his boyishness, his delight in tricks and jests that could be charming – or irritating – to those who knew him. When, for example, a particularly fine political argument was clinched in the Commons by an obscure Ancient Greek quotation, Sheridan stood to answer it, 'admitted the force of the quotation so far as it went, "But", said he, "had the noble lord proceeded a little further and completed the passage, he would have seen that it applied the other way." Sheridan then spouted something, ... which had all the *ais, ois, ous, kon* and *koss* that give the world assurance of a Greek quotation.' His opponent backed down, admitted Sheridan had the right of it, and congratulated him on his memory. 'It is unnecessary to observe that there was no Greek at all in Sheridan's *impromptu*.'[33] Another time, 'coming very late out of a tavern, he fell, and being too much overtaken with liquor to recover his feet, he was raised by some passengers, who asked his name and place of abode, to which he replied by referring to a coffee-house, and hiccupping – "Gentlemen, I am not often in this way – my name is [abolitionist William] Wilberforce!"'[34]

But this giddy, carefree attitude had its downside. Not only was he irrepressible, he was frequently irresponsible, with chaos and crisis following behind him. Allegedly, for example, on the opening night of his new play *Pizarro*, 'Sheridan was upstairs in the prompter's room, where he was writing the last part of the play, while the earlier parts were acting; and every ten minutes he brought down as much of the dialogue as he had done, piecemeal into the greenroom.'[35] Nor was he more organised when it came to money matters, being pursued frequently for debt, evicted for rent arrears and imprisoned when further bills could not be discharged. Professionally and politically, opportunity after opportunity was missed, letters went unanswered, the salaries of his actors unpaid: 'To-morrow was always his favourite pay-day.'[36]

His reliance on the bottle was partially the cause, once missing an appointment with the king thanks to his drinking 'five bottles of port, two of madeira, and one of brandy' with two friends the night before.[37] He would often turn up to debates in the Commons 'so exceedingly drunk he could hardly articulate'.[38] Even as his theatre burned to the ground on 24 February 1809, landing the already spendthrift Sheridan with extra debts of over £400,000 and no way to pay them back, he couldn't avoid a drink and a joke. 'As he sat at the Piazza coffee house, during the fire, taking some refreshment, a friend of his having remarked on the philosophic calmness with which he bore his misfortune, Sheridan answered, "A man may surely be allowed to take a glass of wine by his own fireside."'[39]

There were only two things about which Sheridan was ever serious. The first was the Irish cause. Like the British Americans, the United Irishmen – so called because they crossed the sectarian divide – had wanted simple liberties and freedoms, such as equal trade rights and an independent parliament, while remaining closely linked with Britain. But thanks to the paranoia and distraction of the government in London, and sectarian and agrarian troubles in Ireland, any hope of a workable, peaceful accord soon faded. Instead, increasingly repressive measures encouraged the United Irishmen to ally with Catholic agitators and revolutionary France. In late May 1798, Ireland erupted in open rebellion. The response was swift and brutal. By September the rebellion was over, with tens of thousands of rebels, loyalists and civilians killed, and within three years Ireland – lubricated with bribes of money and title – had been brought under even tighter British control, the newly 'free' Irish parliament abolished and the whole country merged with Britain to form the United Kingdom. The maintenance of the Union, as a later politician observed, would not be 'by moral agency, but through the agency of force'.[40] Throughout, Sheridan offered support to all caught up in it, speaking on their behalf in the Commons, giving testimony in court, pushing for reform and standing out against oppression.

The second thing about which he was serious, and then only in retrospect, was the love of his life, Eliza. Upon first entering the marriage state, officially, the couple had been almost deliriously happy. They had become the toast of the town, spending indiscriminately, holding lavish parties, dreaming and drinking heavily. But as their debts increased, their fidelity diminished. Divorce was mooted but avoided – despite Sheridan being caught with the governess just after he'd begged for forgiveness – although they both continued their obvious affairs, including a dalliance between Eliza and the later William IV. By 1791, when Eliza began a relationship with Lord Edward Fitzgerald, an Irish aristocrat and United Irishman who later died of wounds received while resisting arrest in the rebellion, the Sheridans were married in name only. The following year, Eliza gave birth to her lover's daughter, Mary. Just a few sweet, short months later, Eliza succumbed to tuberculosis, a guilt-ridden Sheridan attending her to the last breath. Her dying wish was that he accept the baby girl as his own, which was willingly granted. Sheridan became besotted by the tiny creature who looked so entirely like her mother, pouring all the love he might have bestowed on his wife on his adopted daughter. Yet that relationship, too, ended in tragedy, the little girl dying before she was eighteen months old, during a house party held by her father.

By the beginning of the nineteenth century, Sheridan was a fading man. His theatre gone; his wife and adopted child dead, his second wife and string of mistresses not filling the void; his creative juices dry; his wit broken; his parliamentary seat lost; and his income reduced. When he died, on Sunday, 7 July 1816 – exactly twenty-four years after Eliza's funeral – bailiffs were hovering near his bedside, ready to carry him off to prison in blankets. Even after his passing, he was not safe:

On the forenoon of the day fixed for [his] interment, a gentleman dressed in deep mourning entered the house, and requested . . . a last look of his departed friend . . . The lid of the coffin was removed – the body unshrouded, and the death-chilled frame revealed to view. The gentleman gazed for some minutes upon it, and then fumbling in his waistcoat pocket, produced a bailiff's 'wand', with which he touched the face, and instantly declared . . . that he had arrested the corpse in the king's name, for a debt of £500.[41]

It was a more salubrious crowd that packed Westminster Abbey and the streets around it, patiently waiting for the funeral procession to pass by on Saturday, 13 July. It was a performance in its own right, exactly as Sheridan would have wanted. Among the pallbearers and mourners were two princes, half the House of Lords, the bishop of London, and several past and future prime ministers. Richard Brinsley Sheridan, 'the last of the giants', was buried in Poets' Corner. But he would rather have been buried next to his party comrade Charles James Fox.[42]

※

Charles James Fox has to be one of the most remarkable politicians of the late eighteenth century – and not just for extreme hairiness and lack of grooming. Spending only a year in high government office in total, throughout the entirety of his political career he made opposition an art form. He detested George III, whom he blamed for wrecking his political aspirations, and the feeling was mutual, the king believing Fox to be responsible for leading his son, the future George IV, into a debauched lifestyle.

There was good cause for the king's dislike, because Fox didn't live by the same rules as other men. Having enjoyed a faulty degree of indulgence as a child – in 1763, at the age of fourteen, his father, the former paymaster-general Lord Holland, took him to France and paid for both a serious gambling session and a 'lady' to relieve Fox's virginity – he was never able to operate with the necessary restraint. Just a year after the Paris trip, he was asked to leave Eton school for being 'too witty to live there – and a little too wicked'.⁴³ Expulsion did nothing to reform him. On his grand tour across the Continent a few years later, there was a string of women, leading to all sorts of scrapes. Arriving late to meet a friend at Genoa, his excuse was that he had whisked a jeweller's wife off to the mountains with the intention of conveying her to England. Within a few days, however, his infatuation had passed. Returning, he 'made it up with the husband, bought off assassination, and here I am'.⁴⁴ Rumours circulating around Europe, and eventually published in a book in 1785, suggested instead that he had murdered the cuckolded spouse. Along with these escapades came sexually transmitted disease, about which he likewise felt no shame, instead composing witty Latin ditties on the topic for the amusement of his friends. Not until he was thirty-five did he enter into his first stable relationship, with a famous courtesan and former lover of the Prince of Wales, Elizabeth Bridget Armistead. They would later be married – to the shock and disapproval of society.

Women were not his main preoccupation, however:

> From his cradle to his coffin, he was a gamester, without positive avarice, except while he was engaged, from a pure unadulterated love of play . . . Every object he contended for was a stake to be won, and made him, in the hazardous pursuit of it, just as prodigal of honour as of fortune, when he had nothing else to risk or to forfeit. Next to the delight of winning he had none but in losing, and on that desperate principle, the more he lost the better; as if there were some elevation or enjoyment in excess of any kind.⁴⁵

Fox's lifestyle – playful and performative in the extreme – inevitably led to debt. Between 1772 and 1774 Lord Holland bailed him out of gambling arrears to the tune of £120,000 (about £20 million today); between 1781 and 1784 Fox faced bankruptcy twice; in 1793 his friends raised £61,000 to give his finances some stability. When he died, in 1806, he still owed £10,000. Mutterings questioned the wisdom of throwing good money after bad: as Horace Walpole said, 'It is a strange way to correct vice, that of furnishing fresh means to gratify it!'[46] Other gossip thought the sins of the father were being visited on the son. After all, Lord Holland, it was rumoured, had made an illegal fortune out of embezzlement and corruption during his time in the government. It was, therefore, only correct 'that the money . . . should come back into circulation as payment for his son's debts'.[47] That might well be true, but Fox's friends had no such charge to answer, and still they suffered. Those who stood surety for tens of thousands of pounds of debt became liable themselves, forced to mortgage properties and impoverish their own families. One was forbidden to talk to Fox about money without a chaperone. Yet 'Charles bore both the sufferings and resentment of his friends with triumphant and impudent insensibility', and perhaps even more astoundingly, his friends didn't mind.[48]

Nor were they willing to sacrifice only their incomes for Fox, but their careers too. Fox had entered the Commons underage, thanks to some string-pulling by his father, and his fine speeches and quick wit soon started drawing the crowds. Within no time, he began to collect a circle of disciples around him, people who would willingly assume his opinions and arguments on any topic. Devoted to his father, Fox initially bore all the family's political conservatism, attacking the populist Wilkes, and supporting the Tories. These leanings, after all, suited the determinedly Stuart name of the great-great-grandson of Charles II whose family were proud to have served Charles I.* But after the death of Lord Holland in 1774, and the destruction of Fox's political dreams through the machinations of George III between 1782 and 1784, he began to forge his own radical path, supporting civil liberty, religious toleration, an amount of Irish home rule, the attack on Hastings, and American complaints.

But most of all, Fox supported the French Revolution. Believing the French to be following their own 'Glorious Revolution' against oppression, he greeted its initial outbreak in 1789 with praise and admiration.

---

* On his mother's side, Fox was descended from Charles II and his mistress Louise de Kérouaille, Duchess of Portsmouth. It was, however, his paternal grandfather, Sir Stephen Fox, who had served Charles I.

According to Fox's new reformist agenda, Britain's involvement in the Revolutionary Wars was founded upon a dreadful conspiracy between George III and William Pitt the Younger's government, to take the country back to the tyranny of the Stuarts. It was 'the cause of kings': despotism attempting to claw back control.[49] For a while he seemed to have a point. With the country bankrolling its allies, funded in part by a raft of new taxes (including in 1799 the 'temporary' income tax, with the top rate set at a painfully high 10 per cent) that fell 'with terrible weight . . . on the middling ranks of the people', ideas of *liberté, égalité, fraternité* found fertile ground.[50] Social unrest grew and the Navy, the very foundation of British security, mutinied. The government responded in the only way it knew how: the suspension of habeas corpus and a range of new legislation clamping down on dissent and 'sedition', morphing and expanding the definition of 'treason' until it was nothing short of meaningless. The 'Pittite Terror' had begun, and who was to say when, if ever, it might end.

Even as the situation in France gradually, and then quickly, slid into a bloodbath, Fox looked for excuses: although appalled by the massacres of the Terror and the execution of the French royal family in 1793, he considered it reaction to undue outside pressure in the first instance, and Louis XVI's two-faced dealings with the revolutionaries in the second. And even three fruitless meetings with the new Emperor Napoleon Bonaparte following the 1802 Peace of Amiens couldn't convince Fox that France had veered off course. He never considered, as one biographer put it, 'that a man like Bonaparte who achieves power by military force might only retain power by exercising it'. Instead, Britain was 'the only potential aggressor'.[51]

It was only after Fox had become foreign secretary in the short-lived 1806–7 Ministry of All the Talents that the aggressive character of the French regime began to dawn on him, at last realising that 'our bed of roses is not very comfortable'.[52] It might, in a way, have been a small blessing that by the time Fox understood that peace was not possible – that, in fact, his whole career might have been based on false assumptions about revolution and its followers – he was too ill to care. After eating 'his former opinions daily and even ostentatiously', he died on 13 September 1806.[53] His post-mortem showed a hardened liver, thirty-five pea-sized gallstones and seven pints of transparent fluid sloshing around his abdomen. Fox's legacy lasted longer. Not only did he inspire the political mythology that fuelled nineteenth-century Liberalism; more importantly – for him, certainly – his name lived on. Every Whig, from kings to actresses, proudly and prominently displayed his statue or bust, his name was whispered almost as a talisman for any radical cause, and every year for over a century new disciples to his cult would convene in clubs across the country to honour his birthday. Guests were invited to speak, 'the miseries and sufferings of Fox's career would then be tearfully rehearsed' and glasses would be reverentially raised in a resounding toast.[54] To many, Fox hadn't just been the man of the hour; he'd been the man of the century.

Chapter Eight

Officers and No Gentlemen 1802–32

Dramatis Personae

36. Sir Eyre Coote (1759–1823)

    Queen's County 1802–06
    Barnstaple (Devon) 1812–18

37. Andrew James Cochrane-Johnstone (1767–1833)

    Stirling Burghs 1791–97
    Grampound (Cornwall)........................ 1807–08
    Grampound (Cornwall)........................ 1812–14

38. Lord Thomas Cochrane (1775–1860)

    Honiton (Devon) 1806–07
    Westminster (Middlesex) 1807–14
    Westminster (Middlesex) 1814–18

39. William Pole Tylney Long Wellesley (1788–1857)

    St Ives (Cornwall)................................. 1812–18

Wiltshire	1818–20
St Ives (Cornwall)	1830–31
Essex	1831–32

The wars fought against Napoleon during the first fifteen years of the nineteenth century spawned an army of British national heroes. Daring people performing feats of derring-do would become part of the country's consciousness, an integral part of its citizens' collective character, and an essential prop for government. From the Jack Tars of 'Nelson's Navy' to Arthur Wellesley, Duke of Wellington, the man who eventually defeated Napoleon at Waterloo, they all won a place in the pantheon of British demigods – and in the hearts of every living Briton. But mixed in with those rightly hailed as British 'saviours' were those who, while often still protected by government, deserved no such acclaim.

Sir Eyre Coote was one of those men. Starting as an ensign, he had shipped out to America in 1776 and, fighting with distinction at the battles of Brooklyn, of Brandywine, and of Monmouth, New Jersey, had steadily worked his way up through the ranks. Taken prisoner at the Siege of Yorktown, he returned to England in 1782 and served first in his native Ireland, and then against the French in both the West Indies and on the Continent, where he was once again taken prisoner, before heading off to Egypt. By 1802 his distinguished service had given him the honour of a knighthood of the Bath, a seat in the Irish parliament and then, after the Union, a place representing his Irish constituency at Westminster. So respected was he that when he made a request – such as the 'cushty' governorship of Jamaica – it was duly granted. Looking forward to an easy, well-paid life in the tropics, he'd set out with optimism and determination at the end of 1805, arriving in his new province at the beginning of the following year.

It was not to his liking. Despite having land and the slaves to work it, providing a tidy side-profit to top up his official salary, Jamaica was not the dream it had promised to be. For a start, the soldiers and slaves were restless. Writing home, Coote warned of possible mutiny and insurrection, a nervous tic prevalent in societies where a significant portion of the population lives under extreme coercion, but not necessarily a paranoid one, with the last great Jamaican slave revolt of 1760 still in living memory.

Clamour had been growing against the slave trade for decades, accelerated by the new notions of liberty and equality. In 1794 the French had outlawed slavery, before reintroducing it in 1802 under Napoleon. Too late, however, to keep their wealthiest and most productive West Indian colony of Saint-Domingue, which had risen in revolt in 1791 and declared independence as Haiti thirteen murderous years later. For the British, religious objections to slavery mixed with philosophical ones and were cemented by high-profile cases, such as the 1781 journey of the slaver *Zong*, during which more than 130 sick slaves were mercilessly and unceremoniously lobbed overboard in an insurance fraud. But British law, as with British politics, was based on property: accordingly, slaves were considered chattels and so inviolable. And then there were economic problems: Britain's commercial success, and therefore her status in the world, came from the colonies – built on the backs of slave labour. To tamper with the trade, so the planters fretted, was 'econocide'. Nevertheless, moves towards emancipation started being made. In the beginning, there were small steps to improve the lot of slaves, particularly during their desperate Middle Passage from Africa to the Americas. In 1807 the Abolition of the Slave Trade Act – pushed by Charles James Fox, whose funeral monument shows a grateful kneeling slave at his feet – banned British ships from trading in slaves. That, however, did nothing for those already in the system. It would take until 1834 for a partial ban on ownership to be implemented, and a further four years to achieve complete abolition, at a cost of £20 million – £2 billion today – in compensation to the former owners. The slaves themselves were expected to be content with becoming unpaid apprentices, obliged to work forty-five-hour weeks for their former owners for between four and six years – although their 'employers' were responsible for ensuring the 'newly freed' slaves had 'food, clothing, lodging, medicine, medical attendance, and such other maintenance and allowances' as custom demanded.[1]

Yet it wasn't the unsettled state of slave ownership that decided Coote against staying in Jamaica. Instead, it was that his 'health is unfortunately so much impair'd by the effects of the climate', with fevers and headaches his constant companions.[2] So, abandoning his slaves and the natural child he'd fathered upon one of them – whose descendant would, several generations later, be United States secretary of state Colin Powell – he returned ready for his next adventure in the Netherlands, without a backward glance or a stab of regret. By 1814, he was a general and once more an MP, after heavily bribing his Barnstaple electorate.

By 1815, however, he might have wished he'd stayed abroad. It had started off as any normal Saturday morning in November. He got up, breakfasted and dressed, and made his way to Christ's Hospital School in Horsham, Sussex. There, he'd had some conversation with six boys, aged between fourteen and fifteen, and was just finishing up when the school nurse walked in. Next thing he knew, all Hell had broken loose.

Admittedly, it didn't look good. He was, after all, still in a state of undress, hastily buttoning his breeches as she intruded. Scanning the scene, her anger and revulsion were readily apparent as she demanded, 'Who are you and what are you doing here?'

'I am merely a gentleman. I have heard many fine things about this school, and wished to talk to the boys about it. Now, if you will kindly move out of my way and let me pass.'

That was the last thing Nurse Polly Robinson was prepared to do. Quickly locking the door, she swept toward Coote, formidable in that moment. 'You, sir, appear to be no gentleman.'

'You don't know who I am, or what I am. I demand you let me leave, or it will be trouble for you.'

'Who you are I do not care, but what you are I plainly see.' Without shifting her gaze, she instructed one of the boys to run for the porter.

Unable to daunt the nurse, Coote tried a different tack. 'Are you a mother?' he asked. When she replied in the affirmative, he replied: 'I am also a father.'

'Worse and worse!' she roared.

It wasn't the reaction he'd hoped for. Bribery seemed not to work either, the bank notes in his hand swatted away contemptuously. Getting desperate, physical intimidation seemed the only remaining option. 'Hear me, Madam. Let me go, or I will use force.'

'Don't talk to me of force. Before you should go, I would knock you down.'

It never got to a test of strength, as at that moment the porter arrived. Quickly taking charge of the situation, he marched Coote to the steward's office. Still refusing to give his name, it seemed for a second that Coote would be committed to the local prison, but a bit of name-dropping of friends in high places, and the promise to return on Monday, at least spared him that indignity. It did not, however, spare him the subsequent investigation.

As each boy was questioned over the following days, the enormity of Coote's actions became clear: how his visits had been happening for at least two years; how he would conceal his name, and hide away from the sight of adults; how he would enter into conversation with boys, asking them 'how often the master flogged, and if we had any rods', and then, 'if they liked being flogged', and next, 'if any of us would be flogged, he would give us some money'. Paying them half a shilling per two lashes, he would whip them, stopping occasionally to run his hands over the boys' naked flesh, fondling them, slapping them with bare hands. And then, when no further boy would consent to spanking, it would be his turn. He would pull his breeches down, lean against a desk, arse exposed, and encourage them to return the favour.[3]

The school and the local magistracy were appalled, but Coote hadn't actually broken any existing laws. What's more, he had some form of defence to offer up: two of his own three daughters had just died, and his brain, already addled from too much sunshine, was further disturbed by their loss – he said. Admittedly, the authorities would need to overlook the awkward fact that the visits spanned too great a time for their cause to be temporary insanity, and to ignore that 'when the aforesaid discovery occurred, he seems to have had such possession of himself as to be fully sensible of the indecency of the proceeding, and capable of adopting the most grounded and prudent means to avoid further disclosure'.[4] Yet further investigation would bring disrepute down on both the school and Coote, and the more-than-uncomfortable truth was that his societal and military rank was too high for him to be laid low. Instead, the authorities suggested a donation of £1,000 to the school – money that was eventually returned as being inappropriately demanded.

Word did, of course, leak out. The following year, a military inquiry expelled Coote from the Army and stripped him of his honours. If only the same decisive action could be said of Parliament, but Coote remained an MP until the next general election – two years later – despite him having taken refuge on the Continent. And then, when the election came around, the electors of Barnstaple invited him back, pledging their 'best and warmest support' for his 'manly, honourable, independent, and upright conduct'.[5] Wisely, he chose not to stand.

*

It was small consolation to the Army that Coote's dreadful behaviour had not cost the military, or the country, more severely: the war was over, soldiers were already being dispersed and expenditure was being pruned. It was not as lucky with another one of its misbehaving officers. Andrew James Cochrane-Johnstone had seen far less active service than Coote. Joining the Army at the end of the American war, he had served in India before becoming governor of Dominica in 1797. Cochrane-Johnstone, however, took well to the West Indies, quickly settling into a horrific regime of bribery and brutality.

It wasn't that Cochrane-Johnstone easily slipped into the life of a sugar baron, with an estate consisting of about two hundred slaves. It wasn't that he made the most of 'perquisites': raising money for private use on the regimental account, neglecting to pay soldiers under his command, not bothering to provide training or serviceable weapons. Nor was it even that Cochrane-Johnstone abused military authority by targeting resident civilians: James Ryrie, for example, was 'illegally arrested by an armed military detachment . . . confined in a military fort and guardhouse', and 'insulted, beaten, and maltreated'.[6] Another local man, Etienne La Caze, was dragged from his house at pistol point, thrown into a squalid prison, and guarded with drawn bayonets, again for no reason. Instead, it was the way he 'employed or directed to employ soldiers of the 8th West India [Black] regiment in manual labour, on his own lands, and on other works', for his own profit, and 'neither paid nor directed them to be paid for their labour, contrary to his duty, and to the injury of the service'.[7] He had used soldiers, protected and employed by the British Army, as slaves.

Small surprise that the 8th West India – who in 1801 were commended for their honour and gallantry in the capture of the Leeward Island of St Martin, but who were now slogging away in fields, clearing land for Cochrane-Johnstone's ever-increasing estates, draining swamps and chopping trees – finally snapped. On the night of 8–9 April 1802, the company stormed Fort Shirley, took defensive positions on the surrounding hills, and imprisoned the survivors within. Three days later Cochrane-Johnstone marched a newly arrived regiment into the fort, and into a close-range gun fight. Some mutineers escaped, seeking refuge with fugitive slaves in the mountains; many more were mown down. Thirty-four were hanged at court martial.

Recalled by the Army, Cochrane-Johnstone submitted to his own court martial and was acquitted, in theory. In reality, his career in the Army was over, and he would never receive another command. But there were other military uses for a man such as Cochrane-Johnstone. While technically still an MP for the notoriously venal borough of Grampound in Cornwall – until he was expelled from the House in 1808 for having incorrect property qualifications – he used his contacts to become a gunrunner engaged in supplying weapons to the unofficial resistance armies against the French. Guns considered 'totally unfit for service' were procured in Birmingham at 17s. each and shipped to the Spanish junta in Mexico for a cost of 63s. apiece.[8] Bringing back the payment of 3 million Mexican dollars, intended to be donated to the Russians in their fight against Napoleon, he instead filched from the kitty and dabbled in his own smuggling ring. Another time, he filled his ship with Spanish goods as forward payment for weapons that never arrived. In 1808 he was charged with defrauding the Crown of revenues from their newly captured Danish acquisitions in the Caribbean but absconded before he could be punished. With so many fingers in so many pies, he should have been filthy rich, yet he just couldn't keep hold of his pilfered cash, spending it chasing down one bad investment after another. But in 1814, Cochrane-Johnstone pushed his schemes just a touch too far.

Early in the morning of Monday, 21 February 1814, the residents of the Ship Inn in Dover were roused by the sound of knocking. The man responsible, 'attired in a red military uniform with a grey great coat', 'said he had just been landed on the beach from France with the most important despatches that had been brought to the country for these twenty years'.[9] Asking for a chaise and four as soon as possible, he sat down with pen, ink and paper to compose an urgent letter to the port admiral. Once completed, a local boy was found and sent, letter in hand, to deliver it. The message was glorious: that 'the Allies obtained a final victory; that Bonaparte was overtaken by a party of Sacken's Cossacks, who immediately slayed him, and divided his body between them. General Platoff saved Paris from being reduced to ashes. The Allied sovereigns are there, and the white cockade [the badge of the French Bourbon royal line] is universal, and immediate peace is certain.'[10]

As soon as the carriage arrived, the messenger was off, but news of the 'great victory' travelled to London much faster than he ever could. By ten o'clock, it had reached the stock exchange, immediately prompting a boost in shares and government bonds that were raised even higher as reports circulated of 'a post-chaise and four, the horses decorated with laurels, and in it three gentlemen dressed as French officers with white cockades in their hats . . . As they went along the occupants of the chaise scattered little paper billets inscribed with *Vive le Roi! Vivent les Bourbons!* This seemed to give the stamp of certainty.'[11]

Still, a few 'hard-headed, incredulous people' remained unconvinced.[12] Determining to remain doubtful until word of peace and British victory was received through the proper channels, they sent messengers to Whitehall.

The response was not to the liking of those who had invested heavily in the surging stocks that morning: Napoleon had not been killed; Britain was still at war. Frantic selling of those same shares and bonds quickly reduced the market to its pre-opening levels. The only winners, apart from those who had let their heads rule their hearts, were the ones who had bought in the weeks before and then sold while the markets were still high. Among them was Andrew James Cochrane-Johnstone.

It didn't take long for fingers to begin pointing. After all, Cochrane-Johnstone, who was known to be a debt-ridden villain, had made almost £5,000 (£400,000 today) in just a few hours. Indicted for this 'fraud of the most impudent and nefarious description', he once again absconded and made his way back to Dominica via France and Portugal.[13] There he discovered that much of his estate had been sold to satisfy creditors, but still managed to transfer the bulk of his chattels – including his slaves – to Demerara, where he set up a coffee plantation that, like much of the rest of the colony, was swept up in the massive slave rebellion of 1823. His degenerate ways didn't change and he never returned to Britain, dying in France in 1833 – the year that the Abolition of Slavery Act was passed in Parliament.

※

Birds of a feather flock together. Or, at least, that's what the Admiralty and government strongly suggested to the jury that tried Cochrane-Johnstone's nephew, the MP Lord Thomas Cochrane. It is true that he had made about £2,000 out of the rumours of Napoleon's demise, and who could contest an admiral who loudly trumpeted that the whole family 'are not to be trusted out of sight, they are all mad, romantic, money-getting and not truth-telling'?* It didn't help that Cochrane junior was known to be impulsive, once seriously considering blowing up half of Piccadilly to save a friend

---

* The Admiralty had spent ten years chasing another uncle through the courts for embezzling £9,000. Basil Cochrane was cleverer than Cochrane-Johnstone, however, and came away with a further £1,000 after eventually winning the case. Cited in R. G. Thorne, 'Cochrane (Afterwards Cochrane Johnstone), Hon. Andrew James', *HP*, 1790–1820.

from arrest. But possibly the greatest condemning factor, as far as the plaintiffs were concerned, was that for the previous two decades Cochrane had led a one-man crusade against abuses within the military.

Cochrane had always known that he was meant for life at sea, and time was to prove him a fine sailor. In Britain's long struggle against Napoleon, the Navy was its first defence. Not only was it essential for protecting Britain's borders and colonies, it was also necessary for ensuring Britain's life blood – trade – remained flowing while staunching that of France and her allies. So, there were plenty of rich pickings for a man such as Cochrane to hurt the nation's enemies and to line his own pockets, legally, when given half a chance: in one encounter he bested an enemy Spanish frigate four times the size of his own little 'sloop', while a three-month tour off the Azores in 1805 allegedly netted him £70,000 (about £7 million today) in prize money – after the Admiralty had taken their share.

Sadly, he was rarely given that chance. The problem was that Cochrane did not fit well with Admiralty culture. He was cheeky, if not downright insolent, to superiors, and he always thought he knew best. The fact that he was often proven correct did him no favours. To top it off, he couldn't bear corruption, was not afraid of doing an honest day's work alongside the tars – British seamen – and campaigned, constantly and noisily, for naval reform. His behaviour was not, therefore, designed to make him friends in high places, but it did endear him to his crews: one of his many boasts was that, in all his decades of service, he had only ever had to press-gang sailors once – although that incident had landed him in court on charges of assault.

Trouble therefore followed him around like a loyal dog. At a costume ball with French royalists in Malta in 1801, he turned up dressed as a tar only to be told that his costume was not permitted. His good-humoured arguments were met with 'a brusque answer' and a still firmer invitation to leave. Lord Cocky, having none of it, was still stubbornly refusing to go when the master of ceremonies seized him by the collar to march him out, 'in return for which insult he received a substantial mark of British indignation, and at the same time an uncomplimentary remark in his own language'. 'In an instant all was uproar', the unflinching fists of this irate captain gathering a crowd of cheering onlookers to the brawl, which was stalled only when the French watch overpowered Cochrane and carried him to the guardhouse.

Once realisation dawned that Cochrane was no common seaman, they let him free, 'but the officer who had collared' him 'demanded an apology for the portion of the fracas concerning him personally. This being of course refused, a challenge was the consequence.' They met the next morning behind the ramparts. Cochrane was barely scraped as the shot passed through his clothes; his opponent was more seriously wounded in the thigh, but 'not materially hurt'. As Cochrane later surmised, 'It was a lesson to me in future, never to do anything in frolic which might give even unintentional offence.'[14]

Yet it was a lesson that he roundly failed to apply as he continued to confront and challenge authority. In 1809, for example, when his battle plan had nearly wiped out the entire French fleet at Basque Roads, he refused to be included in the vote of thanks issued by the House of Commons – of which he was a member – to the overseeing admiral. Technically, he was right to do so: the admiral, while disingenuously claiming the honour of the victory, had hung nine miles back from the battle and refused to commit any ships, leaving Cochrane and a few lesser vessels to the hazard of (mainly successfully) attacking alone. Politically, however, it was unwise. The ensuing court martial of the admiral, with odds stacked heavily in favour of the defendant, scuppered Cochrane's brilliant naval career: he had, allegedly, libelled a senior officer. From thereon in, he would need to seek his fortune and fame elsewhere.

At least it gave Cochrane more time to pursue his crusade against higher-ups in the Navy and Whitehall. His speeches in the Commons tore into shreds the government's strategy of spending a fortune on propping up tyrannical, but anti-French, regimes with troops on the Continent, rather than better utilising the Navy to blockade and destabilise the enemy. If they didn't want to do this, Cochrane suggested in one particularly noteworthy speech of 1810 – in which the total cost of sinecures and perquisites of government officers was compared with that of payouts to those who had lost their livelihoods and lives in service to the nation – perhaps they could put the funds towards paying decent compensation to wounded sailors and their relatives.

It was after this embarrassment to the ministry that Cochrane was ordered back out to sea until the furore he'd created had died down. He refused, for he still had his own mission to fulfil. Determining to furnish his arguments in the Commons with more evidence, in 1811 he visited Malta as a private citizen to find written proof of the corrupt practices of the local Admiralty board. There was a further motive, however. In the previous decade, Cochrane had experienced directly the board's underhand practices when he'd had to deliver many of the prizes he'd captured to the island. There, he'd witnessed how his portion of the prize money had dwindled (and in one case been wiped out to the point where he was actually indebted to the Admiralty), with officials purloining items and money, charging excessive administrative costs for what amounted to consulting themselves, and excusing other unauthorised astronomical fees listed on a hidden bit of paper – the Georgian equivalent of the modern twenty pages of small print – by explaining that their victims had been pre-warned.

So, he returned to the scene of the board's crime to demand, firstly, a readjustment of his prize money based on the government-approved fees; and, secondly, a copy of the table of fees that should, by law, have been hanging in a public area. Both requests were, of course, denied, but after a thorough search of the premises, he found and nicked the board's table of fees, giving it to a friend for safe keeping.

Just in time. The local Admiralty court, not wanting their practices investigated, sent a line of officers to arrest Cochrane. To the first one he simply shrugged, saying that as the officer was illegally appointed, 'I would treat him as one without authority of any kind, so that he must take the consequences, which might be more serious to himself personally than he imagined.' The good gent thought better of the task and backed away. But others were volunteered. '[T]o the great amusement of the fleet in harbour', officials followed Cochrane around the streets like shadows, but dared not go near him. Resignations followed until, eventually, one man was appointed according to the rule book. Cochrane was at a meeting of naval officers when the newly appointed deputy marshal was announced at the door. Entering without any signal of politeness, he turned to his quarry and declared him under arrest.

'Not without me seeing proper credentials,' Cochrane demanded.

A slightly disconcerted marshal pulled a piece of paper from his pocket and handed it over for inspection. It was just what Cochrane needed: a signature on a document showing that those higher up had been improperly appointed, proving they were illegally holding several positions at once to line their own pockets at the cost of both the Navy and Britain's war effort – proving, indeed, that the whole court could be implicated further in scam and fraud. Cochrane couldn't, therefore, refuse the warrant, but tucked it away and declared everything to be satisfactory.

Pleased to be, at last, getting somewhere, the proud marshal said, 'You will accompany me to an inn, then. There you can remain on parole.'

'I will do nothing of the kind. If you take me anywhere it must be to the town gaol.'

Somewhat bemused, the marshal changed his order, but judging by the faces of the officers in the room, he could tell he was walking into a trap.

'No,' Cochrane retorted. 'I will be no party to an illegal imprisonment of myself. If you want me to go to gaol, you must carry me by force, for assuredly I will not walk.' With a triumphant look he plopped down in a chair and folded his arms, accompanied by a chorus of huzzahs and laughs.

Not sure what else to do, the marshal retreated to summon a carriage. When that arrived, it became blindingly obvious that Cochrane would refuse to board of his own accord, so they next had to wait for a party of Maltese soldiers to appear. Some head-scratching later, Cochrane was lifted, chair and all, carried to the transport and placed gently inside.

His new quarters were not actually too bad, 'the best the place afforded . . . situated on the top storey of the prison, the only material unpleasantness about them being that the windows were strongly barred'. Cochrane was just settling in when the gaoler, 'a simple worthy man', knocked at the door and asked what he would like for dinner.

'Nothing! I thank you, but as you are no doubt aware, I have been placed here on an illegal warrant, and will not pay for so much as a crust. If I starve to death, the Admiralty court will have to answer for it.'

The poor chap looked absolutely aghast. Standing around, not sure what to do with himself, he eventually took his leave and quit the room. About an hour later, he was back. 'I have spoken to the marshal,' he explained. 'An account has been set up with a neighbouring hotelkeeper, to supply you with whatever you choose to order.'

A carte blanche: excellent! 'Good man! In that case, I will have dinner for six brought to me and be sure that whatever is prized in Malta, as well in edibles as in wines, is put upon the table. Anything remaining will, of course, be left to you to dispose of in whatever way you deem fit.'

That, and a note to the hotel master 'to keep his counsel for the sake of the profits, had the desired effect; and that evening a better-entertained party . . . never dined within the walls of Malta gaol'. And so it continued. Day after day, parties of officers congregated to toast Cochrane, 'avenging their own wrongs at the expense of their plunderers'. But it couldn't continue forever. The authorities were, after all, holding Cochrane without charge or trial, all the while keeping him from sitting in the Parliament to which he belonged. Unable to find anything that would stick, they at last tried the simple expedient of asking him to hand back the paper. But even if Cochrane still had the document, there was no way he would do as requested: he was being held illegally and he wanted the fault to be officially acknowledged, so he wouldn't quit prison without a trial.

A trial it would therefore be. On 2 March 1811, over a fortnight since his initial detention, Cochrane accordingly attended the courthouse. The charge: that he had been seen to take the table of fees from the Admiralty court and put it in his pocket. A 'series of interrogatories' followed, the court hoping that Cochrane would somehow incriminate himself. It didn't work. While continuing to claim his innocence, he managed to point out the numerous laws the court had broken. That approach failing, and not seeing any other route for the court to avoid criticism, the judge next asked him to abscond while on bail. Refusing that course, on the grounds that it would be accepting the legality of his detention and therefore turning him into an outlaw, he was returned to prison.

That evening, as Cochrane's friends dined on the best food and wine Malta had to offer, a crisis conference was held. The problem was becoming bigger than a one-man battle against the court. As the most senior naval officer in the room commented, 'Lord Cochrane, you must not remain here; the seamen are getting savage, and if you are not out soon they will pull the gaol down, which will get the naval force into a scrape.' There was, however, another option: escape. This Cochrane readily assented to. After all, an escape denied the right of the court either to hold him or to convict him. Once the basic premise had been set, the details followed smoothly. Cochrane's servant would be supplied with files and rope; Cochrane himself would cut through the iron bars of the window; and a boat would be available on the first favourable night to take him, and his table of fees, to England.

Four nights of bar-filing later, everything was prepared. Holding one 'last symposium at the expense of the Admiralty court', the gaoler was encouraged to drink until he couldn't stand. At midnight, Cochrane made his move. First his bedding, and then he, were lowered from the window. A decent knot – he was, after all, a sailor – allowed him to unhook the rope thereafter, thus concealing the escape until morning. Bidding *adieu* 'to the merriest prison in which a seaman was ever incarcerated', he turned to the harbour where 'several brother-officers assembled to take leave of me'. And he was off. There was uproar the next morning, and in the following weeks, as every inch of Malta was searched for Cochrane. Rewards were offered, but no one – despite most of the port knowing – uttered one word to incriminate him or any of his abettors.[15]

This in itself was a win, but a greater victory was to follow. Upon his return to the House of Commons, 'His lordship ... produced the copy of a proctor's bill in the island of Malta, which he said measured six fathoms and a quarter, and contained many curious charges.'[16] Unrolling it with a flourish, and no small effort – for it seemed to be the length of the House – Cochrane listed all the abuses, all the charges, all the corruption that riddled the foreign Admiralty courts. The information was now part of the public record; the court would have to be more careful in the future.

Stung once again, government and Admiralty bided their time, waiting for the opportune moment to exact their revenge. Their chance came – three years later – by way of Cochrane's uncle's manipulation of the stock market. It wasn't just that Cochrane had made money from the scam – accidentally, so he claimed – it was that a gentleman fitting the description of the messenger who delivered the news of Napoleon's 'death' was seen to visit Cochrane's house on the same day. Upon his honour, Cochrane did what he could to help the inquiry, even divulging the name and purpose of his visitor. But the establishment was determined to bring him down. With a judge and prosecution using every trick to bias proceedings – hearing the defence's case throughout the night and into the next morning, when everyone was too exhausted to string together a coherent sentence; using the single testimony of a criminal who had only just been in court for cruelty himself, and who was later transported to the new penal colony in Australia for theft; sending witnesses who could attest to the truth of Cochrane's story off to sea; amending or ignoring any evidence that ran counter to their purpose – a guilty verdict was inevitable.

Unlike his uncle, Cochrane was in court to receive his sentence: a £1,000 fine, a year in prison and an hour in the pillory – the latter remitted only for fear of London's reaction. Following quickly on the heels of the verdict was the removal of Cochrane's honours, and his expulsion from the military and Parliament. But his Westminster constituents, fond of their man-of-the-people, were having none of it and, Wilkes-style, returned him to Parliament at the by-election.

Armed with the knowledge of his innocence and the support of the electorate, and believing himself to have every right to attend the Commons, Cochrane again escaped prison. Making use of inky night once more, he clambered out of his upper-storey window and onto the roof. Attaching a length of cord between the roof and the spikes of the outer wall, he slowly, hand over hand, pulled his way across the void below. Reaching the wall, and perching 'somewhat discomfited' astride the spikes, another length of cord provided the means of his descent.[17] It should have been easy: he was, after all, used to shimmying up and down rigging. But ships' ropes are sturdier than his bit of cord and, with Cochrane still twenty feet above ground, it snapped. He tumbled the rest of the way, and was knocked out on landing. Coming round, he wincingly checked he was still in one piece: no broken bones, no pools of blood. But it hurt like the devil and standing, let alone walking, was not an option. So, as with all best prison breaks, he crawled to freedom covered in all the filth of the London streets until, stinking and bruised, he reached the house of a family friend.

Four days later – on the same day that Napoleon escaped Elba to begin his final 'Hundred Days' campaign that would end at Waterloo – a letter was received by the Speaker of the Commons: 'it is my intention, on an early day, to present myself for the purpose of taking my seat and moving an inquiry'.[18] On 21 March 1815 Cochrane was discovered sitting patiently on the benches of the Commons. His recapture was, therefore, easy. Refusing to walk once more, 'he was carried out of the House on the shoulders' of the attending constables and returned, now in close confinement, to gaol.[19] It was dreadful: after three weeks a doctor was called, reporting, 'His pulse is low, his hands cold, and he has many symptoms of a person about to have typhus or putrid fever.'[20] With the establishment unwilling to murder a national hero, Cochrane was moved to a slightly better cell for the rest of his term. This one, at least, had daylight.

Finally released after Waterloo and the payment of his fine – using a £1,000 bank note scrawled with the message 'I submit to robbery to protect myself from murder, in the hope that I shall live to bring the delinquents to justice' – Cochrane was then fined an extra £100 for his escape. He refused to pay, and was returned to prison.[21] Once again, the good people of London came to his aid, raising a penny subscription to cover the fine and legal costs. Thereafter Cochrane attended Parliament, reading out petition after petition in favour of electoral reform, insisting that 'the House doth not, in any constitutional or rational sense, represent the nation', and campaigning against corruption and abuse in all its forms.[22]

Nevertheless, in 1818 he announced his resignation from these parliamentary wars, to embark instead upon real ones. Banned from employment in the British Navy, he turned his sights on Chile, helping to liberate the state from the Spanish, while hoping to rescue the defeated Napoleon from exile in St Helena to install him as the new master of South America. The former dictator died in 1821, before the plan could be fulfilled, but that didn't stop Cochrane from fighting for 'freedom' wherever he and the expanding markets for British goods were required, next in Peru and Brazil and then in Greece – often seizing his employers' treasuries to reward his men when payment was not forthcoming – before returning to Britain to continue his own battles.

At the very last, he succeeded. By the time Cochrane died in 1860, he had been promoted to admiral, restored to his honours and was admired by the then queen, Victoria. He was even granted a state funeral. His legend outlived him: the people's favourite, the enemy of malversation and venality who sought to rectify abuses in the Navy and in Parliament, the *loup des mers* and 'one of the most splendid naval commanders that ever paced a quarter-deck'. His daring deeds would be immortalised by Patrick O'Brien in the *Master and Commander* series and by C. S. Forester as Horatio Hornblower.[23]

✺

The Navy wasn't the only branch of the military where corruption reached to the highest echelons, and the lands and seas of Europe not the only fields of action. During the first quarter of the nineteenth century, private wars and public battles of a subtler stamp were waged not only for control of territory, but also for hearts and minds. Perhaps nowhere can this be seen better than in radical MP James Paull's struggle against the Wellesley clan.

Paull liked a fight. Falling in with London's radicals in the first decade of the nineteenth century, he was one of a group of MPs who denounced the whole back-patting, self-congratulating and self-sustaining system, and who would, at length, win reform of Parliament. His battles, however, were not limited to the Commons – although sometimes that's where they started. Something of a serial challenger when it came to duels, he was permanently injured in one arm from a contest fought with an MP in the 1790s and was hit in the legbone after falling out with another MP on the campaign circuit in 1807.

His success at gambling was equal to that of his duelling, once losing £90,000 – over £8 million today – in one night. Needing to refill his bank account, he had gone to India in 1802, the source of his initial fortune. But India was changing. Culturally, there were now many more restrictions, not only on how Britons behaved with each other, but also on how they mixed with the locals. More was to follow as the new governor-general started to make his presence felt. In 1790 the East India Company had controlled only a (comparatively) small part of the subcontinent – less than 10 per cent – but the nationalistic, Francophobic Marquess Richard Wellesley had his sights set on something he viewed as far greater. Just as militaristic as his now-more-famous younger brother Arthur, the marquess intended the whole of India for the British, and as governor-general he very nearly succeeded in his goal. By 1803 Arthur could crow to his brother, 'Your policy and our power have reduced all the powers in India to the state of mere cyphers.'[24] They would remain so for the next 144 years.

As part of his diplomatic manoeuvrings to attain this aim, the marquess needed to appease both the small, breakaway Indian states and the Company directors back in London who, quite frankly, had no idea what was happening half a world away. One of those areas that needed tidying, which nabobs had been exploiting for years, was the practice of private trading with states not fully subsumed by the Company, a practice that was a nuisance to those individual states and to the Company, with British employees pretending to be princes refusing to pay duties, treating the local population appallingly, and running roughshod over treaties and agreements. So when Paull attempted to return to his old ways, he was none too pleased to find those routes now blocked.

Returning home disappointed, Paull pushed for an inquiry – Hastings-style – into the practices of the marquess and another of the Wellesley brothers. He might well have had a case. After all, Lord Richard Wellesley – when not womanising – had been operating what amounted to a racket, demanding protection money, engineering complaints, and goading independent states into war in the hopes of provoking what would later be termed 'regime change'. But Paull's vendetta was personal and treated as such – especially as his lordship was a particular friend of one of the leaders of the Ministry of All the Talents and greatly admired by the Prince of Wales. Despite Paull calling for evidence across 1805, and despite the initial backing of a number of radicals – and their newspapers – nothing was to come of it. Instead, suspiciously as Paull saw it, Parliament was dissolved. With a new Parliament, all the work Paull had done, all the 'numerous facts never intended to see the light', all the articles of impeachment, 'all the proceedings with respect to Lord Wellesley, and . . . all the accusations against him' were destined to fade, never to be pursued again. As Paull wrote, it appeared that the 'wanton aggression and tyranny', the whole conduct of Lord Wellesley towards India and its rulers, 'was such as the government of England approved of'.[25]

In the two subsequent elections, Paull tried – and failed – to win a seat: in November 1806 he lost to Richard Brinsley Sheridan; in May 1807, to Lord Cochrane. With his name blackened and his petitions considered 'false and scandalous', Paull instead sought solace in his habitual gambling.[26] Debts mounted further and, on 15 April 1808, after suffering particularly heavy losses at the table and with his duelling wounds plaguing him, he took a razor to his throat. His final request, 'that his body would be conveyed back to the East Indies and blown up', was ignored.[27]

The two Wellesley brothers may well have escaped censure, but another of the Wellesley clan was not so lucky. In some ways William Pole Tylney Long Wellesley was not like the rest of his family – he hadn't even served in the military. Where his war-hero uncle, Arthur, Duke of Wellington, would rather resign than see an extension of the franchise to include marginally more people in the new-fangled electoral register, Pole – henceforth so called for the sake of convenience – was whipping up the crowds to demand it. And this wasn't the only cause for which he was deemed radical, championing relief for the poor, abolition of slavery and partial religious liberty.

There was, after all, desperate need for reform. Politically, the limited franchise and 'rotten boroughs', where a handful of electors would return two MPs, led to the packing of Parliament with 'placemen' – technically government officials but whose only real responsibility was to support ministers in debates – and therefore a strong bias towards the government. Moreover, the very justice and legitimacy of Parliament was beginning to be questioned: when an estimated 96 per cent of the adult population could not vote at all, and the large industrial areas in the North and Midlands were completely unrepresented, it seemed deeply unfair that some men had multiple votes. By this calculation, MPs could not possibly have the best interests of the population as their guiding principle.

This belief was exacerbated as the country descended into social and economic crisis. Demobilisation at the end of the wars led to unemployment; the economy slumped as demand and purchasing power reduced; bad harvests and the protectionism of the Corn Laws, which banned foreign imports of corn unless domestic prices hit an astronomically high ceiling, created famine and social unrest; industrial and agricultural 'advancement' destroyed livelihoods and communities, and started the rise of the machines. With so much to complain about, it was only natural that the unenfranchised multitude campaigned for democracy, and perhaps only natural too that government would respond in extreme fashion, using soldiers to kill at least eleven and wound over five hundred at the peaceful Mancunian rally in 1819 that became known as the Peterloo Massacre.*

The counterbalance to protest and sedition, as one historian of the period has shown, was 'to expose the government as corrupt in all its branches, to prove that the liberties of Britons were endangered or

---

* The reported numbers vary between sources. David Cannadine, *Victorious Century: The United Kingdom 1800–1906* (New York: Viking, 2017), p. 131.

extinguished, and to persuade people that the only solution was a changed political system.'[28] This is what the reform-minded authors and philosophers, as well as a clutch of politicians, attempted to do, and this is likewise what Pole – and Lord Cochrane – worked towards. It is almost unbelievable, then, that Pole has been described as 'one of the most odious men ever to sit in parliament'.[29] If only he had extended his concern for the faceless masses to his own family.

※

Pole's first wife, Catherine Tylney Long, had everything going for her: youth, good looks, a pleasant manner and, most appealingly of all, an inheritance valued at £1.5 million (plus £300,000 in personal effects). She was the toast of the town, and the sparkle in the eye of the Duke of Clarence, the future William IV. For a whole season at Bath, he assiduously courted her, and a more perfect marriage alliance could not have been imagined.

But in the background there was a Pole-shaped clothes moth, drawn towards Catherine's bright exuberance, flittering around her, pretty enough but damaging when left to its own devices. To Catherine, Pole at first was little more than an amusement, distracting but not to be taken seriously. His perseverance, however, paid off and, despite his avarice being clear to all around, in March 1812 Catherine chose Pole over the future king. With her hand came all her wealth, minus £13,000 per annum 'pin money'.

The honeymoon period was over quickly. By the 1818 Wiltshire election the signs of disharmony were enough that Pole felt compelled to combat rumours of his dissipation and dalliances. *That* election cost him a reputed £32,000 – some of which went on 130 gallons of punch – raised through borrowing at 16 per cent interest on the couple's much reduced income, everything else having already been digested by 'the great yawning gullet' of Pole.[30] It was no surprise, then, that within three years the couple's debts and accumulating interest had forced them to flee to Paris.

That's where Catherine's problems started in earnest. Renewing an old acquaintance with Mrs Bligh – reputedly the natural daughter of Arthur Wellesley, and therefore Pole's cousin – Pole fell into an 'illicit intercourse' with the lady, who moved out of her husband's house and into the Pole family home. The unwelcome *ménage à trois* continued until Catherine put her foot down: either Mrs Bligh would leave, paid off with an annuity from Catherine's private income, or Catherine would return to England. Promises upon his honour flowed freely, but Pole had no honour. In July 1824 Catherine and her three children were back in England, leaving the errant husband shacked up with someone else's wife. Back home, she began divorce proceedings, requesting also that her children become wards of the court as protection from their mercenary father. But Catherine never saw it through to completion: her health collapsed and she died in September 1825 at the age of thirty-five. Her dying wish, perhaps aside from regretting her choice of partner, was that Pole should have nothing to do with the children, who were left in the care of her sisters.

It was a good job Catherine had made preparations, for she was barely cold in the grave before Pole attempted to get his grubby claws into the children, or more precisely into their inheritance. Petition and counter-petition were submitted to the courts, while Mr Bligh launched a case against Pole for criminal conversation. Damages of £6,000 were awarded to Bligh, the entire court rising in applause at the verdict. It didn't help Pole's custody case. Nor, as the judge pointed out, did it help that 'Neither the Duke of Wellington, nor Lord Maryborough, nor the Marquis Wellesley' – in other words, all of Pole's family festooned in military honours – 'think it proper ... that this gentleman ought to be intrusted with the care of his children.'[31] Pole's behaviour towards his wife was shown to have been 'without kindness or affection'; instead he'd treated her 'in an unfeeling and insulting manner, though he was aware that she laboured under a disease in which mental agitation was highly dangerous'. Furthermore, 'the adulterous connection between him and Mrs. Bligh ... implied a total want' of all moral principle. '[L]oose and profligate', he had also shown 'grossly improper conduct ... towards his children'.[32] Under such circumstances, Pole could never have custody.

Mrs Bligh was soon divorced and the adulterous couple married. Yet if the new Mrs Pole Tylney Long Wellesley thought her second husband would treat her any differently from Catherine, she was much mistaken. Within a few years, they too had permanently separated, Pole leaving the former Mrs Bligh to scrape by on poor relief while he frittered away money that by court order should have supported his wife and child. By now unsuccessful in politics, Pole at last faded into obscurity in Manchester, surviving on handouts from the second Duke of Wellington. He died suddenly in July 1857, while eating an egg. The final word on Pole Tylney Long Wellesley could be left to his obituarist: 'A spendthrift, a profligate, and gambler in his youth, he became a debauchee in his manhood, and achieved the prime disgrace of being the second whom the court of Chancery deprived of paternal rights . . . Redeemed by no single virtue, adorned by no single grace, his life has gone out even without a flicker of repentance.'[33]

Pole was reprehensible: the way he treated his wives and his children, the manner in which he chose to live his life, is distasteful now and was scandalous in his own time. Yet arguably he was no worse than the rest of his family – he just wasn't as decorated. He was no hero, and so the country was less inclined to look the other way. It didn't need men like Pole, who appeared the exact opposite of the new national narrative that focused on progress, on victory, on the military, commercial and industrial might of the Empire. Because, with the coming age of Victoria this would be the country's focus, and for the rest of the nineteenth century it would be full steam ahead.

Chapter Nine

Full Steam Ahead
1832–67

Dramatis Personae

40. George Hudson (1800–71)

    Sunderland (Durham) 1845–59

41. John Sadleir (1813–56)

    Carlow (Co. Carlow) 1847–53
    Sligo (Co. Sligo) 1853–56

42. James Sadleir (1815–81)

    Co. Tipperary 1852–57

43. Joseph Myles McDonnell (1796–1872)

    Co. Mayo 1846–47

44. James Thomas Brudenell (1797–1868)

    Marlborough (Wiltshire) 1818–29
    Fowey (Cornwall) 1830–32
    Northamptonshire North (Northamptonshire) 1830–31

For some of the middle class, the Great Reform Act of 1832 really did make it feel as if progress were afoot. Small landowners and substantial tenant farmers were enfranchised, perhaps doubling those with the vote to about 7 per cent of the adult population – although for the first time women were specifically excluded from the franchise – and fifty-six of the rotten boroughs were removed to make way for new constituencies in the counties and industrial heartlands. It wasn't far enough for the Chartists, who emerged as a working-class urban movement thereafter, demanding universal male suffrage, a secret ballot, equal electoral districts, payment of (and abolition of the property qualification for) MPs, and annual elections. But it would take a very long time before their demands were satisfied – we still don't have annual general elections – and the middle years of the nineteenth century continued to see MPs pushing on, feathering their own increasingly industrial nests at the expense of everyone else, even when they had risen from similar stock.

In 1845, when George Hudson won the by-election to the new constituency of Sunderland, he had come a long way from his origins – both geographically and metaphorically. The younger son of a Yorkshire farmer, Hudson had left a local lass pregnant and reliant on payouts from the parish while he had followed his dreams and his feet to the county town. Inheriting first a York drapery business through his apprenticeship and connections and then a windfall of £30,000 from a great-uncle, he was propelled into the first ranks of the city's mercantile community, and it had been full steam ahead from there. Next to come was election to local office, but what really powered him upwards was revolution – not of the French, American or Haitian sort, but of something equally as potent: transport.

For almost a hundred years, methods of travel had been moving apace. From the impassable lanes and the consequent over-reliance on river and coastal transports at the beginning of the seventeenth century, advances had been made and journey times cut. First came the roads. The first turnpike trust was established in 1663, using private funding, toll charging and local initiative to improve routes, and more soon followed. But roads remained limited: vehicles were still horsedrawn, capping their speed and capacity, and travel was still expensive, particularly when taking freight long distances. But enterprising individuals were considering other options, and the solution seemed simple: connect the main rivers with one another to make an extensive, fully navigable network of waterways. In 1759 the first modern canal was commissioned, and within a few short years they had become the primary man-made means of transporting freight.* But there were other methods being developed too. As *The Times* later wrote, George Stephenson's locomotive, first introduced in 1814, was one of the most important inventions of the era:

> Yet for many years this great discovery was but little applied in the country which produced it. In the United States it was seized upon at once, and in a rough way the Americans intersected all the North-Eastern States with railways. Here there was a tremendous conservative influence against it. England was too beautiful a country to be cut up by iron abominations. Railways would ruin the coaching interest, annihilate our unrivalled breed of horses, put an end to hunting and other country sports, produce a democratic mixture of classes, poison the air and destroy vegetation by the noxious effluvia of the locomotives. Almost every nobleman and gentleman was ready to oppose the construction of any such works in his neighbourhood, unless, indeed, he was enormously compensated for the land taken, and then his scruples vanished wonderfully. Our seats of learning and chief schools protested energetically against the sacrilege of bringing a railway within miles of them. The consequence was that for ten years after the principle was scientifically demonstrated the advance made was small: some main lines were authorized, but beyond this all was timid, tentative, and feeble.†

---

* There is, however, some competition (rather like the older Oxford colleges) over which was the first and when it was started.
† Stephenson wasn't, in fact, the first person to invent a locomotive. That title goes to Richard Trevithick, in 1804, but unless you're from Camborne, he tends to be forgotten. *The Times*, 16 December 1871.

George Hudson was none of those things. Seeing an opportunity, he jumped on board. In 1833 he heard about a scheme to link York to the Leeds–Selby line, bought 500 shares, became the largest shareholder and in 1837, after the necessary Act of Parliament had passed, became the new chairman of the York and North Midland Railway Company. More schemes and more companies followed until, by 1844, the newly crowned 'Railway King' controlled over 1,000 miles of track – a whopping 20 per cent of the country's lines.

That same year, president of the Board of Trade William Gladstone attempted to introduce state control to the now rapidly burgeoning railway system. It wasn't just the crazy speculation that was concerning him – by the middle of the century, £250 million had been invested in various schemes – but the growing number of accidents and fatalities.[1] Passenger railway transport had been marred since the beginning: the opening ceremony of the Liverpool and Manchester Railway – the first in Britain to run a scheduled, fully steam-powered, inter-urban passenger service – witnessed two collisions and one death, of MP William Huskinsson. But now, so bad were some of the lines that the satirical magazine *Punch* suggested 'commuting' dates with the hangman's noose to train journeys: the end result would be the same.

Hudson, however, travelled to London and convinced the government to back off. It wasn't difficult to persuade the investigating committee. With over one hundred MPs themselves acting as directors for railway companies, and many more holding some financial interest, there were – once again – too many vested interests involved. Ultimately, therefore, Gladstone's 1844 Railway Regulation Act became more of a gift to the companies than a safety net for the public: anti-monopoly controls were watered down and recommendations to ban members with conflicting interests from involvement in relevant legislation, along with making any future legislation apply to existing railways, were removed completely. But it was a fantastic way for Hudson to launch his career in national politics.

By this point fabulously rich, with an estate in North Yorkshire and, shortly, a gawdy new-build in Knightsbridge (which now houses the French

Embassy), everyone who was anyone flocked to Hudson. 'The choicest aristocracy of England sought his presence. Foreign potentates sued for his society . . . The minister paid his court, and the bishop bent in homage.' Even Madame Tussaud had his waxwork on display. And no wonder, for despite his excruciatingly nouveau-riche manners and unpolished accent, everything Hudson touched seemed to turn to gold: 'in the city he was idolised. When his name graced an advertisement, men ran to buy the shares.'[2] When the Duke of Wellington visited, concerned that a relative had made a bad investment in a company not owned by Hudson, the Railway King started speculating in the same shares, artificially raising the price. Once they'd reached a suitably colossal level, he advised Wellington's elderly sister to sell, making both of them a handsome profit. But a closer look showed that, like the people duped through stock-market manipulation, investors had put their money in fool's gold.

The problem was that Hudson had overextended himself. Growth was achieved only by the promise of more growth, of subsuming more companies and building more tracks, even when no funding was available. It was unsustainable, and the greater Hudson's empire grew, the more it tottered. Desperate to keep rivals at bay, Hudson resorted to underhand practices, utilising his place in the Commons to hold up bills for other companies and bribing fellow members to protect his monopoly, running services at a loss so others couldn't compete, employing agents to dig up dirt on challengers. To keep interest in his own projects high, he promised dividends at 10 per cent. To fund them, costs and corners were cut. Turnover was recorded as profit. Salary and training budgets were slashed and children employed, at a cheaper rate, to work the points, causing yet more accidents. At the inquest into one such fatal collision, the jury found that the driver – who, it seemed, had never kept a job – had received only three weeks' training before being let loose unsupervised.

Answering those criticisms, Hudson claimed he was the victim of industrial sabotage, thus giving him both the excuse to cut salaries further and the kudos of refusing to kowtow to collective bodies of workers: he could now claim that he was not a disreputable business owner at all, but a champion against the trade union movement. When these tricks didn't cover the promised sums, Hudson started drawing on the capital to pay dividends, assuming future acquisitions and income would fill the gap. And the financially minded started to notice.

The more they dug, the more dodgy practices they unearthed. For Hudson had not just resorted to tricks to pay shareholders, but also to line his own pockets. One favourite device was to invest in a new company before amalgamating it into another already owned, falsely inflating the share price and pocketing the additional cash. So, the York, Newcastle and Berwick line discovered that the purchase price of the Great North of England company should have been about £16 a share, instead of the £21 they had paid. After a faltering attempt at denial, Hudson was forced to admit that at least 2,800 of those shares had belonged to him: a quick profit of £14,000 (over £1.5 million today).[3] Caught out, he offered to return the extra with interest, but that was missing the point: it was the principle, rather than the money, that was at stake. Not just this, but false expense claims, raising prices after signing contracts, taking undeclared 'fees', insider trading, profiting from illegal purchases between companies: all these and more he constantly practised.

As evidence built, his world collapsed around him. Unwilling to face his accusers, Hudson sent letters of resignation to his various boards. Never one to avoid the bottle, his drinking became more than usually excessive. Newspapers reported his 'extraordinary and disorderly conduct' as he once again attended the Commons sozzled, while fellow MPs joked that he should join a temperance society.[4] The crowds of people who had flocked around him when at his peak now made no pretentions at friendship. Jokes about him, his wife, his background and behaviour were shouted aloud rather than whispered behind hands.

Required to repay the entirety of the £750,000 he had embezzled, Hudson's debts mounted. His position as MP protected him while Parliament was in session and, luckily for him, his Sunderland constituents did not care about him fleecing the great and the good, returning him to Parliament twice more. But in 1865 he was arrested before the vote was called, spending three months in prison before the loyal raised a subscription providing £600 per annum for him, and compounding his debts. At last curbing his lifestyle to fit his income, Hudson died of angina six years later. At the time of death, 'The former millionaire's effects were valued at less than £200.'[5]

※

Sadly for the good people of Britain and Ireland, Hudson was not the only MP happy to make a killing on the railways. John and James Sadleir were brothers born to a wealthy banking and farming family in Co. Tipperary. Following tradition, by 1839 they had founded their own bank, the Tipperary Joint Stock Bank, with nine branches across Munster and Leinster. Through John's contacts and training as a solicitor, he became chairman of another bank, the London and County, involved in railways with interests as far afield as Italy and Sweden, as well as in a Californian mining company and a weekly newspaper. Not content with merely mercantile pursuits, the brothers turned to politics, helped by the local power wielded through the Tipperary Bank – and their ability to give, or withdraw, loans at whatever rate they fancied – and became the beating heart of the nascent Independent Irish Party or the 'Irish Brigade', campaigning for religious rights and agrarian reform.

Ireland in the 1840s needed all the help it could get. Already poor and struggling under a convoluted and subdivided system of land ownership that gave absentee landowners the lion's share while the majority of rural Irish tenants scraped by with extortionate rents on less-than-subsistence plots, Ireland went into a tailspin when the staple potato crop failed over successive years between 1845 and 1849. As agriculture collapsed and impoverished and spendthrift landlords became unable to pay poor relief, thousands were evicted from what were barely more than hovels anyway: 90,000 in 1849 and 104,000 in 1850.[6] Out of a population of 8 million, about 1 million were to die of starvation or famine-related diseases; perhaps another 2 million emigrated, particularly to the United States. Government, hundreds of comfortable miles away in London, was slow to act. Initial moves, including the repeal of the Corn Laws that caused a monumental split in the Tory-turned-Conservative Party, helped little. When London eventually pulled its finger out, over half of the 'relief' was in the form of a loan that was later remitted in exchange for income tax.* The state was, quite simply, not set up to provide the major levels of intervention necessary. With so many people starving, and the underdeveloped economy battered to within an inch of its life, there was no way the hated new and already overstretched Poor Law system – designed to make relief so meagre that it incentivised the unemployed into work – could function. Tipperary alone had a workhouse population of 1,100 in February 1848, with a staggering 15,000 more surviving on outdoor relief.[7]

But by 1853, John was facing the real possibility of being able to effect change in Ireland when he joined the British government as junior lord of the Treasury, even though a significant portion of the Independent Irish Party ostracised him for breaking an oath not to take an office that was, in their eyes, tantamount to climbing into bed with the devil. But this hoped-for change never came to pass: within a year he was forced to resign. The cause was his 1852 election to the usually Conservative Carlow. During the campaign, one of his rich supporters had doubted Sadleir's suitability and accordingly switched allegiance, taking the votes of his subtenants with him. Vengeance was sweet. John got hold of the man's debt through the Tipperary Bank, had writs of execution drawn up – with the forged signature of a man then on his deathbed – and had his former supporter arrested for debt. Others refusing to vote for John were physically – and spiritually, thanks to the involvement of priests – threatened by a Sadleir-funded mob, or simply kidnapped. The British government hoped to hush up the affair, but the victims continued launching annoying, and vocal, lawsuits. The resultant outcry echoed around the United Kingdom, observers condemning John for 'the most unheard-of and Satan-like plot against the political virtue of Catholic Ireland'.[8]

---

* At least Ireland received something, however. Western Scotland's suffering was just as bad, but the relief was considerably less.

Obviously none of this was good news for John. He did at least retain his business interests – for a while – but the rest of his empire was soon to collapse alongside his political capital. An overdraft of £288,000 had been drawn on Tipperary Bank, bringing it teetering to the brink of insolvency. Debt led to fraud, with forged shares and forged deeds, using seals lifted from original documents. A rush injection of cash – raised on non-existent railway shares – did nothing to support the crumbling edifice. In a final desperate measure, a month before the bank went bust the brothers forged a statement to encourage more people to purchase shares in the defunct business. It didn't help, although it did ruin another round of investors. As the blinkers fell away, the scale of John's losses became clear: £1.5 million, of which two-thirds was spent on disastrous stock-market speculations – including traceable gambles of £120,000 on a failed venture in sugar, £35,000 on a hemp transaction, and £50,000 on an iron business.[9] By 15 February 1856, Tipperary Bank drafts were being refused. It was too much for John.

Just before midnight on Saturday, 16 February 1856, John Sadleir left his house in Gloucester Square, Hyde Park. He had dressed well, with a 'raised silk plush waistcoat, fancy tweed trousers, grey lambs' wool socks, walking shoes, buckskin gloves, black silk neckerchief, and a fancy shirt', finished off with a frock coat and a hat from Christy's of Bond Street.[10] Walking four miles almost due north, he arrived at his one-time favourite watering hole and lodging place of Jack Straw's Castle tavern, on the edge of Hampstead Heath. But he didn't enter, instead turning towards the parkland and making his way 'a considerable distance from the public road'.[11] Settling down on a small mound, he took his hat off and placed it carefully on the cold ground next to him. Then, pulling a silver jug out of his pocket, he emptied into it some powder – opium – before uncorking a bottle marked 'Essential oil of bitter almonds', tipping in the whole half-pint. Perhaps he took a moment to pause, to reflect, to watch the world go by on that lonely February night, before he downed the lethal concoction.

At about ten o'clock on Sunday morning something caught a donkey drover's eye as he searched the Heath for a wayward charge. He didn't have to approach too closely before the shape became form, and he turned on his heel and ran to the local police station. When he returned with an officer, the body of John Sadleir – identified by the helpfully placed note in his coat pocket – was found to be stone cold, hardened by rigor mortis. As the corpse was moved to the nearest workhouse, an investigation was swiftly started, although there was never really any doubt that it was anything other than death by suicide. Indeed, the four notes he'd left for family and friends at home confirmed *felo de se*: wilful self-murder.

Some perhaps saw this act as the coward's way out. After all, his notes made very clear that he knew how heinous his crimes were, lamenting, 'To what infamy have I come step by step – heaping crime upon crime – and now I find myself the author of numberless crimes of a diabolical character and the cause of ruin and misery and disgrace to thousands – aye to tens of thousands.' He couldn't stand to see the consequences: 'Oh, how I feel for those on whom all this ruin must fall – I could bear all punishments but I could never bear to witness the sufferings of those on whom I have brought such ruin – It must be better that I should not live.'[12] But, equally, he was a Catholic – the Catholic Emancipation Act having been passed after bitter disputes and three unsuccessful attempts by a Tory government in 1829 – and a dedicated one at that. And in the Catholic faith, suicide was the ultimate crime – damning the soul to eternity in Hell. He would have known that his body would receive no Christian burial, that it would not be laid to rest in sanctified ground.

Not that his remorse helped those picking up the pieces. For a start, the inquest found him to be of sound mind when he killed himself. As such, he had committed a felony and the state could therefore claim everything he left behind – if, that is, he'd left anything other than misery and debt. But he wasn't exaggerating when he wrote that he had been the ruin of many a poor boy, farmer, tradesman and widow, as well as investors and companies – John Sadleir having 'perfected the technique of insulation by using others in such a way that it was difficult to trace any course of events directly' to him.[13] James Sadleir had cooked the Tipperary Bank's books in an effort to cover his brother's frauds, but the shareholders soon found that they, too, would suffer as they were forced to contribute to a relief fund for those affected. In fairness, the shareholders needed to pay for their laissez-faire attitude, having been happy to sit back, never wondering why the brothers refused every external audit or why they were still paid a 6 per cent dividend, plus a bonus 3 per cent, during an economic crisis.

At least those who could prove that they had previously tried to leave were given something of an easier time – although many still ended up paying thousands in compensation. Even relatives had not escaped, discovering instead that John, acting in his capacity as land agent, had mortgaged their lands, issued fraudulent receipts, understated rents, and bankrupted owners while he spent the proceeds. Any hope of reparation would only come after years of complicated legal wrangling. Indeed, 'Protracted legal battles ensured that the lawyers were the real beneficiaries of the Tipperary Bank crash', for surely no one else was.[14]

James Sadleir, however, was not yet willing to admit defeat. Expelled from the Commons on 16 February 1857 – the first to be so since Cochrane-Johnstone forty years earlier – and with eight counts of fraud and conspiracy chasing him, he escaped to Zurich, surviving on a small annuity from his in-laws. But in June 1881, he stood his ground during a robbery. Unwilling to give up his gold watch, he was murdered.

❄

Understandably, it was not only the Sadleirs who were elected on a platform of Irish rights during this period of industrial and social turmoil. Joseph Myles 'Big Joe' McDonnell represented Co. Mayo for the briefest of moments – between 1846 and 1847 – failing to get re-elected thereafter because of an enormous expenses bill. But more than that, he represented a dying breed: a country gent and landlord of the old tradition, dolling out hospitality and whiskey in enormous measure, fighting against the encroaching cloud of steam and smog, holding on to the old ways of life with a grim and increasingly desperate grip. And in the 'time-honoured' customs of Ireland, he stood up for his country, his religion and his tenants. He sought to improve Catholic rights and the dreadful working conditions in the factories springing up seemingly in every community, to overturn the Act of Union and to repeal the Corn Laws, and to block the Irish Coercion Bill that took repressive measures against anyone with the temerity to complain about starvation during the Famine.

Not that McDonnell was always the strictest Catholic himself. During his election campaign, he 'was caught by a horrified supporter eating meat on Friday'. The news swept round his constituents and before he could say 'Amen' he was being booed. But 'Big Joe was equal to the occasion'. Climbing on stage, ducking eggs as they whizzed past him, he pulled a piece of paper from his pocket. '"Does anyone here", he roared out in a voice of thunder that dominated the tumult . . . "know the handwriting of His Holiness Pope Pius the Ninth?"'

> There was a moment's pause. No one seemed to know the handwriting of His Holiness. Without waiting for an answer, Joe read the letter at the top of his voice: 'My Dear Joe, I am well pleased to hear you are fighting for the old faith down in Mayo. You are neither to fast nor abstain while the good work is in hand. With kindest regards for yourself and the boys that are helping you, I remain, Yours very sincerely, Pope Pius IX.'

'A roar of applause followed the name, and Big Joe was once more the popular hero.'[15]

But this wasn't the reason he was best known. Rather silent in Westminster – mainly because his attempt to smuggle bagpipes into the House was blocked by friends – he was anything but elsewhere. At home, he kept an 'open-door rollicking hospitality', where any guest walking across the threshold of Doo Castle would emerge, possibly days later, crawling, hiccoughing, belching, and with a rather sore head.[16] For McDonnell was a prodigious drinker: rumour had it that he could drink twenty-one tumblers of punch, among other tipples, every night after dinner. As soon as the ladies retired from the table, the men would be locked inside – the key thrown through the window – and subjected to hour upon hour of drinking games, with a 'pint of salt water ... the penalty for refusing a bumper of claret at every round of the decanter'.[17]

It was not, however, a cheap way to live, and 'Joe always abounded in creditors.'[18] Aside from the protection that Parliament gave him, however, there were other, novel ways of avoiding his responsibilities. When a Dublin wine merchant, for example, became a bit too insistent about payment for the canal boat of wine Big Joe had ordered, he was cordially invited to dinner. The usual practice ensued, with the merchant locked inside, happily necking his own wines. He didn't even notice when night turned to day and then back round again. But as the hours wore on and the wine went down, the limits of his endurance were reached, and he began to suspect he would never receive any payment for the shipment. So, making the most of a moment of relative sobriety, he found Big Joe in his study. 'Mr McDonnell,' he said, 'may I have a word with you?'

'Certainly, my dear boy, certainly. Only too delighted.'

'Well, I am a little embarrassed, and you may help me out. I have an order from a very old customer for some of the vintage wines I have supplied to you; unfortunately I have none in stock, so I thought you might perhaps let me have some back. I would allow you of course the full price in your account.'

'That's kind of you, very kind indeed.'

'I would not inconvenience you for the world, but it seems to me that the gentlemen I have met here would just as soon have whiskey punch as those wines.'

'As soon have it!' interrupted Joe. 'They would a great deal sooner have it, if they could get it.'

'Then in the name of goodness, why not let them have whiskey punch instead of costly wine?'

'My dear sir,' whispered Joe confidentially, patting the merchant's knee, 'where do you think would I find the ready money for the lemons?'[19]

Pliable wine merchants were not McDonnell's only concern. Belonging to the class of asset-rich, cash-poor landowners known as 'Sunday men', Big Joe would barricade himself within the confines of his estate during the week – when the bailiffs were active – only to emerge on Sunday, their day off. When he did, by necessity, have to venture out during daylight hours, there was always the risk of being cornered and chased, like a fox gone to ground, into the nearest hole – that safe haven once being the house of the attorney who had issued his warrant. Regardless, thanks to traditions of hospitality, the attorney wined and dined the impromptu guest, and then entertained him at cards until gone midnight. Only after a handsome win did Joe make moves to leave, saying, 'It is Sunday morning now, and I have already kept that poor fellow of yours too long waiting outside in the cold.'[20]

Things never improved. The country was moving on. Populations were abandoning rural areas in droves, heading for the new and growing industrial towns. In England and Wales, the percentage of people living in the countryside had dropped from about 50 per cent of the population in 1850 to only 20 per cent by the end of the century.[21] Over roughly the same period in Ireland, rural population declined from 85 per cent to about 66 per cent.[22] Compounding this, thanks to the Famine and subsequent emigration, the entire Irish population had shrunk by about a third during the second half of the nineteenth century.[23] For landowners such as McDonnell, it was a sorry state of affairs. Their way of life, and their income, had changed forever. When McDonnell died, still in debt, in 1872, the family didn't even have enough money to pay for gravediggers. The job was performed instead by some of their tenants 'out of respect and liking for the big man'.[24]

❄

The British countryside was not the only area changing thanks to the Industrial Revolution. The mastery of steam and new manufacturing techniques also enabled Britain to rule the waves – and extend and control its colonies – as never before. Across the Far East, around Oceania and the Pacific, and down through Africa, the tentacles of British settlement and conquest reached into almost every corner. It really was a case of charging onward – although some in the Army would take it very much too literally.

Lord James Brudenell had undergone the standard training for an aristocrat: a stint at Harrow, then at Oxford, the Grand Tour, followed by time in the Commons (where it took him twelve years to make a maiden speech). From there, he had joined the British Army, rising in the service through connections and purchase. This was also perfectly normal, but the price – reputedly over £35,000 for the command of the 15th Hussars – was not. And no wonder, for he would never have received promotion otherwise.

By nature violent and overbearing, from the start Brudenell had shown 'an injudicious zeal in the enforcement of military discipline', resorting to court martial for the slightest infraction, using it as one of a host of bullying tactics – denying leave, niggly fault-finding, criticising in public, putting unusual and unnecessary charges to officers' accounts and then fiddling others to give the appearance of mismanagement – against men towards whom he took an immediate and immovable dislike.[25] A regimental doctor was reprimanded for leaving church by the wrong gate; one officer was arrested for locking a door and not handing over the key; another officer because Brudenell's secretary had neglected to update a parade time. The latter officer was arrested again, and subsequently court-martialled, for, basically, taking too long to write a letter. At the trial the jury was unimpressed, finding that Brudenell's 'conduct has been reprehensible in advancing such various and weighty assertions, to be submitted before a public tribunal, without some sure grounds of establishing the facts'. His practices – secretly recording private conversations, asking men to report on their superiors – were not just dishonourable, but 'in every respect most dangerous to the discipline and the subordination of the corps, and highly detrimental to that harmony and good feeling which ought to exist between officers'.[26] This judgement, given in 1833, might have ended his career: Brudenell was disgraced, removed from the lists, and put on half-pay. But his friends in high places eventually, in 1836, had him reassigned to the 11th Light Dragoons, who had spent the last seventeen years serving in India.

Despite only spending four weeks of his first two years with the regiment stationed in the North-Western Provinces (now Uttar Pradesh),

Brudenell was assiduous in asserting his particular brand of discipline. Suddenly, the army prison cells were full, 'not one was left unoccupied, and most had two tenants. In less than a month his lordship had eight courts martial and more than a hundred men on the defaulters list'.[27] An old soldier who became tipsy celebrating the news that the regiment would shortly return home was flogged, despite pleas and convention otherwise. That incident encouraged 158 men to volunteer to stay and risk death from disease rather than serve under Brudenell a moment longer. Furthermore, between his 'assumption of command in October 1837 and the summer of 1840, an unprecedented 19 officers either sold out or exchanged into other regiments'.[28]

Things didn't improve upon his return to England. Indeed, they may have become worse, particularly as Brudenell was now Earl of Cardigan. At a regimental dinner, one of Cardigan's officers, Captain Reynolds, had the temerity to order an undecanted bottle of wine for the table. The next morning, Reynolds found he had more than a hangover to deal with. A verbal warning not to treat the mess 'like a tavern or pothouse', delivered through the medium of another captain, soon became a spat, and before Reynolds knew it, he was under arrest.[29] His cousin, another Captain Reynolds, was then cashiered for sending Cardigan a disrespectful note complaining of the commander slandering the two cousins in public.

The press gobbled it up, the story fitting their campaign for military commissions to be granted on merit rather than purchase. Cardigan was a prime example of why the time-honoured practice didn't work. Here was a man who, without skill or experience, by 1840 had been raised to the rank of lieutenant-colonel. He had never seen battle. He had terrorised his officers and soldiers. He had participated in any number of dishonourable practices.

But it could be dangerous to complain about Cardigan in print. After all, he had hunted down the editor of one newspaper and attacked the poor man with a horsewhip. And another instance ended with Cardigan being tried for intent to murder after this letter appeared in the *Morning Chronicle* on 4 September 1840:

Gentlemen,

I feel it necessary to call your attention to the following facts, in which I am sure you will agree with me the honour of our profession is concerned. Lord Cardigan some time since grossly and wantonly insulted an officer at the mess-table (desiring him to hold his tongue); and, when called to account, pleaded his privilege as commanding officer. He again wantonly insulted the same officer, and charges were sent in against his lordship for 'conduct arbitrary, unjust, and offensive to the feelings of a gentleman'; but 'superior authority' declined permitting an inquiry ... Lord Cardigan has now insulted the senior captain of the regiment – *a private insult*; and when called upon for redress, has again claimed his privilege as commanding officer, and placed Captain _____ in arrest for resenting such insult. Many a gallant officer has waived the privilege which nothing but wealth and an earldom obtained for Lord Cardigan.

The Army are supposed to be peculiarly tenacious of their honour, and to regard with repugnance any violation of it. I therefore sincerely trust, gentlemen, that you will aid in calling for an inquiry, and that it may no longer be imagined that a commanding officer may outrage every gentlemanly feeling of those under his command with impunity.

I have the honour to be, Gentlemen,
Your obedient servant,
An Old Soldier[30]

It didn't take Cardigan long to work out the author: former officer Harvey Tuckett, a friend of Reynolds, now working for the East India Company – which, having lost its commercial function in 1833, was now nothing more than a quango for British rule on the subcontinent (until the 1857 Mutiny, when India would come under direct control of the Crown). It was an obvious challenge, and one readily accepted. But satisfaction was not obtained. When the pair met on Wimbledon Common on the afternoon of 12 September 1840, Tuckett's shot went wide. Cardigan's second shot, however, was true, entering Tuckett's body through the hip and lodging next to the spine. He had only just fallen when a local parish constable arrived, placing everyone under arrest, and taking Cardigan's pistols – that had, dishonourably, been secretly rifled and made with hair-triggers to give unfair advantage – into custody at the same time.

The Old Bailey, the Central Criminal Court of England and Wales, did what it could to help Tuckett by throwing out the charges against him. But Cardigan was a peer of the realm and, as such, was too good for any old court of justice. His case was, instead, referred to the House of Lords.

It was a whitewash. Before any witnesses were called, the attorney general stated that he believed 'Lord Cardigan [did not hold] any grudge against Captain Tuckett – any personal animosity, any rancour or malignity . . . I am willing to believe that his only object was to preserve his reputation, and to maintain his station in society as an officer and a gentleman.' The pistols were discounted because the prosecution held 'the most firm conviction that nothing but what was fair and honourable was intended'.[31] But that, ultimately, was neither here nor there. Because Cardigan's defence had an ingenious plan: claim that Tuckett wasn't in fact Tuckett.

With English law insisting on the victim's name being firmly established to prove the indictment, it was a brilliant approach. Every witness, every bit of evidence confirming Tuckett's identity was discounted as circumstantial, denying common sense but remaining true to the letter. Therefore, the only possible way to verify the victim's identity was for Tuckett to give evidence in court, an impossibility because Tuckett would then also incriminate himself – and the charges against him had already been dropped. Judgement for Cardigan could only fall one way – the way he, and his class, chose. Of the 120 peers who stood to give their verdict, only one was brave enough to qualify his answer: 'Not guilty legally.'[32]

Public reaction was predictable. As *The Times*, a usually moderate paper, stated:

The extraordinary termination of the proceedings of the highest court of criminal judicature in Lord Cardigan's case reflects deep disgrace upon the present state of the English law, and suggests very grave doubts as to the manner in which the officers who represented the Crown on this occasion have discharged their duties ... Evidence, perhaps the clearest and the most convincing ever submitted to a court of justice, was produced to show that on the day in question the prisoner had deliberately, and with premeditation, fired a loaded pistol at one of Her Majesty's subjects, and wounded him.

Yet he was acquitted. 'How was this?' *The Times* cried. 'Could the members of that august tribunal be so forgetful of their honour as to conspire for the purpose of shielding one of their order from the consequences of his actions, at the expense of decency, truth, and justice?' 'What earthly difference could it make in a moral or social ... point of view, whether that British subject was rightly or wrongly described in the indictment?' How embarrassing that

> a court of ermined peers paraded before the eyes of foreign ambassadors and distinguished men, who doubtless expected to witness some august spectacle of justice ... might learn how much more important names are considered in British jurisprudence than things; how omnipotent quirks, and quibbles, and pettifogging objections are in Westminster Hall; how infinitely more serious a matter it is with us to preserve the technical rules of evidence and pleading than to vindicate the laws of God and man![33]

'We lament it especially,' they continued the next day, 'because an opinion ... prevails, that in England there is one law for the rich and another for the poor.'[34]

A few in the Commons also felt uneasy. On 13 May 1841 a motion was made 'That a humble address be presented to her Majesty, praying her

Majesty to institute an inquiry into the conduct of the right hon. the Earl of Cardigan, during his command of the Eleventh Hussars, with the view of ascertaining how far such conduct has rendered him unfit to remain in her Majesty's service.' It was glaringly obvious, so the MP promoting the motion declared, 'that the noble earl . . . appeared to labour under a failing which rendered him totally unfit to command others; and that was a total want of command over his own temper.' The facts bore it out: 'in two years . . . the Earl of Cardigan had held 105 courts-martial. In the same two years he punished in the defaulters' list upwards of 700 men. During the same period, 90 men were placed in Canterbury gaol.'[35] The motion was rejected.

And Cardigan continued to be tolerated. Admittedly, he failed – twice – to be elected to the prestigious United Service Club and was refused both the lord-lieutenancy of Northamptonshire and his impertinent requests to join the Order of the Garter. But as Britain and France drifted to war with Russia in 1853 over interests in the failing Ottoman Empire, Cardigan, eager for a first-ever taste of action, saw his chance for glory and snatched it with both hands. Writing to the commander-in-chief, he offered his services and was granted command of the Light Brigade of Cavalry – fittingly on April Fool's Day. But Cardigan's commanding officer would be his despised brother-in-law, the Earl of Lucan. If any man were more detestable than Cardigan, it was this man, who had tyrannised Cardigan's sister until the two separated. These appointments, blind and idiotic, were destined to cause trouble. As one commentator said, the 'moment the government of the day made the monstrous choice of . . . Lord Cardigan as the brigadier of the Light Brigade of the Cavalry Division, knowing well the relations between the two officers and the nature of the two men, they became responsible for disaster; they were guilty of treason to the Army – neither more nor less.'[36]

Not only, then, was Cardigan grossly underprepared for active service in Crimea, he was also appallingly placed. Furthermore, although he was known to be a good horseman, particularly on the hunt, for someone in charge of cavalry he had very little care for horses. As early as his first command, comments had been made about cruelty to mounts as well as their men. Over-long and too-frequent drills had exhausted the horses, turning them weak and thin and lame. The constant rubbing of too-large covers and saddles made matters worse, leaving half the horses of the troop with sore backs.

Cardigan never changed. Encamped in Bulgaria en route to Crimea, he led a 200-strong squadron on a reconnaissance mission. Setting off on 25 June 1854, each horse burdened with 25 stone in weight, across parched plains that offered no solace of shade or water, Cardigan kept his troops out for over double the length of time ordered. In fact, 'because he was enjoying himself', he ignored direct orders to return, prompting two search parties and wasting Army resources in an attempt to find him.[37] Seventeen days and three hundred miles later, they arrived back at camp. As one witness to their return recorded,

> They have . . . lived five days on water and salt pork; have shot five horses, which dropped from exhaustion on the road, brought back an araba [wagon] full of disabled men, and seventy-five horses, which will be . . . unfit for work for many months, and some of them will never work again . . . a piteous sight it was – men on foot, driving and goading on their wretched, wretched horses, three or four of which could hardly stir. There seems to have been much unnecessary suffering, a cruel parade of death, more pain inflicted than good derived.[38]

For that bit of foolhardy machismo, Cardigan was promoted to major-general.

However, the tight discipline Cardigan imposed on his men meant that, outside Balaclava on 25 October 1854, they decided theirs was not to reason why, theirs was but to do and die. Pointed at the wrong artillery, along what any imbecile could see would be a valley of death, the brigade walked, then trotted, then at last galloped 'full steam ahead', unquestioningly, suicidally, with cannon to the right of them, cannon to the left of them, into the jaws of Death.[39]

For hell had opened upon us from front and either flank, [wrote survivor Private Wightman] and it kept open upon us during the minutes – they seemed hours – which passed while we traversed the mile and a quarter at the end of which was the enemy. The broken and fast-thinning ranks raised rugged peals of wild fierce cheering that only swelled the louder as the shot and shell from the battery tore gaps through us, and the enfilading musketry fire from the infantry in both flanks brought down horses and men... 'Close in! close in!' was the constant command of the squadron and troop officers as the casualties made gaps in the ragged line, but the order was scarcely needed, for of their own instance and, as it seemed, mechanically, men and horses alike sought to regain the touch.

We had not broke[n] into the charging pace when poor old John Lee, my right-hand man on the flank of the regiment, was all but smashed by a shell; he gave my arm a twitch, as with a strange smile on his worn old face he quietly said, 'Domino! Chum', and fell out of the saddle. His old grey mare kept alongside of me for some distance, treading on and tearing out her entrails as she galloped, till at length she dropped with a strange shriek.... It was about this time that Sergeant Talbot had his head clean carried off by a round shot, yet for about thirty yards further the headless body kept the saddle, the lance at the charge firmly gripped under the right arm.

... I saw Captain White go down and Cardigan disappear into the smoke. A moment more and I was within it myself. A shell burst right over my head with a hellish crash that all but stunned me. Immediately after I felt my horse under me take a tremendous leap into the air. What he jumped I never saw or knew; the smoke was so thick I could not see my arm's length around me. Through the dense veil I heard noises of fighting and slaughter, but saw no obstacle, no adversary, no gun or gunner, and, in short, was through and beyond the Russian battery before I knew for certain that I had reached it.

Over more minutes that felt like hours, they managed to capture the guns. But the cannon could not be held. There were simply too many Russians, and too few survivors of that first, crazy charge.

> we were all . . . wearied and weakened by loss of blood; our horses wounded in many places; there were enemies all about us, and we thought it was about time to be getting back. I remember reading in the regimental library of an officer who said to his commander 'We have done enough for honour'. That was our humble opinion too, and we turned our horses' heads.

Surviving the gauntlet once was a miracle, but those men now fleeing had to take their chances again. Some made it all the way back to the British lines. Private Wightman, however, did not. His horse, 'riddled with bullets' at last could take no more, dying during the second run. Wightman, already injured in the knee, had taken more bullets across the forehead and through his shoulder. Now, struggling to free himself from the deadweight of his fallen steed, he was attacked by a Cossack, who 'stabbed me with his lance once in the neck near the jugular, again above the collarbone, several times in the back, and once under the short rib; and . . . through the palm of my hand'. Luckily for Wightman, he was taken prisoner and survived his wounds. Many others did not, including the man who, with a bullet lodged in the back of his head, had carried him on their forced march to the Russian camp.[40]

Out of the 670 men of the Light Brigade who had started the charge, each mounted, 158 men and 335 horses had been killed or captured; a further 120 men had been grievously injured.* The charge was futile; the battle a strategic defeat that had no impact on the outcome of the war that ended, in 1856, with a victory for the British, French and Turks. Unlike many of his men, Cardigan had not tarried long at the front. Perhaps

---

* No one can agree on the actual numbers. These are those given in the Official Return. See the discussion in David, *The Homicidal Earl*, p. 415.

realising, at last, that glory in war was not all it was cracked up to be, he retreated before the brigade had even reached the guns and immediately launched into tirades about his officers' insubordination. The 'hero', who demanded unthinking loyalty and obedience, valued his own life far above those of the brave men before him. Nevertheless, he was initially worshipped back in Britain, where he continued as he always had: intolerant, bad tempered, extravagant. When he died, from injuries sustained falling from his horse, he left over £300,000 of debt. He also left a legacy, and a taste of what would come next: of a nation pushing forward without forethought or control, and an example that, given the right connections and an outward show of virtue, the powerful could evade censure in many a circumstance.

Chapter Ten

'Rule by Virtue'
1867–1910

Dramatis Personae

45. Benjamin Disraeli (1804–81)

    Maidstone (Kent) … … … … … … … … … … … 1837–41
    Shrewsbury (Shropshire) … … … … … … … … 1841–47
    Buckinghamshire … … … … … … … … … … … 1847–76

46. Sir Edward Bulwer-Lytton (1803–73)

    Lincoln (Lincolnshire) … … … … … … … … … 1832–41
    Hertfordshire … … … … … … … … … … … … 1852–66

47. William Ewart Gladstone (1809–98)

    Newark-on-Trent (Nottinghamshire) … … … … 1832–45
    Oxford University (Oxfordshire) … … … … … 1847–65
    Lancashire Southern … … … … … … … … … … 1865–68
    Greenwich (Kent) … … … … … … … … … … … 1868–80
    Midlothian … … … … … … … … … … … … … 1880–95

48. Henry Labouchère (1831–1912)

Windsor (Berkshire) 1865–66
Middlesex 1867–68
Northampton (Northamptonshire) 1880–1906

Benjamin Disraeli was not your usual Victorian Conservative politician. An upfront fun-loving, philandering, Byron-worshipping novelist with homosexual leanings, 'Dizzy' was the grandson of a Jewish Italian immigrant and was bullied mercilessly as a child. But it seemed not to do him any harm. Without the benefit of public schooling or university education, he had nevertheless clawed his way up through politics, climbing over both self-inflicted hurdles and popular prejudice with a remarkable, determined self-confidence, to become worshipped as one of the great men of the age.

And what hurdles they were. Already an outsider, he had been baptised at nine to escape restraints placed on Jews, but his eagerness to advance – one could almost call it his sense of destiny – had turned the precocious puppy into an oddity, even in the cut-throat worlds of his chosen professions: literature and politics. As a young man, his renowned verbal 'hits' accompanied by a 'surprising disdain for the law of libel', had led to duelling challenges and court cases aplenty but few respectable allies.[1] Nor had he helped himself by his infatuation with other men's wives, for – as he wrote – 'there is no fascination so irresistible to a boy as the smile of a married woman'.[2] Following his heart rather than his head, he formed attachments to all manner of inappropriate people: the wives of doctors, of lawyers and of family friends.

In literary circles, a certain disrespect for societal norms could be expected, but by 1832 Dizzy was exploring a career in politics, attracted by the shifting sands of reform and the promise of acclaim, and a politician should always have an outward show of virtue. It was not, therefore, the done thing to share a mistress with a prospective political patron, regardless of how much access it gave him to the politicos and need-to-knows, or to party funding. Nevertheless, by 1837 the new connections had given him the necessary leg-up – at the expense of his lover's reputation, which finally crumbled absolutely when she switched her affections to an Irish painter.

Glory was not the only draw of politics, however, for Dizzy was dizzy about finance. The Commons, of course, brought protection from debt, and office brought both salary and pension, something he sorely needed. It had begun in 1825 when, believing money was power, he had dug into the mania for South American mining. Investing heavily with borrowed money, and publishing pamphlets at his own expense that scoffed at the nay-sayers, he lost everything when the companies turned out to be chimeras, existing only on paper. Still, he didn't learn his lesson. More money was borrowed as he turned to railway speculation and, fantastically, punts on 'Swedish turnips' and 'Naples biscuits' to make his millions.[3] Each project sank without a trace.

Yet despite his straitened circumstances, Dizzy didn't stop spending, on prostitutes, on 'peacock finery', and on foreign travel.[4] In 1830–31, for example, he had splashed out on a tour of the Near East, where he smoked kif, caught venereal disease and delighted in 'being made much of by a man who was daily decapitating half the province'.[5] He strove to catch attention, and he succeeded, his consumptive-chic pallor contrasting with 'a thick heavy mass of jet black ringlets' and 'gorgeous gold flowers of a splendidly embroidered waistcoat. Patent leather pumps, a white stick, with a black cord and tassel, and a quantity of chains about his neck and pockets, served to make him, even in the dim light, rather a conspicuous object.'[6] It seemed as if Disraeli actively courted debts, even as – or possibly because – he feared arrest for them: 'they were the source indeed of his only real excitement, and he was grateful to them for their stirring powers.'[7]

No wonder, then, that his dual needs for success and protection involved him in some dastardly, underhand schemes to safeguard his political position. From the time he was a young man, Disraeli had got on famously with another writer and politician, Sir Edward Bulwer-Lytton – too well, as Sir Edward's estranged wife Lady Rosina publicly suggested, among a whole host of other accusations. So, in 1858, when the pair were offered positions in the minority Conservative Cabinet, and had to recontest their seats as law dictated, they needed everything to go smoothly. Lady Rosina Bulwer-Lytton had other ideas. Turning up at her husband's Hertfordshire by-election, she

> announced herself as the wife of the Right Hon. Sir E. B. Lytton, stated that she had come according to a promise made by her to confront her husband, and to expose the wrongs which she said he had inflicted upon her . . . Recognised as soon as observed, her voice was nearly drowned by the shouts of Sir Edward's supporters, but Sir Edward's eye caught hers, and his face paled. He looked like a man suddenly attacked by paralysis. Those near him say he trembled exceedingly. For a few moments he retained his position in front of the hustings, but turned his back on the unwelcome visitor. Then he suddenly disappeared below the hustings' platform, while his wife cried 'Coward', and he . . . escaped into the residence of the gentleman on whose grounds the election took place. Lady Lytton continued to address the audience assembled for more than a quarter of an hour . . . It is needless to say that the event described has caused the greatest possible excitement in Hertfordshire.[8]

Unable to affect the outcome of Lytton's election, two weeks later Lady Lytton travelled to London on the promise, at Dizzy's suggestion, of receiving some of her unpaid allowance. It was not Lytton waiting for her, however, but policemen, nurses and the keeper of a lunatic asylum. Immediately restrained, she was bundled into a waiting coach and 'carried to one of those miserable abodes of the most hapless of human beings – "a madhouse"' in Essex.[9]

Lady Lytton might have been disappeared, but that didn't make the problem go away. Her friends, already committed to her cause, had the anti-Conservative press onside. As the *Morning Chronicle* reported, there is . . . a firm belief that Lady Lytton is the subject of a horrible and appalling injustice and wrong; that, while perfectly sane, she has been shut up in a lunatic asylum merely in order that a woman who has, no doubt, been a constant cause of annoyance to her husband, may be prevented for ever from giving him similar trouble, or in any way again molesting him . . . that she has been made, for some reason or other, the victim of an atrocity.[10]

After just three weeks, public pressure was so high that she was released on condition that she retreat abroad. This she acceded to, but it did not count a jot against her ongoing letter-writing campaign: in December of that year she wrote to the prime minister, 'Indeed if you would study the propensities of your loathsome colonial secretary [Lytton], and chancellor of the Exchequer [the financially inept Disraeli], you would make one king of Sodom, and the other king of Gomorrah, they having run the gauntlet of every vice.'*

Beyond political status, there was one other way for Disraeli to alleviate his financial distress: a suitable marriage. After a few misfires, in 1839 his aim hit true with Mary Anne Wyndham Lewis, widow of his fellow Maidstone MP. According to the embittered Lady Lytton, it had not been love at first sight, with Disraeli venting the full force of his acerbic wit against that 'insufferable woman'.[11] 'Under-bred', Mary Anne's penchant for extravagant dress and opening her mouth before engaging her ill-educated mind invited ridicule: in polite Victorian society one should not talk about conjugal relations around the dinner table, nor lecture the future Napoleon III on his terrible boatmanship. Yet she nevertheless had enough sense to question Disraeli's motives for proposing, tarrying for several months before she was finally convinced that his addresses displayed more affection than affectation, and answered in the affirmative.

---

* To be fair to Lytton, his wife does read as if she's raving mad. See Rosina Bulwer-Lytton, *A Blighted Life: A True Story* (London: The London Publishing Office, 1880); cited in Daisy Hay, *Mr and Mrs Disraeli: A Strange Romance* (London: Chatto & Windus, 2015), p. 190.

For the first two decades, the relationship was tempestuous. Mary Anne was jealous – with good reason – while Dizzy, often unavailable and frequently dissembling, was forced to sneak around to hide debts so enormous that his wife's fortune could do little more than dent them. But as the couple grew older, and the stress of indebtedness was removed by a timely inheritance, Dizzy became less of a rascal and more of a good egg. By the last decade of their marriage, they were absolutely devoted to one another. Their relationship was lauded as the perfect example of Victorian marital bliss: she, an angel in the house, always available to support and care for her husband; he, the strong and successful man who protected, guided and adored his wife. So much had he grown to love and respect her that when Dizzy resigned as prime minister following electoral defeat in 1868 and was offered a peerage, he made the socially awkward request that it be instead presented to Mary Anne in her own right. Yet Dizzy's devotion was so touching there was no way the queen could refuse. As the new Viscountess Beaconsfield (pronounced *Bee*consfield) told her friends, 'Dizzy married me for my money, but if he had the chance again, he would marry me for love.'[12]

By the time of his resignation in 1868, when Dizzy at last had 'climbed to the top of the greasy pole', he was becoming a national institution.[13] The dangerous opportunist had been transformed from his early days as an unsuccessful radical into a pillar of the Conservative Party. The metamorphosis was reciprocal: just as the party had changed him, so he had changed the party. In the heady days of 1844, when the Corn Laws were still a hot topic and the powerful feared the popular demands of the Chartists, Disraeli had unleashed vitriol on the party that was to become his home, swearing that 'A Conservative government is an Organised Hypocrisy', and deriding it as 'a party without principles'. 'There was indeed a considerable shouting about what they called Conservative principles; but the awkward question naturally arose, what will you conserve? . . . Conservatism assumes in theory that everything established should be maintained; but adopts in practice that everything that is established is indefensible.'[14]

By the 1870s and his second premiership, Disraeli had reshaped the entire political spectrum and brought the party out of the past and into the future with his 'one-nation Conservatism' (coined from his novel *Sybil*). His concern for a better representation of the people in elections, for the breakdown of society, for the age's all-consuming materialism, for the increasing gap between rich and poor, induced him to introduce a range of political reforms and social measures to improve education, sanitation and the slums, to protect workers and decriminalise the work of trade unions. Dizzy the desperate dandy had become one of the two great politicians of the Victorian era.

※

The other political giant was Dizzy's arch-rival: William Ewart Gladstone, the 'Grand Old Man' of the Liberal wing of Parliament – constituting Whigs, radicals and repeal-minded Conservatives. The two were, in some ways, similar. They were of a comparable age, they had both switched party allegiance – Gladstone began as a Tory and he and Dizzy had, for a while, inhabited the same benches – and they were both chancellor of the Exchequer and prime minister multiple times. Indeed, Disraeli refused to hand over the traditional chancellor's robes to Gladstone, them having once been worn by his hero Pitt the Younger, and to this day they hang in the National Trust-owned Hughendon in Buckinghamshire. The two politicians were also both, in their own way, outsiders. For while Gladstone had, unlike Dizzy, gone the traditional route of Eton and then Christ Church, Oxford, his family were new money – and, by the 1830s, not very respectable money at that.

As the abolitionist movement had gathered pace during the Napoleonic War, Gladstone's father, John, had started buying estates from owners looking to disentangle themselves from the whole sorry business of slavery. By the time slave ownership was abolished, John had purchased almost 3,300 slaves, making him one of the biggest owners in the West Indies. And when abolition compensation was paid to those owners, he received a whopping £120,000 (£14 million today) from the government.[15] Not yet tired of paying workers a pittance – or nothing – to make his fortune, he thereafter returned to using indentured labour on both his East and West

Indian estates. No wonder, then, that upon William Gladstone's first entry into the Commons in 1833, the 'People's William' was an outspoken campaigner for even greater reparations in the planters' interests.

Like Disraeli, Gladstone also had a voracious sexual appetite. The problem for Gladstone, however, was that he had been brought up in a restrictive, deeply religious family (with which the whole issue of slavery was, seemingly, felt to be compatible). 'The conjuncture of these two considerations', historian Roy Jenkins has wryly observed, 'must necessarily have introduced some urgency into his desire for matrimony.'[16] It might also explain why he was unsuccessful in his first forays into the marriage market, making two unsolicited proposals in a strikingly Mr Collins-like manner, only relenting when warned off by the ladies' fathers and brothers. Amazingly, it was third time lucky for Gladstone, who discovered a Charlotte Lucas willing to consider the author of 'a letter proposing marriage including a sentence of 140 words all about the Almighty'.[17]

Even so, his lusty horn was not quite sated, particularly when his wife was unavailable thanks to her frequent pregnancies, illnesses or visits to her sister. Use of 'pornography' – mainly limited to Restoration poetry and the more salacious classical authors – was one palliative, for which he beat himself up mentally and physically, recording in his journal, 'I read sinfully, although with disgust, under the pretext of hunting soberly for what was innocent; but – criminal that I am – with a prurient curiosity against all the rules of pious prudence.'[18] Not only this, however. His religious leanings led him down a hard path. Having taken a secret oath with other religious enthusiasts in the 1840s, Gladstone made it his enduring task to 'rescue' prostitutes. No matter what pressing political business there was, Gladstone would prowl the dark alleys of Covent Garden, Whitechapel – the stomping ground of the still-unidentified Jack the Ripper – and other poor areas, looking for 'fallen women' to 'save', providing them with money, taking them for meals and even bringing them back to Downing Street.

Most of these women were minor infatuations, but one lady in particular caught Gladstone's eye. Laura Bell was born in Co. Antrim around 1830.

'Rule by Virtue' (1867–1910)

Vivacious and strong-willed, Laura could find no enticement interesting enough to keep her in the provinces, and as soon as she was able, she made her way to Belfast. Despite the parlous economic state of Ireland, and the rest of the United Kingdom, the town still had much to offer and Laura soon found employment in a department store. But the wages weren't high – certainly not enough to meet the needs of a girl with aspirations. So Laura turned to the 'oldest profession' for a bit of extra on the side. Apparently she had a natural talent. Before she could catch her breath, she had squirrelled away a tidy sum and was making her way to the much grander city of Dublin.

But how to stand out from the crowd in Ireland's capital? Her youthful good looks helped: 'She had a small doll-like face, piquant and provocative, big blue eyes, a strawberry-and-cream complexion, cascades of glorious golden hair, the most shapely pair of shoulders . . . and a soft and persuasive voice. She was, in short, well armed for her attack upon male susceptibility.'[19] That was a natural advantage, but her pretty face and figure needed to be seen. With a flash of marketing genius, Laura purchased a barouche, a luxurious carriage with collapsible hood that second-hand could cost £250 (which would need a modern income of £340,000 a year to purchase) and headed to Phoenix Park.* A wealthy, attractive girl driving around in public by herself was bound to attract the right sort of attention, and before long she had a list of respectable clients, including the father of Oscar Wilde, with his 'insatiable appetite for young ladies'.[20]

But as with Belfast, the charms of Wilde and Dublin could not hold Laura's attention for long. At twenty, she closed her Dublin shop and set her sights on that Mecca for her profession: London. For despite the prudish veneer of nineteenth-century society, London had a thriving sex industry: one investigator reported 80,000 ladies of 'easy virtue' within the confines of the city, many – but by no means all – working from the brothels that

---

* This calculation is based on *Measuring Worth*'s 'Labour value': the average wage that a worker would need to purchase the item. This is, therefore, different from the standard RPI comparison used for much of this book.

constituted one in every sixty houses.[21] Laura, however, was determined to be no brothel-dweller.

Implementing her two-pronged strategy, she found employment in the mourning section of Jay's Regent's Street department store, providing a reputable facade for her perhaps less-than-respectable schemes. A shop selling mourning clothes and accessories might be thought an unlikely place to hook up with clients, but it fulfilled its purpose. In May 1850, not long after Laura had reached London, Prince Jung Bahadoor of Nepal landed on British shores. Acting as his country's emissary to a United Kingdom desperate to create a buffer state between India and Russia's supposed territorial advances, he was treated and wined and dined and courted and entertained beyond all imagining. Occasionally, however, he found that his wardrobe was missing some vital ingredient. That is what took him to Jay's, and that is how he met Laura. In little more time than the length of a simple transaction, Laura had conveyed her availability – for the right price.

For the next three months the prince lavished every bit of time and money he had on her, gifting Laura fine clothes and jewels, trinkets and keepsakes – as well as a Belgravia townhouse. It was like a fairytale: the poor but plucky Irish girl who struck it lucky and lived happily ever after. But it wasn't a fairytale and, too soon, Bahadoor had to return home. According to legend, however – and despite having already reputedly spent £250,000 on his beautiful lover – he had one more gift to give. The prince, one likes to think on bended knee, presented Laura with a ring: a pledge that, if ever she needed anything, all she had to do was send the request, along with the ring, back to him. Her wish would then be fulfilled. So the story goes, when Indian sepoys mutinied in 1857, prompting two years of rebellion, Laura made use of the promise and asked the prince to support the British. This he did, although far too soon for Laura's supposed request to have reached him. The romantic, however, would like to believe that Britain's long relationship with Nepal since then has more to do with a prince's fondness for a call girl than the flattery, and finances, received from a blandishing British state that had, without even a shrug, reimbursed him for his dalliance.

While Laura suffered the fate of every courtesan in being left by her prince, she was thenceforth set in her profession. Using the same tactic as Dublin, she invested in a light, open-top carriage drawn by two white horses, with a 'tiger' (a boy dressed in striped livery whose job it was to hand her in and out) in the back, and 'rode in spanking style' through Hyde Park.[22] For a while she was the talk of the town, escorting the likes of Napoleon III to the opera, delaying 'her entrance until the last minute' before sweeping in, 'with the grace and assurance of a prima donna, which invariably caused every eye in the house to be fixed upon her'.[23]

One client was especially charmed by her. Arthur Thistlethwayte was the grandson of the Bishop of Norwich and so smitten was he that when he went to fight in the Crimean War, he begged his brother to take care of Laura. He didn't come back. 'Having bravely distinguished himself, and escaped unhurt in the two hard-fought battles of Alma and Inkerman, [he] lost his life from fever and exhaustion', aged twenty-two.[24] So he never learned that his brother, August Frederick, had been all too eager to fulfil his promise, marrying the girl as soon as Arthur was out of the country.

It was not a happy union. Laura Thistlethwayte would forever be deemed spoiled goods, never allowed into polite society – and certainly not into the company of ladies. Even when she adopted the fervent Evangelicalism that was sweeping the country, the Victorians wouldn't welcome their very own Mary Magdalene. And so she lived a social half-life, hosting all-male dinner parties that cost a fortune and infuriated her husband. The couple – or, rather, Laura – ran up significant debts, perhaps having concluded that affection of any kind needed to be purchased. Husband and wife continued in this fashion, in and out of debtors' court, her spending and him stressing, until 1887. August Frederick had a habit of summoning servants by firing a pistol into the ceiling. On 7 August, however, he missed. And shot himself in the head instead.

By that point, Laura had – emotionally at least – moved on, having met Gladstone during her soirées. To him, she was irresistible. Not only did she have a shady past, but she was still beautiful, and also now, apparently, reformed: she ticked all the boxes. She was utterly captivating. One lady who saw her preach on 'the plan of salvation by faith in a risen Saviour' noted:

> after a time curiosity got the better of discretion, and people flocked from all parts of the country to hear her discourse ... Mrs Thistlethwaite, beautifully dressed ... poured out an impassioned address, not eloquent nor convincing, but certainly effective. She spoke with great facility, and with a good deal of emotion in her voice, and an evident air of sincerity and personal conviction. This, added to the remains of very great beauty, an influence largely increased by her great generosity to the poor people, made a vast impression on her congregation, and after the first meetings she succeeded in producing all the effects of other revival preachers, and many conversions were supposed to have been the result of her ministrations.[25]

Soon she was Gladstone's 'Dear Spirit', his regular correspondent and frequent guest, with a 'weighty word', 'love', issuing from her in an unguarded moment – a word Gladstone considered unwise to reciprocate.[26]

It is unlikely that anything physical happened – he was far too uptight for that – but there was no doubt he knew his relationship to be wrong. He kept their conversations hidden from his wife, and later decided to burn the 'box of Mrs Thistlewayte's older letters' because '[t]hey would lead to misapprehension'.[27] He went into panic when he thought he would be subpoenaed as a witness in debtors' court, knowing that Laura's extravagant presents to him – including a ring inscribed 'L. to W. E. G.' that he wore for the rest of his life – would be cast in a compromising light.

The same self-knowledge held true for his other ladies, as was obvious from his diary. For a start, there is clear evidence of sexual attraction and infatuation, calling the objects of his attention 'lovely beyond measure', admitting that his interests were 'carnal' and that he 'trod the path of danger'.[28] Nor did he believe that his visits were helpful in any way, pondering that in the eighty or ninety women he met, 'there is but one of whom I know that the miserable life has been abandoned *and* that I can fairly join that fact with influence of mine'.[29] And then there was the penance he inflicted upon himself, indulging in post-perambulatory self-flagellation. In 1849 he had bought himself a whip, which he used every time he was touched by temptation. Indeed, so much did he trust in this form of 'punishment' that he had 'been seduced into a neglect of other rules', and vowed to leave it alone, for 'reliance on one remedy or safeguard only induces forgetfulness and remissness as to others'.[30] He banned himself from taking Holy Communion for two weeks instead. The conclusion must therefore be that his primary goal in seeking out these women – however respectfully he cloaked it – was titillation.

Other members of Parliament considered his peccadillo somewhat singular. For such a strait-laced man – the jest was that 'Gladstone's jokes are no laughing matter' – to pursue his 'lovely ladies' was a curious sort of scandal, with Dizzy allegedly quipping, 'When you are saving fallen women, save one for me.'[31] But parliamentarians weren't the only people aware of his nocturnal strolls. In 1853, an unemployed young man reckoned he could improve his circumstances by blackmail when he saw Gladstone talking to two 'ladies of the night' near Haymarket. Gladstone refused the deal and led the young chancer to the police station instead. Several conversations with police officers, a collection of evidence, and two court appearances later, the blackmailer was sentenced to twelve months' hard labour, reduced to two at the request of the victim. Thereafter, Gladstone decided that 'These talkings of mine are certainly not within the rules of worldly prudence', concluding that the whole experience had 'been sent to teach me wisdom'.[32] It didn't. By the 1880s, Gladstone's gallivants had caused enough of a stir that members of his Cabinet were flipping coins to see who would lead an intervention.

It was desperately required, because the politics of the last two decades of the century were difficult enough without the prime minister's very particular fixation entering the mix. After a period of relative calm in Ireland, parts of the country were once more becoming restless. A bungled nationalist Fenian uprising in 1867, combined with Fenian action – and shootings – in Britain, led to coercion, arrests and the suspension of habeas corpus, but also to an acknowledgement in Westminster that something needed to be done to improve the lot of the Irish. By the time another agricultural crisis hit in 1879, only baby steps had been taken to this end: the disestablishment of the Protestant Church of Ireland, an attempt to found a university system acceptable to Irish Catholics, and an ineffectual fiddle with tenant rights.

It was with renewed vigour, then, that Gladstone returned to the issue with his resumption of the premiership in 1880, after six years as Dizzy's Opposition. With pressure mounting, and obstructionist tactics bringing Commons business to a standstill – on one occasion Irish MPs forced the House to sit continuously for forty-one hours – the political world divided on how best to remedy Ireland's multiple economic, agricultural, social and religious problems. Two Home Rule Bills granting Ireland limited self-rule, but under the umbrella of the British Empire, came and went – the first defeated in the Commons by thirty votes; the second when it reached the Lords – setting up a world of problems for the next century and beyond, as the majority of Ireland would violently seek a more definite and permanent split from Britain. By 1894, an exhausted Gladstone retired from politics, his quest 'to pacify Ireland' having instead created an unhealable breach in the Liberal Party.[33]

Nevertheless, when he died in 1898, Gladstone was still a popular man, with the area around Westminster Abbey packed for his funeral with up to 100,000 weeping spectators. Gladstone's supporters and family continued to insist that the Grand Old Man's contacts with the women he met on his night-time walks were purely innocent, philanthropic events. They even won a libel case in 1927 to that effect, with the jury concluding 'the evidence that has been placed before them has completely vindicated the high moral character of the late Mr W. E. Gladstone'.[34] But then again, the family had withheld the evidence of his diary.

※

It is therefore unsurprising that Gladstone's moonlit excursions were not more frequently referenced in the newspapers, even in the determinedly modern gutter-press-style rags like *Truth*. *Truth* stuck to no rules: emerging from an age when newspapers presented facts and left the reader to form an opinion alone, this weekly pushed its editor's views with as much vitriol and satire as possible. The public gobbled it up. From a launch in January 1877, with capital of just £1,000, it rapidly gained a following of 30,000 sales a week, playing audiences – and the libel courts – superbly.[35]

The founder was as unconventional as the paper. Henry Du Pré Labouchère, 'Labby', has been called the least Victorian of all Victorian politicians.[36] Asked to leave Cambridge – where he'd whiled away his time attending the races at Newmarket and 'don-baiting' – after a practical joke went awry, his father attempted to teach him a sense of responsibility by sending him to supervise the family's South American business interests. Labby loved it there, for all the wrong reasons. Trekking across jungles and mountains, falling in – and then out – with local bandits and tribes, and engaging in as many love affairs as possible, he was a free spirit. So free, in fact, that night after night he would watch a visiting circus, purely for the chance of seeing a particular girl perform. Then, one day, he decided to try his luck backstage.

He didn't get very far before he was roughly challenged by the proprietor.

'I have formed an honourable attachment for one of your circus riders,' Labby explained. 'I am here merely to kiss the hem of her garment as she passes by.'

Romantic notions were beyond the owner. 'Get to hell out of this, you damned loafer!' he roared back.

Labby didn't need to be asked twice. He turned and fled, but he hadn't given up. It seemed that a different approach was needed, so, waiting until the owner was in a better mood, Labby presented himself in another guise: 'I would like to join the circus.'

'Very well. What's your line?'

When need arose, Labby could be an exceptionally quick thinker. 'I specialise in standing jumps,' he explained. And he proceeded to show that he could, indeed, jump.

Perhaps thinking that the circus needed another clown, unbelievably Labby was employed. The 'Bounding Buck of Babylon' henceforth travelled with the circus, collecting entrance fees and then, dressed in a fillet – a sort of hat, often paired with a wimple, associated with unmarried women in the Middle Ages – and pink tights, he would amaze audiences by his ability to jump up and down on the spot.[37]

Possibly because his legs grew tired, or possibly because he fell out of love with the circus girl as quickly as he fell in, at some point Labby became bored of his pink costume and began to wander on his own. In California, during the Gold Rush in 1853, he participated in a jury that condemned a man to be hanged by lynch law; in Minneapolis, he met members of the Chippewa tribe, journeying with them to their hunting grounds west of Lake Superior and secretly watching their rituals; in New York he became a convinced republican. Back in Britain, and without consultation, his family decided he'd had enough of the itinerant lifestyle – particularly when they were funding it – and signed him up to the diplomatic corps. It was with good grace that he took up his position in Washington in 1854.

His diplomatic postings were a success, for him at least. There was enough variety and challenge to keep Labby entertained, whether it was sending a rapidly decomposing corpse in a box labelled 'This side up – with care' backwards and forwards between Washington and New York, or playing whist badly with the American secretary of state, or having someone down on his luck sign an imaginary trade treaty. From Washington he went to Turkey, to Russia, to Germany and to Sweden – where he fought a duel 'to establish an Englishman's right not to fight duels. To be killed was bad enough, he reflected, but to be killed paradoxically was still worse.'[38] But, perhaps his time in the circus having never truly left him, he also jumped at the chance to abscond whenever possible, visiting Venice, Palmyra, Jerusalem: wherever fancy and the Fates would take him. Nevertheless, even this career couldn't hold his interest forever. In 1864, while in Germany, Labby received another posting, this time to Buenos Aires. Writing back, he accepted the position, on one condition: that he be allowed to fulfil his duties from his current location. After ten years in the diplomatic service he was, at last, fired. Labby, however, didn't care, for he was turning his attention to another path: politics.

Considered a joker, and unable to stay in the chamber for twenty minutes together without nipping out for a cigarette, this 'Christian' member for Northampton (the other MP being a self-professed agnostic, who had – Wilkes style – been expelled by, and re-elected to, the Commons several times) nevertheless campaigned against some serious issues – notably what was delicately described as the 'White Man's Burden' to civilise the world, but what was in reality the populist, opportunistic imperialism eponymously labelled 'Beaconsfieldism'.

By the end of the nineteenth century, Britain was 'uncomfortably squelching in too many imperial quagmires.'[39] The Empire was, simply, too large. Even by the middle of the century, 60 per cent of all ocean-going tonnage was registered in the United Kingdom, and to protect its economic interests the Empire 'in a fit of absence of mind' acquired yet more land.[40] The never-ending search for a buffer state between India and expansionist Russia tied up troops in Afghanistan. Australian interests, along with those in the Far East – particularly after the energy and money expended in the Opium Wars – 'had to be' defended by the annexation of Upper Burma, as well as parts of Borneo and New Guinea. And in 1879, following Disraeli's purchase of shares in the Suez Canal to guard the passage to India, the British and French jointly took control of Egypt's astronomical levels of international debt, provoking a nationalist and religious backlash that led to Britain's indirect control of the country. Sudan, technically part of Egypt, rebelled against the 'Westernisation' that came with this control and rallied under unofficial religious leadership. Preferring to take the hint rather than stick it out, the government sent the obsessively devout General Gordon to oversee an evacuation of British citizens and their allies. Instead, he dug in and got himself – and those he'd been sent to protect – slaughtered. The resultant territorial and commercial one-upmanship rose to hysterical levels, and suddenly every European nation wanted a slice of the pie. The 'Scramble for Africa' had begun. This push for land and power would finish, via the fields of Flanders, in the furnaces of Auschwitz-Birkenau.

And then there were the two British south African territories of Cape Colony and the Colony of Natal, settled uncomfortably close to the Dutch Boers in the Transvaal and Orange Free State. Already important as waypoints for any ocean voyage to India, the Empire's drive to 'protect' these territories became more urgent once rumours spread of substantial deposits of gold and diamonds in the rich African soil. In 1877, the British had occupied the Transvaal, but in 1880 the Boers rose up and reminded Britain – and the rest of the world – that Britain was not, after all, invincible. The First Boer War was the country's first defeat since 1783.

For some politicians, then, South Africa was a pressing issue. Cecil Rhodes – millionaire, head of the British South Africa Company and, from 1890, prime minister of Cape Colony – and his friends made it more so. In 1895, under pretence of protecting the rights of recently arrived British gold-diggers in the Transvaal, and backed by colonial secretary Joseph Chamberlain (whose family had extensive contracts supplying the military), Cecil's friend, Dr Leander Starr Jameson, illegally rode into the state hoping to trigger a rebellion among the expatriate British employed there. It didn't work. When news of the 'Jameson Raid' arrived in Britain, Labby devoted considerable time, in the Commons and in print, pushing for an investigation. It was another whitewash – as it always would be with Chamberlain on the committee rather than examined by it. Evidence was withheld, witnesses refused to divulge, and Labouchère was kept firmly under control. The resultant report was an anaemic travesty. Undaunted, Labby published his own grim minority report. Out of the eleven members on the panel, he alone signed it.

As Britain descended into the Second Boer War in 1899, Labouchère was one of the few not to greet it with glee, his warning that the war would cost a hundred million pounds – as it turns out, an underestimate of 50 per cent – met by 'a burst of laughter and ironical cheering'.[41] MPs thought it would be a quick and glorious war. Three years later, when the Treaty of Vereeniging was signed in 1902, the war had instead cost the lives of 7,882 British soldiers in action and a further 14,210 from disease.[42] This was nothing, however, compared to the civilian death toll. About 28,000 Boer women and children, and a further 15,000 Africans, perished through malnourishment, unsanitary accommodation and epidemic disease in British concentration camps.[43]

But despite his heroic stands in and outside of Parliament, Labby was often not a paragon of virtue. Indeed, at times he would have been better keeping *Truth*'s original working title, *Lyre*. For a start, for all his chasing after financial villains, he was happy to turn a blind eye when the rogue was a friend. Gladstone, for example, made a small fortune out of the Egyptian bond market, and doubled the worth of his investment (which in 1882 represented more than a third of his portfolio), as a direct result of his intervention in the country. But that was studiously ignored by the newspaper.[44]

Nor was Labouchère above utilising his position to help himself. Many enemies attempted to unmask him. Some took direct measures. Mr Abbott, for example, was a stockbroker whose speculator-client was exposed by Labby in another newspaper, *The World*. Passing Labby in the street one day, Abbott decided the most sensible action to protect his own name would be to attack the author. Accosting him, Abbott offered a challenge: 'You know that you write in *The World*, and if anybody were to attack me in that way in any other newspaper, I would show you what I should do.'

'If you are attacked in a newspaper unfairly, I presume you would bring an action for libel,' replied Labby, 'and if it was unfair, you would get very heavy damages.'

'I should not go into courts. I know what newspapers want: they always want to go into courts; it is a free advertisement for them. I should horsewhip the man.'

That sounded like a threat, and Labby could never resist poking a bear. 'I reply to you in the words of Dr Johnson: "I shall not be deterred from unmasking a scoundrel by the menaces of a ruffian."'

'I presume you mean that for me?'

'Well, it looks like it. You were just now talking about horsewhipping. Here I am. Horsewhip me.'

That stumped Abbott, particularly as he had no whip. Looking around at the growing audience and not sensible enough to consider that, with one bluff called, bluffing again was unlikely to work, 'he went through all the motions with which nervous pugilists try to impress their antagonists; he rolled his body about, adopted a crouching posture, clenched his fists and sawed the air with them'.

Labby called his bluff again. 'Why do you not begin?'

Having to do something, Abbott weakly flailed towards the journalist, punching at rather than through him, and lightly made contact with Labby's arm. Like for like, as much as possible, Labby poked his cane at the outraged man's top hat, attempting to knock it off. 'Abbott caught his arm; he caught Abbott's arm; and in this embrace they leaned against a wall, breathing hostilities. Wondering what to do next, Abbott glanced about him and noticed a small boy who was taking a keen interest in the proceedings, "Do you happen to have a horsewhip about you?"'

'Hadn't you better take my stick?' Labby suggested.

No coherent answer forthcoming, Labby instead addressed the crowd. 'Is there a policeman here?'

The policeman, hovering at the edges and hoping to enjoy the spectacle as much as the next person, was pushed forward. 'I give this man in custody for an assault,' Labby said to him, and off they went to the nearest station. Abbott was charged and bound over for £500 to keep the peace. And as Abbott's stock-market dealings crashed, Labby's reputation flourished.[45]

But then, in 1897, an allegation stuck. Labby was often accused of recommending shares that he himself possessed, and to that he had a simple answer: 'What greater proof can I give of my belief in the shares I write up than buying them? Or what stronger evidence can there be of my disbelief in a share than my selling it?'[46] However, these new accusations were on an entirely different level. Henry Hess was a journalist not dissimilar from Labouchère. Like Labby, he excelled in uncovering fraudulent and corrupt business dealings; and, like Labby, he often found himself in court as a result. But unlike Labby, he was a loud proponent of British rights in South Africa. It was this, rather than the printed slanging match between them, that led Hess to publish letters that showed this 'self-constituted censor of public morals ... has, for too long, posed as a public benefactor, whilst committing the same faults which he deplores in others.'[47]

The letters were damning. In them, Labby explained how he wrote articles to send shares down, so that 'a lot of people sell at 56, 57, or lower if possible'. At a suitably low price, he would purchase and then circulate rumours that would 'send them up again. It seems to me that this can be renewed several times.'[48] At another time he used malicious libel to 'bear' (or bring down) the market, and committed perjury in court.

These were weighty accusations, but nothing happened. Other papers passed comment on Labouchère's resolute silence – a silence enforced on both sides once Labouchère obtained a gagging order – but, as Labby knew, the public was easily distracted. Three years later, everything was forgotten: he was re-elected by Northampton in 1900, and then retired to Italy of his own free will in 1906.[49] Hess, on the other hand, suffered bankruptcy and ignominy when he was found guilty of similar financial misdealings in 1909 and sentenced to twelve months' imprisonment.

For all the fun, the clowning, the appearance of virtue, Labby was, therefore, not so different from his contemporaries, putting on an outward show but driven by, if not greed and resentment, a belief in his own importance and self-worth. A radical Liberal who scoffed at female suffrage and who was instrumental in increasing the penalties of the Criminal Law Amendment Act 1885 under which Oscar Wilde suffered so publicly, his attacks were also targeted to suit his phobias.* And first and foremost was his antisemitism. In 1875 Labby had no fixed opinion about Jewish people; if anything he favoured them as a group. But within the space of a few years, his opinions flipped and then crystallised. With increasing frequency, the targets of Labouchère's vitriol were Jewish, or perceived as such. The 'alien' and 'Jewish' financiers of the British South Africa Company were to blame for the Boer Wars, not the Anglican Cecil Rhodes; the actions of *D'Israeli*

---

* To be fair, it has been suggested that his contribution to the Criminal Law Amendment Act was intended as a wrecking motion rather than as an 'improvement'.

were excoriated, while those of the good Christian Gladstone were overlooked. *Truth*'s 'tired clichés and familiar boilerplate continued to resonate' into the twentieth century. Eventually, 'the journal which Labouchere had originally conceived as a crusading organ for progressive causes became instead an apologist for Nazism and a haven for home grown fascists'.[50] Fifty years later, the consequences of Labby and others' unthinking, casual racism would reverberate around the world.

Chapter Eleven

Led by Donkeys 1910–45

Dramatis Personae

49. David Lloyd George (1863–1945)

    Caernarvon Boroughs (Caernarvonshire) … … … … … 1890–1945

50. Rufus Isaacs (1860–1935)

    Reading (Berkshire) … … … … … … … … … … 1904–13

51. Sir Oswald Mosley (1896–1980)

    Harrow (Middlesex) … … … … … … … … … 1918–24
    Smethwick (Staffordshire) … … … … … … … 1926–31

52. Ignatius Trebitsch-Lincoln (1879–1943)

    Darlington (Co. Durham) … … … … … … … … 1910

Members Behaving Badly

It was grandeur on an unprecedented scale, 'marked by every outward sign and symbol of imperial pomp and magnificence which the resources of the oldest and greatest of European monarchies and the widest and most mighty of world empires ... are able to furnish'. King Edward VII had died of pneumonia on 6 May 1910, aged sixty-eight. Now, two weeks later, it seemed that the world had turned out to witness his final journey, from Buckingham Palace to Westminster Abbey, and then on to his last resting place at Windsor. 'All branches of both services' – the Army and the Navy – were there, dressed in their finest, 'together with the forces of the Dominions and the Indian Army.' Immediately behind the coffin rode the new king, George V. On George's right was his cousin, German Emperor Wilhelm II. To their rear followed 'such a group of kings and heirs ... as never yet graced the funeral of a British sovereign'. Further back still marched 'deputations from the armies of nine European Powers, including those of Austria-Hungary, Germany, Russia, and Spain, and from the German, the Russian, the Spanish, and the Swedish Navies'. All this, crowed *The Times*, 'will remind us how wide are the limits, how vast is the population, how immeasurable are the resources of the states over which the king-emperor bears rule and which his sway unites. It will recall to us the things ... which, if we are not unworthy of our fathers, are destined to draw them more and more closely together in the future.'[1]

As Britons lined the streets to watch this grand procession march slowly past, it probably didn't occur to them that they were witnessing more than just the last journey of a king, that they were also seeing the death throes of every certainty of the previous century. For within a decade, and led by myopic politicians, Britain would have more to mourn than a monarch. Each pillar supporting her dominion – financial, industrial, military, colonial – was rotting and crumbling, and by 1916 Britain would face the ruin of her former glory.

For a start, things had stepped up in Ireland, and Easter 1916 gave future Irish generations another Rising to remember. Although the failure of this short-lived, Dublin-centred rebellion against British rule was a foregone conclusion – being strategically flawed, reliant on outside help, confused and lacking in basic resources – it became the final straw that collapsed the camel of the United Kingdom of Great Britain and Ireland. Over the following six years, talk of Home Rule would become cries of 'Freedom' and local guerrilla tactics were countered, violence for violence and terror for terror, by the paramilitary Whitehall-sponsored Black and Tans, until the country – minus the tricksy northern counties – emerged as the Irish Free State. Britain's empire was irrevocably shrinking.

And then there was the Great War, the belligerents led by the men who had come together in mourning just a few short years before. By 1916 the localised conflict that should have been over by Christmas 1914 had engulfed much of the planet and raged for two murderous years. Britain and France were bogged down in trenches stretching from the North Sea to the Alps, and had settled in, with their trench foot and lice, for years of grinding attrition. The most recent colossal push to overrun the German defences at the Somme had ended in literal quagmire. Seven miles of ground – at most – had been gained at the cost of 204,253 French, 419,654 British, and somewhere between 450,000 and 680,000 German casualties.[2] Elsewhere, the attempt to take the Central Powers of Austria-Hungary, Germany and Turkey in the rear by throwing men at the disease-ridden, arid, mountainous and inhospitable Gallipoli peninsula had finished – after the sacrifice of hundreds of thousands dead and wounded – in ignominious defeat and withdrawal. And Russia was a teetering mess, ready to break – as it did the following year – and release German troops to flood the Allies in the west. It seemed a hopeless case.

The military weren't the only ones stuck in the mud. Back in London, the government appeared in no hurry to win the war. Believing, just as they had one hundred years ago when Lord Cochrane approached the Admiralty with ideas for new and formidable weapons, there was something ungentlemanly about modern warfare, they followed a deliberate policy of keeping the fighting Tommies undersupplied. While the Germans mowed down British troops with sixteen machine guns per battalion, Lord Kitchener, secretary of state for war, insisted on a maximum of four for each British counterpart.[3] Nor were supply processes in place even if there had been the will. In 1915, while the Army cried out for 200,000 high-explosive shells a day and the government instead provided 150,000 per month, the prime minister lay practically horizontal, watching his Cabinet fight their own little wars rather than the one that mattered. Gumption had followed strategic and tactical ability out of the room.

David Lloyd George, however, was not like other ministers. Acting initially in his role as chancellor of the Exchequer, by 1915 he was rectifying the supply problem through bloody-minded determination and making as much of a nuisance of himself as possible. Unauthorised, he improved machine-gun manufacturing and supply by instructing his staff to 'Take Kitchener's maximum; square it; multiply that result by two; and when you are in sight of that, double it again for good luck.'[4] By 1916, and now with a particular remit for munitions, he was working with the press, with labour and the trade unions, with business, even with suffragettes, to ensure a workforce capable of turning the economy into one geared solely for the purposes of war. And it was starting to pay dividends. As he told the prime minister in one of his many unsent resignation letters, 'When I came in we were manufacturing in this country 70,000 shells a week; that is about one-sixth of what we spend now in a single week of ordinary trench warfare activity. The whole ammunition reserve was under 75,000; we produce more than twice that per day now.'[5]

To say, therefore, that Lloyd George wormed and schemed his way to leadership of a coalition government of Liberals, Conservatives and a smattering of Labour representatives at the end of 1916 might be too harsh. Perhaps it was destined: Lloyd George's friend, the owner of the *News of the World*, recorded in his diary that before the war, 'L. G. ... showed me a letter he had received from a palmist and soothsayer, who stated, among other things, that L. G. ... would be protected by unseen spirits until he had accomplished a great mission he was destined to perform.'[6] The 'Welsh Wizard' had certainly proved his mettle since, and many in the Commons and beyond believed him to be the only man able to improve British prospects. So when the former prime minister, Herbert Asquith, was manoeuvred into standing down, Lloyd George had few problems forming a Cabinet of his own, despite the disgust of many of his former fellow Liberal colleagues, and a tainted past.

It wasn't just that Lloyd George was an absolute cad, who couldn't keep it in his trousers. A familiar story by now. Having early on found married life to be tedious, particularly when his wife was in a delicate condition, the 'greatest Bible-thumping pagan of his generation' sloped away for sermons, political rallies and temperance meetings – and a string of mistresses, including one who became pregnant and was subsequently bought off by Lloyd George's representatives during his first election campaign.[7] As his disinherited son later complained,

> His entire life, including the fifty-three years of marriage with my mother, was involved with a series of affairs with women, some innocent, some romantic, some deeply obsessive, some cynical and worldly, and most of them fruitful. To portray his life without taking into account this side of his personality is like failing to depict Beethoven's handicap of deafness during the composition of his greatest works.[8]

There were wives of friends, there were village girls and society ladies, there were secretaries and all manner of other staff, even a beekeeper. 'The ladies came and went and I have not the least doubt that some of them really exercised a perfectly proper occupation. But one day, after a rather mellowing dinner, as I was leaving amidst a girlish chorus of farewells and looked a little hazily at the confusing array of variedly pretty faces, I remarked ... "if all you ladies were laid end to end, I wouldn't be the least surprised."'[9]

One girl in particular, however, made it through to the end. Frances Stevenson was young enough to be Lloyd George's daughter – indeed, she had been the friend of his eldest, who died too early. This past connection was undoubtedly a reason for Frances being hired as a tutor for his youngest daughter, but there were other enticements. Before long, in a cliché of clichés, Lloyd George had convinced Frances to quit her teaching career and instead enter a different profession, as the minister's 'private secretary'.

From that moment on, this 'second wife' shared Lloyd George with his long-suffering actual wife, until time, disease and age removed the latter, allowing the forbidden couple to marry, but causing an almighty rift between the rest of the family.

Good looks and a magnetic charm undoubtedly aided Lloyd George in his conquests. So too did his impressive power of invention – a skill that could also be put to other purposes. Indeed, one historian has gone so far as to remark that 'no statement of his should ever be accepted unless corroborated from at least one other source'.[10] Lloyd George would spin a web of tales around his poor upbringing, fondly recalling, for example, that 'we scarcely ate fresh meat, and I remember that our greatest luxury was half an egg for each child on Sunday mornings' – an utter fabrication but one that appealed to those parts of the electorate not in the know.[11]

Lloyd George's early relative poverty does, however, account for his chasing of a quick buck. In the 1890s, he speculated on gold in Patagonia, Argentina, fraudulently encouraging others to do the same. There was, of course, no gold, and Lloyd George lost considerable sums of money in the venture. (He also briefly lost his famous moustache, shaved off as a disguise to avoid fighting a duel with an irate cuckolded husband.) But so too did all those people who listened to him. Next, he used insider knowledge as president of the Board of Trade to gain advantage in the stock market. But then, in 1912, another scandal hit the headlines – and nearly brought down the government. At issue was the new investment in telegraphy, its importance highlighted beyond doubt by the sinking of *Titanic* that very year. Out of all the possible companies working with long-distance telecommunications, the Marconi Company was selected to build the first six of eighteen wireless stations across the Empire – and it just so happened that Lloyd George and three other politicians had shares in its sister company.

The official most obviously to blame for the mess was Rufus Isaacs, the solicitor-general, whose brother was a director of Marconi. As with so many other politicians, Isaacs had a chequered past. In the words of his son, in Isaac's youth, 'He was wild; he was idle; he was volatile . . . the terror of his schoolmasters, the scandal of the neighbourhood and the despair of his father.'[12] Aged sixteen, he went to sea as a ship's boy at his father's command to avoid an inappropriate marriage. Seven weeks later, on docking at Rio de Janeiro, he bailed, hiding first in the mountains and then with a 'generously proportioned protectress', who fed him bananas until Isaacs realised she wanted compensation in kind. Deciding 'It was possible to pay too high a price even for food and freedom', 'as soon as her overbroad back was turned he fled precipitously from her wiles.'[13]

By nineteen, having determined the sailor's life was not for him, he had taken a job in the foreign markets of the Stock Exchange – despite being two years underage – and accrued debts of £8,000. Burned, he next turned to the law, and discovered that he had 'a legal mind like a stiletto'.[14] Thereafter he became a trusted member of Parliament and of the government, working his way up to power and prestige, even representing the Board of Trade at the *Titanic* inquiry – for which he charged over £2,400.[15]

His family, however, were still active in the business world. Isaacs was therefore perfectly placed to profit when his brother offered him shares in American Marconi. Ten thousand were purchased by Isaacs, 1,000 of which were sold to Lloyd George. This, on the surface, was fine. After all, the American and the English Marconi companies were registered separately. But given that the two companies shared managers, board members and patents – not to mention their name – any government contract awarded to one was bound to affect the share price of the other. Bad enough, but there was worse: the shares were purchased, at bargain prices, before they were floated. *If* the ministers had been sensible, they would have turned £2,000 into £4,000 overnight and walked away happy.[16] Instead they tried to be clever, selling some shares and making convoluted deals, but mistimed their final sale, on which they eventually made a slight loss.

Word of the dealings naturally leaked. At a debate in Parliament, the government was criticised on two grounds: 'first, that it is a bad bargain, an imprudent bargain; and, second, that it is a bargain which is tainted with corruption.' In itself, the agreement with Marconi contained enough 'to utterly damage the business reputation of any government'. This was compounded, however, by the 'very grave rumours all over the City that people have made money out of this business who ought not to have made money out of it'.[17] The ministers, of course, denied all knowledge. Nonetheless, a select committee was appointed to investigate.

Sometimes, one has to wonder why they bothered. The committee's remit was circumscribed to the point of impotence, but even with limitations its conclusions were too strong for the Liberals. After the 'necessary' redactions, its report became absolutely toothless: Lloyd George et al. had behaved badly; they had been stupid; they were not corrupt. To save the party – and his own power – the prime minister chose to support his ministers. In the subsequent parliamentary vote on whether the House would accept the ministers' 'expressions of regret' and acquit 'them of acting otherwise than in good faith', the Liberals rallied around – as did the Irish Nationalists and most Labour MPs – to win the point 346 to 268.[18] After all, they didn't want to make politics 'intolerable to just the class of men we would like to have in public life' by insisting on strict and honest declarations of conflicts of interest.[19] There were too many skeletons in too many closets for a thorough clean. They all could carry on regardless. But it would not be forgotten, and when the next scandal rocked Westminster, commentators rediscovered their long memories.

✽

The Reform Acts of the nineteenth century had affected more than the number of voters; they had changed the whole nature of electioneering. What at one point had been a small affair, paid for by contesting prospective MPs, had become a national event touching millions. To top it off, there were now limits on the amount candidates could spend in their pursuit of votes, thus placing all expense on the underfunded political parties. So, with election costs soaring in proportion to the number of voters, and legal means to meet those costs reduced, parties turned to another source of income: the sale of honours. The first scandal emerged in the 1890s, when a banker and a linoleum manufacturer, despite having no prior connection with the Liberal Party, were nominated for peerages. Between 1905 and 1914, a further 102 peers were created. As Herbert Gladstone, Chief Whip and son of William, admitted, many were unwarranted, but it was of no concern: 'If the letter of the law has not always been observed ... let everyone ask himself if in tax-rating and other matters, he has always observed the letter of the law.'[20]

The pace really increased, however, when Lloyd George became prime minister. By June 1922, eyebrows that had been steadily rising reached the hairline. That year, the honours list included 30 per cent of peers, 55 per cent of baronetcies, and 30 per cent of knights who had no strong record of public service and who came from 'unconventional' backgrounds.[21] Included was a war profiteer convicted of food-hoarding, a South African mine owner fined half a million pounds for fraud, and a man who had offshored his business to escape taxation. Two were accused of trading with the enemy. Questions began to be asked. As one former Liberal grandee later wrote in *The Times*, if honours were sold 'there would be nothing in the worst times of Charles II or Sir Robert Walpole to equal it. But what amazes me is this: no one seems to think that there would be anything unusual in such [a] sale.'[22]

Nonetheless, a few did find the practice inexcusable and on 17 July 1922 the storm hit. As the Duke of Northumberland attacked in the Lords, providing evidence that 'A knighthood will cost you £12,000 and a baronetcy £35,000', the Commons called for an investigative committee.[23] Yet this would be even more pathetic than the last. Its stated purpose was not for 'exhuming the past ... or to go into specific cases of abuse'. Instead, it would 'recommend the best procedure for the future'.[24] Delve too deeply, and more than the Coalition and Liberals would be exposed. The resultant nine-page report was as flimsy in the hand as it was in its production. Lloyd George, and the system, would escape once again. Kind of.

The final touch for Lloyd George came later. Once the Coalition fell in October of that same year, the Conservative leader donated his half of the honours booty to his party. The other half – about £1.5 million – disappeared into the ether, later to emerge as the Lloyd George Fund. His shocked son represented many when he asked, 'If you're not putting the money at the disposal of the Liberals then what are you going to do with it?'

I found out soon enough: he was buying newspaper properties. He was turning himself into a business tycoon ... In the years that followed, as election followed election, he grudgingly parted with relatively small sums for political purposes, always complaining that larger sums would be wasted because the Liberal Party was neither efficiently managed nor staffed with worth-while candidates. The bitterness in the Party undermined its drive and purpose. Feuds raged; there were mass desertions to the Conservative and Labour ranks.

The cynical farce had become tragedy.

It was the end of the Liberal Party as a major force in politics. It was the end of Lloyd George as an effective political figure.[25]

Lloyd George's politician daughter Megan was the only one of his children to be by his side as he died in 1945.

※

There is no doubt that Lloyd George contributed to the demise of the Liberal Party, but in the interwar period there were other factors at work that, across Europe, turned traditional politics on its head. With the spectre, or promise, of revolution, combining with severe economic depression and shifting geopolitical boundaries, Europe was a tinderbox ready to be lit. In Britain, returning soldiers had been promised a land fit for heroes. Instead they found unemployment, soaring prices, social unrest and a widening gap between rich and poor. With hindsight, we know that Britain avoided the worst of the extremes, but nothing was certain at the time, as negotiation and compromise turned into fear, overreaction and hatred. Of particular concern to the traditional ruling classes was communism, and the increasing demands of the Labour movement, the unions and the General Strike in 1926 set many of the old school twitching. The natural response was a push in the other direction, so as the left became more strident, so too did the right.

Oswald 'Tom' Mosley was one of the new breed of idealists, hardened in the trenches – or behind a desk in his case, having suffered a wound when showing off that benched him for much of the war – and expecting the promised brave new world. Back in London, he combined his wartime office work with an extensive social calendar and became an immediate hit. His good looks and diffident manner, his limp from his wound and his brief stint in the Royal Flying Corps gave him a gallant dash of romantic heroism that attracted ladies like moths to a flame, while his charm recommended him to his conquests' political husbands. By the end of 1918 he was a Coalition MP for the Unionist (Conservative) Party, and in 1920 the whole of the London set, including the royals, turned out for his society wedding to Lady Cynthia Blanche Curzon, daughter of the foreign secretary and later MP in her own right. For a minute, he seemed to be settling down. His politics were reasonable: supporting the League of Nations; aiming for a centrist middle way; pushing for social reform at home that, he believed, could only be achieved through peace abroad. Within a year he was pegged to become a future great of the Conservative Party.

All that changed when he took a stand, ironically given his later exploits, against the use of the paramilitary Black and Tans in Ireland. The Coalition was not happy and, within days, he had crossed the floor to become a member of the fledgling Labour Party. The problem was that the various Labour governments of the 1920s promised much and delivered little, content to 'keep buggering on', as Winston Churchill would say, in the same vein as their predecessors. Ministers slipped into 'the classic case of the Labour leader for whom arrival and acceptance have become ends in themselves'.[26] They lacked the dynamism that Mosley so desperately craved, and the far-reaching Keynesian reforms he suggested were, simply, too dangerous for them. By 1930 he was disillusioned, coming 'to the deliberate conclusion that in real crisis Labour would always betray both its principles and the people who had trusted it . . . The Labour Party could not, by reason of its very nature, be the force the British people desperately needed to save them.'[27]

For a brief while he flirted with his New Party – a young, assertive movement that crossed the political divide, and that pushed a new economic model of public spending combined with import tariffs to boost the home market – but following crushing election defeat, he decided it was not just Labour, but the establishment, that was rotten to the core. Everyone from the top down was either incompetent, scared or corrupted by the system. Even Auntie, the good old BBC, had politically censored him, banning his party-political film because it showed MPs snoring on the Commons' benches. It was time to try something different.

The New Party had already been developing a paramilitary wing, allegedly as protection from communists who kept literally crashing the party. And Mosley already had something of the dictator about him. As one eyewitness recorded,

> He did not know the meaning of humility. He brooked no argument, would accept no advice. He was overbearing and over-confident. He had in him the stuff of which zealots are made. His eyes flashed fire, dilated and contracted like a mesmerist's. His voice rose and fell in hypnotic cadences. He was madly in love with his own words.[28]

It was but one small goosestep for a man like Mosley to become leader of the British Union of Fascists. His black-shirted supporters, anti-communist and antisemitic, showed the same brutal devotion to him that the SS showed to Hitler. Processions and marches attracted initial interest and support, but also violence, which culminated in the Battle of Cable Street in London's East End on 4 October 1936.

It was a particularly fine day, that first Sunday in October 1936. The breeze had stilled, the sun was shining, and families and sweethearts strolled through London to bask in the last of the year's warmth. But they weren't the only ones filling the streets. From early morning onwards, people started to congregate around the East End. Some, turning up in dribs and drabs from across the country and accoutred in cadet-grey or black military-style uniforms complete with red and lightning-flash arm-bands, made their way to Tower Hill; others – anti-fascists and East Enders, greater by a magnitude of thirty – loitered on the roads running east along the north bank of the Thames; another group, some mounted, wore the blue of the Metropolitan Police. All three had established headquarters and first-aid stations. And all around, expectations were high. The air positively buzzed with anticipation. Battle would shortly commence.

Throughout the morning there had been scuffles. The 6,000 police on foot, and the entire London mounted division, did what they could to keep the peace. Some of the surrounding streets were closed, traffic diverted. They knew that 'the whole of the East End was seething, that the streets were chalked with phrases reading "They Shall Not Pass!", that Aldgate was one vast crowd of resentment.'[29]

A newly arriving group of Blackshirts caught some of the waiting gangs' eyes. Like a cat on the hunt, they crept slowly forward, then pounced. 'A chair leg wound round with barbed wire flashed. Then the police – mounted and foot – drew their batons and charged.' 'When the mêlée cleared one man was stretched out on the pavement. Three Blackshirts had blood streaming from their heads. Two of the Blackshirts were taken to the London Hospital. A third had his head bandaged.' An unfortunate 'onlooker', pointing to his bleeding head, told a reporter that he'd seen 'a crowd rushing by and I stopped my car and got out to see what the excitement was. As I did so a policeman seized me by the arm and hit me on the head.'[30] The same scene was repeated, again and again, across the area.

By half past two, 3,000 Blackshirts had assembled, ready to march forward in ranks stretching 600 yards, putting the Establishment's claims of free speech and freedom of thought to the test. One thousand police drew up around the group, necessary protection from the crowds shouting abuse and hurling missiles. And there they waited, tense as a drawn bow, for the leader to arrive. And they waited. An hour later, motorcycles came around the corner. Between them was Oswald Mosley's bullet-proof car. Late and fashionable – in some circles at least – he emerged clad in his 'entirely unprovocative' 'new SS-style uniform of black military jacket, grey jodhpurs, Sam Browne belt, jackboots and a peaked cap; round the left arm was a red-and-white armband'.[31] And like any general at a parade ground, he proceeded to inspect his troops, seemingly oblivious to the turmoil around.

The Metropolitan Police chief was not oblivious. Every entrance to London's East End appeared blocked by the locals. 'The householders had shuttered the windows of their homes, and eight barricades, in which a motor-lorry and several cars were used, were built across the street.' Another report registered 'a dozen flagstones torn from a pathway, oil drums, sheets of corrugated iron, broken iron bedsteads and the sides of wooden sheds' all piled up to prevent passage. Charge after charge was made by the police in an attempt to clear the way for the gathered Blackshirts. The waiting crowd of counter-protesters refused to be cowed. With home-made weapons and projectiles ripped from the pavements, they fought back.[32] It was hopeless: the Blackshirts really could not pass.

With the police busy charging Londoners, Jack Spot, 'King of the Underworld' knew the time was right. He'd been preparing all weekend. The day before, he'd visited a cabinet-maker in Aldgate and asked for a weapon to be made. 'I knew there were times when I had to carry a weapon,' he reminisced years later. 'And I knew this was certainly one of them.' The cabinet-maker didn't disappoint. Jack was presented with a beautifully turned wooden sofa leg, the top filled with lead.

Bludgeon concealed, Jack rounded up his gang of miscreants. There was big Moisha, his ham-like fist clutching a bicycle chain hidden in a jacket pocket. There was Sonny the Yank with his 'ten pounds of King Edward spuds each with two or three razor blades inserted for maximum damage'. 'Some had knuckledusters; many had coshes. Others were armed with old-fashioned, cutthroat razors with a hollow-ground blade that sliced through flesh like butter.' Seeing their chance, they attacked the group surrounding Mosley. Some, Blackshirt and bobby alike, were felled; others fought back. Mosley hid under the seat of his car.

It was a policeman who took Spot down, refusing to let go as he was pushed to the floor. Wrestling together on the ground, Spot's hand injured by the fall, the King of the Underworld pounded at the officer, 'smashed at him, used my knees and my head, and all at once there were more blue figures charging at me'. It took two heavy blows from a truncheon finally to render him unconscious.[33]

The immediate danger had passed, but the East End was still ready to erupt. There was only one thing the police chief could advise. Sending for Mosley, he said, 'As you can see for yourself, if you fellows go ahead from here there will be a shambles. I am not going to have that. You must call it off.'

'Is that an order?'

'Yes.'[34]

There was nothing else for Mosley to do. The procession, which should have toured the East End, instead turned west and marched down the Embankment accompanied by jeers of 'You're going the wrong way!' and choruses of 'The Grand Old Duke of York'. The East End looked as if the Blitz had come early. 'Hours after the march had been abandoned Cable Street resembled a sacked city. Hundreds of windows were broken and across the road lay a layer of bottle glass, iron and broken bricks. At the street corners the barricades had been thrown into a heap.'[35] Eighty-four arrests had been made, hundreds of people – fascists, communists and police – had required medical treatment. In the aftermath, the Public Order Act was passed, effectively bringing an end to the Blackshirts' activities. Very few, at least in public, questioned 'why the fury of the champions of free speech should be concentrated so exclusively not on those who deliberately and resolutely attempted to prevent the public expression of opinions of which they disapproved, but against those who fought, however roughly, for freedom of speech'.[36] One who did so was Lloyd George.

Just two days after Cable Street, and three years after his first wife had died, Mosley married his second wife in Berlin – with Adolf Hitler as a guest. He was not the first, and nor would he be the last, British politician to be taken in by the Führer. Less than a month before, Hitler had received another distinguished guest in the form of David Lloyd George, who returned 'in a state of great elation ... "He is indeed a great man," were his first words in describing Hitler'.[37] And the Great Appeaser Neville Chamberlain, admittedly in a long line of calamitous errors of judgement, two years later believed Hitler 'would not deliberately deceive a man whom he respected'.[38] Yet regardless of his personal opinions, when war with

Germany arrived, Mosley instructed his followers to support Britain while he continued to campaign for peace. This didn't save him from internment from 1940 onwards, or the slide into insignificance thereafter. He finished his days in Paris, living just a few doors down from his friend, the Duke of Windsor, the abdicated King Edward VIII.

※

Mosley is rightly castigated for his Nazi sympathies, but there was another MP who attempted to work even more closely with the far right in Germany: Ignatius Timotheus Trebitsch Lincoln. Born into a large Hungarian Jewish family, while still a teenager he dropped out of drama school, twice, and travelled across Europe, police reports for theft mapping his journey as surely as any train ticket stubs. Stopping in London, where he stole from a kindly Christian missionary, he continued his journey westwards, but not as a reformed Jean Valjean – although he did convert to Christianity so convincingly that in Canada he took a job as a missionary. By 1903, debts and boredom had spurred him onwards once again. Now with a German-born wife and young family in tow, he returned to Britain where his creatively embroidered curriculum vitae soon found him work as a curate in a Kentish village.

He wasn't particularly good at it. At his ordination exams, he came bottom of the class: 'Some of his work very bad. Surely ought not to pass.'[39] But no sooner had he been instructed to buck up his ideas than his father-in-law died, leaving the young family a decent inheritance. Disfrocking faster than a quick-change artist, he squandered his new wealth in the suburbs of London, until necessity drove him to find employment in the welcoming arms of the philanthropic chocolate magnate Benjamin Seebohm Rowntree. Three years of high-living and all-expenses-paid trips around Europe later, during which time he made the lives of embassy and Foreign Office staff a nightmare, he emerged with a name, connections, an unsecured £10,000 loan and the Liberal Party nomination for a seat in Parliament – despite the fact he had yet to be naturalised.

Lincoln's year in the Commons was undistinguished, the 'pinnacle' an unflattering *Punch* cartoon deriding his barely comprehensible accent, which he nevertheless proudly displayed to everyone he met. It was also short. Just ten months after the election, a new poll was called in the hope of making the House of Lords bow to popular pressure. The government won its point: under the threat of a mass creation of peers to force through its wishes – a mass creation that happened anyway in the subsequent decade – from 1911 onwards the Lords could no longer veto the budget or repeatedly reject other public bills. But by then, Lincoln had more material matters to consider.

All his money was gone. To maintain his luxurious lifestyle, and without pausing to consider how much he knew about the subject – or the fact he was a hair's breadth from bankruptcy – Lincoln established and floated an oil company. The plan was not so much 'Drill, Baby, Drill', as 'Pipe, Baby, Pipe', amalgamating existing lines based on an alleged agreement. But no sooner were the contracts signed than the deposits ran dry. The company was liquidated, after Lincoln had syphoned the remaining wealth into another oil venture, which this time did focus on drilling – into nothing. This second business likewise went into receivership, with debts of over £150,000, its assets surreptitiously stripped by a now desperate Lincoln. With barely enough to cover a meagre existence, and unwilling to consider a 'proper' job, Lincoln resorted to forgery – using first the Rowntree name and then that of a former banking friend – to secure finance. And then the Great War hit.

Aware that his misdeeds would catch up with him sooner or later, and filled 'with a bitter desire for revenge', he made up his mind 'to shake England's dust from my feet but not without "getting even"' for the imagined slights and cruelties perpetrated by his adopted country.[40] His strategy: to become a double agent, and thereby destroy Britain and her Navy. Conveniently forgetting, or perhaps misremembering, how he'd previously irritated the Foreign Office, he visited Whitehall and asked his contacts there to put him in touch with military intelligence.

Then he explained his plan, hoping to secure the trust of the British only to betray them immediately to the Germans:

> You will send two or three cruisers ... with attendant destroyers and torpedo boats, on some errand in the North Sea. You will let me know three or four days beforehand. I will notify the Germans and they will naturally send a more powerful squadron to the same vicinity on the same day in order to destroy them ... The Germans will then see that my information was correct. Now we will do this twice more; each time you must be ready to sacrifice some war vessels of old types.

Having lured the Germans into a false sense of security, he went on to explain, the next time, the entire British fleet would confront the enemy in battle and win. As an aside, he would, of course, need detailed plans of the fleet's position and capabilities.[41]

Lincoln called his plan 'audacious'. The War Office had another word for it. They were too polite to laugh him out of the building, but the result was the same.

Unsuccessful in London, the former MP's next stop was German intelligence in Rotterdam, where he appeared convincing enough to be given some harmless information to take back to Britain as a test. Returning to London, he again sought an interview with the War Office and explained, 'I went to Rotterdam because the British Secret Service would not employ me ... I have now obtained certain secret information that I think will prove my claim that I can be of real use to you.' With pride, he revealed the codes and addresses given to him by the Germans.[42] Fobbed off with impressed looks and noises, Lincoln was promised his desired position and sent away.

For almost a month, Lincoln waited and paced. Time was marching on, the consequences of his crimes were stalking closer, and it was only a matter of time before he was caught. Increasingly frantic calls were made to the War Office, to the Admiralty, to anyone who might put pressure on the grindingly slow bureaucracy. At last, he received a telegram: 'Please call and bring your passport. Director of Intelligence.'[43]

He practically sprinted to the Admiralty. But it was with a cool self-assurance that he sauntered into the interview room. That soon faded as the director of naval intelligence spoke. There would be no need for his assistance, Lincoln was informed. He would not be required in any capacity. He would not be paid for alleged services so far rendered. Did he really believe the Secret Service would know so little about his criminal activities? Did he truly consider himself suited to the work of a spy?

It was a miracle Lincoln wasn't seized on the spot. 'Indeed,' he wrote the following year,

> I cannot understand even now why they did not arrest me. However, I kept up the play and finally after a clever tactical conversation, left the room unmolested. They let me go, thinking that they had me in any case due to the fact that all passports in circulation were [soon to be] declared void. Indeed Captain Hall, who at first wanted to keep my passport, returned it to me with the ironical remark: 'All right, you can have it back, it is only valid two more days.'[44]

Two days were all Lincoln needed. The interview over, he visited a former secretary and convinced him to purchase 'about seventy pounds' of 'certain papers, connected with an oil company'. At five o'clock on 30 January 1915, he told his wife he was going to America, kissed her and his children, and walked out of the door. He had abandoned her with just two pounds in her pocket, and a bill for unpaid rent of £75.[45] The family was thrown into abject poverty, the children were withdrawn from school and set upon a harder path: the youngest, another Ignatius, was later hanged for robbery and murder, aged twenty-three.

Arriving in New York, Lincoln had the chance to start a new life. Unfortunately, he just couldn't help himself. The British had been content to forget he'd ever existed, but they could no longer ignore him when he published much-exaggerated, caustic accounts of his exploits as an 'international spy', which undermined their war efforts and were a propaganda gift to the Germans. Extradited for fraud, he remained in a British prison until 1919, when, with his naturalisation revoked, he was deported and made his way to Germany.

If Lincoln had disliked Britain before his imprisonment, he hated the country afterwards. But in Berlin he found a sympathetic *zeitgeist* in the far-right movements of the young Weimar Republic. Stories were shared with condoling friends, plans were hatched, and in March 1920 he found himself responsible for foreign propaganda in the abortive Kapp Putsch. 'Then he really became a spy ... Trebitsch-Lincoln moved from one group of conspirators to another and from nation to nation, betraying one to another in turn, until most of the Western nations would not let him cross their borders.'[46] Eventually deported from Austria in 1921, he made his way to China where he became a Buddhist monk revered as Abbot Chao Kung.

It all went to his head. Believing himself ordained to save the world, in 1934 he made sycophantic overtures to Hitler in the hope of gaining a visa to proselytise for his newly acquired religion. It was not granted: according to the Nazis, Lincoln was a Jew. Then at Christmas 1939, with the Second World War declared but only a small number of battles as of yet fought – in Poland, the Atlantic, and the ongoing Sino-Japanese War – the abbot released an international statement calling for the resignation of all belligerent governments worldwide. If not, he warned, 'the Tibetan Buddhist supreme masters, without prejudice, pre-direction or favor, will unchain forces and powers whose very existence are unknown to you and against whose operations you are consequently helpless.'[47]

Strangely, no one took him seriously. Unable to make an impact as a spiritual superhero for peace, he turned to his old ways as ineffectual supervillain and spy. The schemes started small, like his idea to manage a propaganda-pushing radio station to sway Asian opinion against Britain. Then they became wilder: Lincoln would use his 'immense authority' to bring Tibet into the orbit of German influence and, aside from the usual expenses – which for him, Buddhist or not, would include a suite in the most expensive hotel available – he would perform this service *gratis*. It would be payment enough to sate his 'desire to make himself important, thirst for adventure, and hatred for England'.[48]

The Abwehr, like its British military intelligence counterpart in the previous war, chose to ignore the mad monk. But Lincoln hadn't given up hope. Tracking down a Gestapo colonel in Shanghai, he requested immediate and fast transport to Berlin to consult with Hitler. The Führer would be convinced by Lincoln's powers when 'three of the wise men of Tibet would appear out of the wall', providing 'best proof of the supernatural powers at the disposal of the [Buddhist] Supreme Initiates'.[49] Unbelievably, the Gestapo agent, Josef Albert Meisinger, the dreaded 'Butcher of Warsaw' who had murdered 16,000 Jews, believed the unhinged upstart, despite the fact he was Jewish born. An urgent despatch was sent to Berlin laying out Lincoln's proposals and pushing for the requested audience.

The Butcher was one of the few – aside from Lincoln's band of adoring disciples – who did believe him. And as power within the Nazi regime shifted on an almost daily basis, and as attention focused on other theatres of war, Lincoln once again faded into insignificance. By the middle of 1943, he was living a calmer existence in a YMCA in Shanghai. Every afternoon, this tea-drinking figure 'clad in a black Buddhist robe, with soft Chinese shoes on bare feet and a rosary around his neck', would take a gentle stroll to the Bubbling Well and Jing'an Temple.[50] He would spend his remaining hours in quiet contemplation and spiritual discussion, or regaling visiting company with anecdotes from his past. He died on 6 October 1943, following an operation for a stomach complaint. Rumour persists that the underlying cause was an overdose of the Gestapo.[51]

❊

As the war came to an end in 1945, the world looked ahead to a new era, a time that would guarantee safety for democracy and rights for the average person. The 'Giant Evils' – want, disease, ignorance, squalor and idleness – would disappear from the nation, and the people would no longer be led by the donkeys who had given us two world wars in thirty years; who had introduced a new, and possibly planet-destroying, weapon; who had brought the economy and society to the brink of collapse; and who all the while sought fame and fortune for themselves. Instead, nations would come together in harmony, having finally learned the lessons of the past.

It was wishful thinking. The Second World War, just like those fought before it, had not made the world safer for democracy. The tragedy of that particular conflict, as one historian has recently pointed out, is that through the British-American-Soviet alliance, 'it made much of Europe and Asia "safe" for communism'.[52] By 1950, everyone was back at it: Germany was divided for most of the rest of the century; a 'hot' war was raging in Korea; while a cold one was dividing countries into blocs that refused to understand that debate and compromise achieve more – at less human cost – than blindly following ideology and party politics. And within the space of a few years, Britain was again being rocked by one political scandal after another. It, and the world, were still being led by donkeys.

Epilogue

The middle years of the twentieth century witnessed earthquakes in parliamentary and international politics of devastating proportions. So catastrophic, indeed, that we tried to learn from our mistakes, to remake the world afresh. Perhaps, for a few optimistic moments in the 1940s and 1950s, we thought that we might succeed, but this was not the first time that great upheavals have been a catalyst for attempted political and societal change. The same process happened in the 1640s, the 1660s, the 1690s, the 1720s – you get the picture – with the same ultimate results. Occasionally, progress limped forward, usually at that point where the government – be it based around a monarchy, a democracy, or even a theocracy – began to fear for its own existence. People can only be pushed so far before they snap. However, as one political scientist has explained, 'there was no reason to assume that political development was any more likely than political decay'.[1] And a brief glance backwards over the last three centuries of Britain's politicians suggests if not deterioration, then at least stagnation.

Although the causes, the faces and, to a lesser extent, the names of our political leaders have changed over time, the key characteristics of many MPs have remained the same. A brief look around the globe today will show any number of dodgy politicians: the barely sane and the psychotic; the megalomaniacs and the incompetents; the greedy, for money and for power; the abusive; the underhand. Death and taxes are the two certainties in life, but perhaps to that we should add a third: that among our leaders, our representatives, there will always be some who lean towards the criminal and corrupt.

While no two politicians are exactly the same, and there are no absolute marks distinguishing the bad 'uns from the good 'uns, there are certain features in common when it comes to those members behaving badly. As a biographer of Labby wrote, party politics is 'a dishonest if amusing game, in which a number of men whose brains should have been better employed were engaged in the silly business of obtaining distinctions or the shady business of getting money'.[2] Politicians like wealth and they like power. The greatest distinguishing factor of all, however, comes down to a particular perspective: they take their power and position for granted. In vain did I look for women in the House of Commons in the first half of the twentieth century who deserved to be included in the ranks of the truly dreadful fifty-two. There were none. That is not to say that female politicians are inherently better, far from it: our most recent crop has included some real corkers. It might, however, be to suggest that the women who entered the Commons between 1919 and 1945 understood the value of their position. They knew the importance of their election, and they were determined to show they could do well. And there's the rub. When it is no longer a privilege, but a right – of birth, of wealth, of profession – that is when the problems start.

This is not to say there are no good politicians, that the drivers behind all MPs are mercenary and selfish. Many truly believe that they can make a positive difference in the world, and some do. Others enter with the best of intentions but find themselves corrupted by the system – or discarded by it and so seek 'other courses' for change.[3] As the adage goes, power corrupts – and excrement rises.

So, what to do? Is it, in fact, the system that is to blame, or do a few rotten eggs spoil it for everyone else? Is the notion of a political utopia – in which our politicians actually put aside their own concerns and instead represent the people who elected them – just that: an impractical idea that can never be realised? We've tried varying degrees of absolute monarchy; we've tried republicanism; we've tried military rule; we've tried the leadership of strong men; we've tried more-and-less balanced constitutions. Nothing has a guarantee of success.

Perhaps, ultimately, there is little that can be done and, anyway, I make no pretences at offering a manifesto. After all, there is still an excellent one (with some modern amendments) that has not yet been fully implemented:

Epilogue

THE PEOPLE'S CHARTER;

BEING THE OUTLINE OF AN ACT

TO PROVIDE FOR THE

Just Representation of the People of Great Britain and Ireland IN THE COMMONS' HOUSE OF PARLIAMENT,

EMBRACING THE PRINCIPLES OF

UNIVERSAL SUFFRAGE, NO PROPERTY QUALIFICATION, ANNUAL PARLIAMENTS, EQUAL REPRESENTATION, PAYMENT OF MEMBERS, AND VOTE BY BALLOT.

Whereas, to insure, in as far as it is possible by human forethought and wisdom, the just government of the people, it is necessary to subject those who have the power of making the laws to a wholesome and strict responsibility to those whose duty it is to obey them when made.

And whereas, this responsibility is best enforced through the instrumentality of a body which emanates directly from, and is itself immediately subject to, the whole people, and which completely represents their feelings and their interests;

And, whereas, as the Commons' House of Parliament now exercises, in the name, and on the supposed behalf of the people, the power of making the laws, it ought, in order to fulfil with wisdom and with honesty the great duties imposed on it, to be made the most faithful and accurate representation of the people's wishes, feelings, and interests . . .[4]

Imagine. If all MPs were truly enacting 'the most faithful and accurate representation of the people's wishes, feelings, and interests', rather than considering their own, what might that look like? There's one thing for sure. It would be very different from the schemes and the scandals, the sozzled and the stark naked, the murderers and enslavers, the comedy and the errors of the MPs we've met here. And, perhaps, be all the better for it.

Acknowledgements

There are a number of people without whose advice, support and patience this book would not have been possible. Firstly, I would like to thank everybody at the History of Parliament Trust for their ongoing, thorough and enlightening work, but especially I would like to thank Dr Philip Salmon and (although he has now left) Dr Paul Seaward for the introductions and access they have granted me.

Secondly, the team, particularly my editors Sarah Rigby and Pippa Crane, at Elliott & Thompson have been brilliant. Not only have they taken a chance on a (relatively) unknown author to start with, they have also been unerringly helpful in guiding me through the process, providing inspiration and a shoulder to cry on whenever necessary, while Amy Greaves has been fabulous in her enthusiastic promotion of the book.

There have been many other people who have helped me, professionally and personally, in the writing of *Members Behaving Badly*, whether that be with advice, reading through revisions, or simply by making cups of tea. My gratitude of course goes to my fantastic husband, Toby Kilroy, who has been constant in his support not just over the last two years of writing, but over the last twenty-plus years of marriage. Thank you, my darling. Also, my two teenage boys, Corvus and Leo, deserve a special mention for being understanding enough to allow me to put my work first on occasion. Further thanks must go to Anne and Guy Miller, Mike and Christine Voyce, Simon Thompson, Darren Sharples and his family, Adam Schuch-des Forges, Alex Hippisley-Cox, Kate Vigurs, Mark Piesing, Jackson van Uden, Louise Errington-Thomas and Steve Law, all for being wonderful. Lastly, I would like to thank all good history teachers everywhere. Often, teachers remain unacknowledged, but they can have such a positive impact on young minds. I was lucky enough to have two amazing teachers, so thank you Sue Brookes and Simon Peaple.

Endnotes

Introduction
1. L. S. Woodger, 'Courtenay, Sir Philip' in *The History of Parliament* (hereafter *HP*), 1386–1421.
2. 8 July 1402, A. E. Stamp (ed.), *Calendar of Close Rolls, Henry IV* (London: HMSO, 1929), vol. 2, *British History Online*; https://www.british-history.ac.uk/series/calendar-close-rolls-henry-iv [accessed January 2023–June 2025].
3. 9 November 1402, Christopher Given-Wilson (ed.), *Parliament Rolls of Medieval England, 1275–1504: Henry IV, 1399–1413* (Suffolk: Boydell Press, 2005) [CD-Rom].
4. Ibid., 25 November 1402.

Chapter One: Absolute Power (1603–37)
1. All currency conversions from *Measuring Wealth*; https://www.measuringworth.com/calculators/ukcompare/ [accessed January 2023–June 2025].
2. Menna Prestwich, *Cranfield: Politics and Profits under the Early Stuarts* (Oxford: Clarendon Press, 1966), p. 510.
3. 30 April 1621, *Lords Journal* (hereafter *LJ*).
4. Ibid.
5. Basil Montagu (ed.), *The Works of Francis Bacon* (Philadelphia: A. Hart, 1852), vol. 2, p. 497.
6. John Chamberlain to Dudley Carleton, 24 March 1621, in Norman Egbert McClure (ed.), *The Letters of John Chamberlain* (Philadelphia: The American Philosophical Society, 1939), vol. 2, p. 356.
7. Bacon to James I, 25 March 1621, in James Spedding, *The Letters and Life of Francis Bacon* (London: Longmans, Green, Reader and Dyer, 1874), vol. 7, pp. 225–6.
8. Conrad Russell, *The Crisis of Parliaments: English History, 1509–1660* (Oxford: Oxford University Press, 1971), p. 38.
9. Francis Bacon to George Villiers, 21 November 1616, in Spedding, *Letters and Life*, vol. 6, p. 102.
10. Simon Healy, 'Mompesson, Giles (1584–c.1651)', in *HP*, 1604–1629.
11. Thomas Tyrwhitt (ed.), *The Proceedings and Debates of the House of Commons in 1620 and 1621* (Oxford: Clarendon, 1766), vol. 1, p. 71.
12. Samuel Rawson Gardiner, 'On Four Letters from Lord Bacon to Christian IV of Denmark', 219–69, in *Archaeologia* 41 (1867), p. 234.

13. 22 March 1621, *LJ*.
14. 26 March 1621, *LJ*.
15. London, The National Archives (TNA), PROB 11/312/30.
16. Andrew Thrush, 'Villiers, Sir Edward', in *HP, 1604–1629*.
17. John Chamberlain to Dudley Carleton, 28 June 1623, in McClure, *Letters*, vol. 2, p. 505.
18. Thomas G. Barnes, 'Introduction to Coke's Commentary on Littleton', 1–25, in Allen D. Boyer (ed.), *Law, Liberty and Parliament: Selected Essays on the Writings of Sir Edward Coke* (Indianapolis: Liberty Fund, 2004), p. 22.
19. John Chamberlain to Dudley Carleton, 22 November 1598, in McClure, *Letters*, vol. 1, p. 54.
20. Laura Norsworthy, *The Lady of Bleeding Heart Yard: Lady Elizabeth Hatton, 1578–1646* (London: John Murray, 1935), p. 31.
21. Ibid., p. 24.
22. Ibid., p. 32.
23. 5 July 1604, *The Commons Journal* (hereafter *CJ*).
24. Norsworthy, *Lady of Bleeding Heart Yard*, p. 23.
25. Ibid., p. 45.
26. November 1617, Mary Anne Everett Green (ed.), *Calendar of State Papers Domestic: James I, 1611–1618* (London: HMSO, 1858).
27. Dudley Carleton to Ralph Winwood, 30 May 1616 [OS], in Dudley Carleton, *Letters from and to Sir Dudley Carleton . . . During His Embassy in Holland, From January 1615/16, To December 1620*, 2nd edn (London, 1775), p. 27.
28. Dudley Carleton to John Chamberlain, 24 May 1616, in Maurice Lee (ed.), *Dudley Carleton to John Chamberlain, 1603–1624: Jacobean Letters* (New Jersey: Rutgers University Press, 1972), p. 202.
29. Dudley Carleton to Ralph Winwood, 30 May 1616 [OS], in Carleton, *Letters*, p. 27.
30. Samuel Rawson Gardiner, *Debates in the House of Commons in 1625* (London: Camden Society, 1873), p. 10.
31. Spedding, *Letters and Life*, vol. 1, p. 98.
32. Robert C. Johnson and Maija Jansson Cole, *Commons Debates 1628* (London: Yale University Press, 1977), vol. 2, p. 3.
33. F. A. Inderwick, *A Calendar of the Inner Temple Records* (London: Masters of the Bench, 1898), vol. 2, p. lxix.
34. Barnes, 'Introduction to Coke's Commentary on Littleton', p. 9.

Chapter Two: What's So Civil about War? (1637–60)
1. Edward Hyde, *The History of the Rebellion and Civil Wars in England, Begun in the Year 1641*, ed. by W. Dunn Macray (Oxford: Clarendon Press, 1888), vol. 3, p. 419.

Endnotes

2. Bulstrode Whitelocke, *Memorials of the English Affairs: Or, an Historical Account of What Passed from the Beginning of the Reign of King Charles the First, to King Charles the Second His Happy Restoration* (London: Nathaniel Ponder, 1682), p. 28.
3. Thomas Peyton to Henry Oxinden, 14 May 1640, in ibid., p. 174.
4. William Cobbett (ed.), *Cobbett's Parliamentary History of England* (London: Hansard, 1807), vol. 2, p. 815.
5. Edward Hyde, *The History of the Rebellion and Civil Wars in Ireland*, 3rd edn (London: T. Cooper, 1740), p. 348.
6. Cited in Amos C. Miller, *Sir Richard Grenville of the Civil War* (London: Phillimore, 1979), p. 65.
7. Hyde, *History of the Rebellion and Civil Wars in England*, vol. 3, p. 418.
8. Ibid., vol. 4, p. 67.
9. *A Continuation of the True Narration of the Most Observable Passages in and about Plymouth, from January 26 1643 till this present . . .* (London, 1644), p. 6.
10. Cited in Roger Granville, *The King's General in the West: The Life of Sir Richard Granville, Bart., 1600–1659* (London: J. Lane, 1908), p. 75n.
11. Richard Grenville, *A letter written by Sir Richard Grenville (under his own hand) to an honourable person in the city of London, concerning the affairs of the west* (London, 1646).
12. Cited in Miller, *Sir Richard Grenville*, p. 101.
13. 'Sir Richard Grenville's Narrative of the Proceedings of His Majesty's Affairs in the West of England. . .', 96–109, in Thomas Carte (ed.), *A Collection of Original Letters and Papers, Concerning the Affairs of England, from the Year 1641 to 1660* (London, 1739), vol. 1, p. 107.
14. 'Sir Richard Grenville's Defence against All Aspersions of Malignant Persons', 230–48, in George Granville, *The Genuine Works in Verse and Prose* (London: J. Tonson, 1736), vol. 2, p. 242.
15. Granville, *The King's General in the West*, pp. 207–8.
16. Henry Cary (ed.), *Memorials of the Great Civil War in England, from 1646 to 1652* (London: Henry Colburn, 1842), vol. 2, p. 4.
17. *King Charles his speech made upon the scaffold at Whitehall-Gate, immediately before his execution, on Tuesday the 30 of Jan. 1648* (London, 1649), pp. 5–14.
18. Edmund Ludlow, *The Memoirs of Edmund Ludlow*, ed. by C. H. Firth (Oxford: Clarendon Press, 1894), vol. 2, p. 322.
19. *Mercurius publicus: comprising the sum of forraign intelligence . . .* 29 (12 July–19 July 1660), p. 451.
20. Hyde, *History of the Rebellion and Civil Wars in Ireland*, p. 354.
21. William Cobbett (ed.), *Cobbett's Complete Collection of State Trials* (London: Hansard, 1810), vol. 5, p. 1288.

22. Revelation 16:1–6.
23. Hyde, *History of the Rebellion and Civil Wars in Ireland*, p. 355.
24. Ibid., p. 354.
25. John Thurloe, *A Collection of the State Papers of John Thurloe*, ed. by Thomas Birch (London: Fletcher Gyles, 1742), vol. 5, p. 671.
26. Mark Stoyle, 'The Honour of General Monck', in *History Today* 43 (1993).
27. Samuel Pepys, *The Diary of Samuel Pepys*, ed. by R. C. Latham and W. Matthews (London: HarperCollins, 2016), 8 March 1661, vol. 2, p. 51; 9 September 1665, vol. 6, p. 324.
28. Anna Keay, *The Restless Republic: Britain without a Crown* (London: William Collins, 2022), p. 276.
29. Pepys, *Diary*, 17 November 1667, vol. 7, p. 536.
30. John Aubrey, *Brief Lives*, ed. by A. Clark (Oxford: Clarendon Press, 1898), vol. 2, p. 73.
31. Ronald Hutton, *Charles II: King of England, Scotland and Ireland* (Oxford: Oxford University Press, 1989), p. 57.
32. Hyde, *History of the Rebellion and Civil Wars in England*, vol. 5, p. 177.
33. Ludlow, *Memoirs*, vol. 1, pp. 282–3.
34. Hyde, *History of the Rebellion and Civil Wars in England*, vol. 5, p. 239.
35. C. H. Firth (ed.), *Scotland and the Protectorate: Letters and Papers Relating to the Military Government of Scotland from January 1654 to June 1659*, for the Scottish History Society, vol. 31 (Edinburgh: Edinburgh University Press, 1899), p. 96.
36. Ronald Hutton, *Oliver Cromwell: Commander in Chief* (London: Yale University Press, 2024), p. 331.
37. Monck to Cromwell, 21 April 1655, in Firth, *Scotland and the Protectorate*, pp. 266–7.
38. Monck to Ludlow, 20 October 1659, in Ludlow, *Memoirs*, vol. 2, p. 449.
39. Cobbett, *State Trials*, vol. 5, p. 1291.
40. Ibid., p. 1289.

Chapter Three: A House of Ill-Repute (1660–85)
1. 3 June 1667, Pepys, *Diary*, vol. 8, p. 249.
2. 3 May 1664, in ibid., vol. 5, p. 141.
3. 10 June 1667, in ibid., vol. 8, p. 257.
4. 14 June 1667, in ibid., vol. 8, p. 267.
5. Andrew Marvell, 'Satires of the Reign of Charles II: The last Instructions to a Painter', in H. M. Margoliouth and Pierre Legouis (eds), *The Poems and Letters of Andrew Marvell*, 3rd edn (Oxford: Oxford University Press, 1971), vol. 1, pp. 601–10.

Endnotes

6. 15 November 1664, in Pepys, *Diary*, vol. 5, p. 322.
7. 16 January 1664, in ibid., vol. 5, p. 17.
8. 18 August 1667, in ibid., vol. 8, pp. 389–90.
9. 23 October 1668, in ibid., vol. 9, pp. 335–6.
10. Ibid., p. 336.
11. 12 September 1671, Sir Heneage Finch to his son in Jeremy Treglown (ed.), *The Letters of John Wilmot, Earl of Rochester* (Oxford: Basil Blackwell, 1980), p. 69n.
12. Rochester to John Muddyman, in ibid., p. 70.
13. Ibid.
14. 12 September 1671, Sir Heneage Finch to his son, and Rochester to John Muddyman, in Treglown, *The Letters of John Wilmot*, pp. 69n, 70.
15. 1 July 1663, Pepys, *Diary*, vol. 4, pp. 209–10.
16. Anthony Wood, *The Life and Times of Anthony Wood*, ed. by Andrew Clark (Oxford: Clarendon Press, 1891), vol. 1, pp. 476–7; Robert Sackville-West, *Inheritance: The Story of Knole and the Sackvilles* (London: Bloomsbury, 2010), p. 80. Because of the delight taken by the gossips in the incident, reports naturally differed and were exaggerated. This account is, by necessity, taken from these sensational reports.
17. 1 July 1663, Pepys, *Diary*, vol. 4, pp. 209–10.
18. Sackville-West, *Inheritance*, p. 80.
19. Anthony Wood, *Athenæ Oxonienses*, 2nd edn (London: Knaplock, Midwinter and Tonson, 1721), vol. 2, p. 1100.
20. Ibid.
21. These days this is attributed to Sedley; previously it was believed to have been written by the Earl of Rochester. 'In the Fields of Lincoln's Inn' (1680), in Mark Ford (ed.), *London: A History in Verse* (Cambridge, MA, and London: The Belknap Press of Harvard University Press, 2012), pp. 203–4.
22. Vivian de Sola Pinto, *Sir Charles Sedley* (London: Constable and Company, 1927), p. 319.
23. 1 February 1669, Pepys, *Diary*, vol. 9, p. 435.
24. Historical Manuscripts Commission (hereafter HMC), *Report on Manuscripts in Various Collections* (London: HMSO, 1913), vol. 8, p. 66.
25. 29 July 1667, Pepys, *Diary*, vol. 8, pp. 363–4.
26. J. P. Vander Motten, 'Porter, Thomas', in *Oxford Dictionary of National Biography* (hereafter *DNB*).
27. John Harold Wilson, *The Court Wits of the Restoration* (New York: Octagon Books Inc., 1967), p. 35.
28. Sackville-West, *Inheritance*, p. 89.
29. Ibid., p. 97.

30. William Durrant Cooper (ed.), *Savile Correspondence* (London: Camden Society, 1858), pp. 45–6.
31. Cited in David J. Sturdy, 'Savile, Henry', *DNB*.
32. Peter Cunningham, *The Story of Nell Gwyn*, ed. by Henry B. Wheatley (London: W. W. Gibbins, 1892), p. 111.
33. 1 November 1678, *CJ*.
34. Charles James Fox, *A History of the Early Part of the Reign of James the Second* (London: William Miller, 1808), p. 33.
35. Gilbert Burnet, *Bishop Burnet's History of His Own Time* (Oxford: Clarendon Press, 1833), vol. 3, pp. 37–8.

Chapter Four: House Party (1685–1715)
1. Francis Sandford, *The History of the Coronation of the Most High, Most Mighty, and Most Excellent Monarch, James II* (London, 1687), pp. 77–9.
2. Ibid., p. 94.
3. Laurence Echard, *The History of England, from the Restoration of King Charles the Second to the Conclusion of the Reign of King James the Second* (London: Jacob Tonson, 1718), vol. 3, p. 734.
4. 22 May 1685, *CJ*.
5. J. Kent Clark, *Whig's Progress: Wharton Between Revolutions* (London: Associated University Presses, 2004), p. 218.
6. Eveline Cruickshanks, 'Wharton, Hon. Thomas (1648–1715)', in *HP*, 1660–1690.
7. John Oldmixon, *Memoirs of the Life of the Most Noble Thomas Late Marquess of Wharton* (London: J. Roberts, 1715), p. 29.
8. Ibid.
9. Kent Clark, *Whig's Progress*, pp. 50–1.
10. Oldmixon, *Memoirs of the Life of the Most Noble Thomas Late Marquess of Wharton*, p. 33.
11. John Carswell, *The Old Cause: Three Biographical Studies in Whiggism* (London: Cresset Press, 1954), pp. 56–7.
12. Ibid., p. 207; Bryan Dale, *The Good Lord Wharton: His Family, Life, and Bible Charity* (London: The Congregational Union of England and Wales, 1906), p. 42.
13. Cobbett, *Parliamentary History*, vol. 5, p. 50.
14. Queen Anne to the Duke of Marlborough, 27 August 1708, in Beatrice Curtis Brown (ed.), *The Letters and Diplomatic Instructions of Queen Anne* (New York: Funk & Wagnalls, 1968), p. 258.
15. Daniel Defoe, *A Tour through the Whole Island of Great Britain*, ed. by Pat Rogers (Exeter: Webb & Bower, 1989), p. 22.
16. 8 December 1691, *CJ*.
17. 12 February 1696, *CJ*.

18. Ibid.
19. Narcissus Luttrell, *A Brief Historical Relation of State Affairs from September 1678 to April 1714* (Oxford: Oxford University Press, 1857), vol. 4, pp. 493–9.
20. HMC, *Report on the Manuscripts of His Grace the Duke of Portland Preserved at Welbeck Abbey* (London: HMSO, 1891–1931), vol. 8, p. 59.
21. Tim Blanning, *George I* (London: Penguin, 2017), p. 69.
22. John Stevens, *The Journal of John Stevens*, ed. by Robert H. Murray (Oxford: Clarendon Press, 1912), p. 70.
23. Cited in Leonard Naylor, 'Wharton, Hon. Henry', *HP*, 1660–1690.
24. Abel Boyer, *The History of King William III* (London: A. Roper, 1702), vol. 2, p. 139.
25. Burnet, *History of His Own Time*, vol. 4, p. 85.
26. Ibid., vol. 4, p. 92.
27. Lawrence H. Leder, 'Robert Livingston's Voyage to England, 1695', 16–38, in *New York History* 36 (1955); 2 December 1699, *CJ*.
28. Robert C. Ritchie, *Captain Kidd and the War against the Pirates* (Cambridge, MA, and London: Harvard University Press, 1986), pp. 128–9.
29. Marquis, *Captain Kidd*, p. 119.
30. Ritchie, *Captain Kidd*, p. 163.
31. John Oldmixon, *Memoirs of the Life of John Lord Somers* (London: J. Roberts, 1716), p. 82.
32. Cobbett, *State Trials*, vol. 14, p. 232.
33. Paul Lorrain, *The ordinary of Newgate his account of the behaviour, confessions, and dying-words of Captain William Kidd, and other pirates, that were executed at the Execution-Dock in Wapping, on Friday May 23. 1701* (London: E. Mallet, 1701).
34. Ibid.
35. 8 May 1701, *CJ*.
36. Douglas Watt, *The Price of Scotland: Darien, Union and the Wealth of Nations* (Edinburgh: Luath Press Limited, 2024), p. 83.
37. Ibid., p. 253.
38. Ibid., p. 193.
39. John Sinclair, *Memoirs of the Insurrection in Scotland in 1715*, ed. by Walter Scott (Edinburgh, 1858), p. 3.
40. Edward Gregg, *Queen Anne* (New Haven and London: Yale University Press, 2001), p. 334.
41. Sinclair, *Memoirs*, p. 90.
42. Ibid., p. 81.
43. Ibid., p. 248.

Chapter Five: Capital Offence (1716–46)

1. 'The Blessings Attending George's Accession', cited in Blanning, *George I*, p. 35.
2. 29 November 1710, *CJ*.
3. Blanning, *George I*, p. 69.
4. Daniel Defoe, *The Anatomy of Exchange-Alley: Or a System of Stock-Jobbing*, 2nd edn (London: E. Smith, 1719), pp. 3–4.
5. William Coxe, *Memoirs of the Life and Administration of Sir Robert Walpole, Earl of Orford* (London: T. Cadell, Jun., and W. Davies, 1798), vol. 1, p. 126.
6. Cobbett, *Parliamentary History*, vol. 6, p. 1022.
7. John Carswell, *The South Sea Bubble* (Stroud: Alan Sutton, 1993), p. 103.
8. Thomas Levenson, *Money for Nothing: The South Sea Bubble and the Invention of Modern Capitalism* (London: Head of Zeus, 2020), pp. 173–4, 179.
9. Ibid.
10. Ibid., pp. 227–8.
11. Cited in Charles Wilson, *Anglo-Dutch Commerce and Finance in the Eighteenth Century* (Cambridge: Cambridge University Press, 1966), p. 124.
12. HMC, *The Manuscripts of the Earl of Buckinghamshire, et al* (London: HMSO, 1895), pp. 504–5.
13. Levenson, *Money for Nothing*, p. 188.
14. Archibald Hutcheson, *Some Calculations Relating to the Proposals Made by the South Sea Company and the Bank of England to the House of Commons* (London, 1720), pp. 15, 41; Bank of England, *A Millennium of Macroeconomic Data for the UK* (2024), at https://www.bankofengland.co.uk/-/media/boe/files/statistics/research-datasets/a-millennium-of-macroeconomic-data-for-the-uk.xlsx [accessed November 2024].
15. Levenson, *Money for Nothing*, p. 247; Carswell, *The South Sea Bubble*, p. 170.
16. Alexander Pope to Francis Atterbury, 23 September 1720, in Alexander Pope, *The Works of Alexander Pope, Esq.*, ed. by William Roscoe (London: Longman, Brown and Co., 1847), vol. 7, p. 185.
17. House of Commons, *The Several Reports of the Committee of Secrecy to the Honourable House of Commons, Relating to the Late South Sea Directors, &c* (London: A. Moore, 1721), pp. 12–17.
18. House of Lords, *The History and Proceedings of the House of Lords from the Restoration in 1660 to the Present Time* (London: Ebenezer Timberland, 1842–44), vol. 3, p. 125.
19. Defoe, *The Anatomy of Exchange-Alley*, p. 42.
20. HMC, *Buckinghamshire*, pp. 510–11; Levenson, *Money for Nothing*, p. 162.
21. 8 March 1721, *CJ*.
22. HMC, *Buckinghamshire*, pp. 510–11.

23. Romney R. Sedgwick, 'Stanhope, Charles', *HP*, 1715–1754; Thomas Brodrick to Lord Middleton, 9 March 1720/21, in Coxe, *Memoirs of the Life and Administration of Sir Robert Walpole*, vol. 2, p. 210.
24. Thomas Brodrick to Lord Middleton, 9 March 1720/21, in Coxe, *Memoirs of the Life and Administration of Sir Robert Walpole*, vol. 2, p. 209.
25. HMC, *Buckinghamshire*, p. 511.
26. William Dalrymple, *The Anarchy: The Relentless Rise of the East India Company* (London: Bloomsbury, 2019), p. xxvii; Andrew A. Hanham, 'Craggs, James I', *HP*, 1690–1715.
27. Edward Harley Jr to Abigail Harley, 19 March 1720/21, HMC, *Portland*, vol. 5, p. 619.
28. Alexander Carlyle, *Autobiography of the Rev. Dr Alexander Carlyle, Minister of Inveresk*, 2nd edn (Edinburgh and London: William Blackwood and Sons, 1860), p. 9.
29. Ibid., p. 15.
30. Nick Hervey, 'Erskine [née Chiesley, Cheislie], Rachel, Lady Grange', *DNB*.
31. R. W. Seton-Watson, 'The Strange Story of Lady Grange', 12–24, in *History* 16 (1931), p. 13.
32. Cited in ibid., p. 17.
33. Taken from 'An Account of the Misfortunes of Mrs Erskine of Grange, Commonly Known as Lady Grange', 333–9, in *The Edinburgh Magazine and Literary Miscellany, Being a New Series of the Scots Magazine*, 1 (November 1817), p. 335.
34. Ibid.
35. Ibid.
36. Ibid., p. 336.
37. Ibid., p. 338.
38. Ibid.
39. Ibid., pp. 338–9.
40. David Laing, 'An Episode in the Life of Mrs Rachel Erskine, Lady Grange', 593–608, in *Proceedings of the Society of Antiquaries of Scotland* 11 (1876), p. 602.
41. 'An Account of the Misfortunes of Mrs Erskine of Grange', p. 339.
42. William A. Pettigrew, *Freedom's Debt: The Royal African Company and the Politics of the Atlantic Slave Trade, 1672–1752* (Chapel Hill: University of North Carolina Press, 2013), p. 46.
43. I. F. Grant, *The Macleods: A History of a Clan, 1200–1956* (London: Faber & Faber, 1959), p. 406.
44. Ibid.
45. Ibid., p. 407.

46. Duncan Warrand (ed.), *More Culloden Papers* (Inverness: Robert Carruthers & Sons, 1923–30), vol. 3, p. 141.
47. James Browne, *A History of the Highlands and of the Highland Clans* (Glasgow: A. Fullarton, 1840), vol. 2, p. 464.
48. John Murray, *Memorials of John Murray of Broughton, Sometimes Secretary to Prince Charles Edward, 1740–1747*, ed. by Robert Fitzroy Bell (Edinburgh: Scottish History Society, 1898), p. 428.
49. Warrand, *More Culloden Papers*, vol. 4, p. 78.
50. Cited in Jacqueline Riding, *Jacobites: A New History of the '45 Rebellion* (London: Bloomsbury, 2016), p. 406.
51. David Wemyss, *A Short Account of the Affairs of Scotland in the Years 1744, 1745, 1746* (Edinburgh: David Douglas, 1907), pp. 428–9.
52. Ibid., p. 429.
53. Ibid., p. 430.
54. Ibid., p. 432.
55. Ibid., p. 433.
56. Ibid., p. 434.

Chapter Six: Liberty and Libertines (1746–75)

1. James Boswell, *Boswell on the Grand Tour: Italy, Corsica, and France, 1765–1766*, ed. by Frank Brady and Frederick A. Pottle (Surrey: Windmill Press, 1955), pp. 56–7.
2. D. M. Lowe (ed.), *Gibbon's Journal to January 28th, 1763* (New York: W. W. Norton and Company, 1929), p. 145.
3. Horace Bleackley, *Life of John Wilkes* (London: Bodley Head, 1917), p. 426; cited in Peter D. G. Thomas, *John Wilkes: A Friend to Liberty* (Oxford: Clarendon Press, 1996), p. 208.
4. Thomas Babington Macaulay, *The Essays of Lord Macaulay: Earl of Chatham*, ed. by H. W. C. Davis (London: William Heinemann, 1908), p. 89.
5. Henry Fielding, *The Covent Garden Journal*, ed. by Gerald Edward Jensen (New Haven: Yale University Press, 1915), vol. 1, p. 209 (11 February 1752); Mary Wortley Montagu, *The Complete Letters of Lady Mary Wortley Montagu*, ed. by Robert Halsband (Oxford: Clarendon Press, 1965–67), vol. 1, p. 38; *The London Gazette*, 25 April 1721, p. 1.
6. Horace Walpole, *Memoirs of the Reign of King George III*, ed. by Derek Jarrett (New Haven and London: Yale University Press, 2000), vol. 1, p. 164; John Wilkes, *North Briton* 41 (12 March 1763).
7. Lionel Cust and Sidney Colvin (eds), *History of the Society of Dilettanti* (London: Macmillan and Co., 1914), p. 9.
8. His italics. Walpole, *Memoirs of the Reign of King George III*, vol. 1, pp. 113–14.

Endnotes

9. Patrick Woodland, 'Dashwood, Francis, eleventh Baron Le Despencer', *DNB*.
10. Horace Walpole to Horace Mann, 14 April 1743, in W. S. Lewis, (ed.), *The Yale Edition of Horace Walpole's Correspondence* (New Haven: Yale University Press, 1937–1983), vol. 18, p. 211.
11. Walpole, *Memoirs of the Reign of King George III*, vol. 1, p. 114.
12. Paget Toynbee, 'Horace Walpole's Journals of Visits to Country Seats, &c', 9–80, in *The Volume of the Walpole Society* 16 (1927–8), p. 50; John Almon (ed.), *The New Foundling Hospital for Wit* (London, 1769), vol. 3, pp. 71–5.
13. Walpole, *Memoirs of the Reign of King George III*, vol. 1, p. 114.
14. Ibid., p. 117.
15. John Wilkes, *The North Briton* 17 (22 September 1762).
16. John Almon (ed.), *The Correspondence of the Late John Wilkes* (London: Richard Phillips, 1805), vol. 3, pp. 38–9.
17. Ibid., vol. 1, p. 124.
18. Ibid., p. 129.
19. Cited in Arthur H. Cash, *John Wilkes: The Scandalous Father of Civil Liberty* (New Haven and London: Yale University Press, 2006), p. 151.
20. Walpole, *Memoirs of the Reign of King George III*, vol. 1, p. 206.
21. Ibid., p. 209.
22. Almon, *The Correspondence of the Late John Wilkes*, vol. 2, pp. 15–17.
23. Lewis Namier, 'Martin, Samuel', *HP*, 1754–1790.
24. Walpole, *Memoirs of the Reign of King George III*, vol. 1, p. 210.
25. 19 January 1764, *CJ*.
26. Bleackley, *Life of John Wilkes*, p. 185.
27. Cited in Thomas, *John Wilkes*, p. 72.
28. Cited in ibid., p. 79.
29. Bleackley, *Life of John Wilkes*, p. 198.
30. *St James's Chronicle* 1214, 8–10 December 1768.
31. J. A. Cannon, 'Middlesex', *HP*, 1754–1790.
32. Cited in Thomas, *John Wilkes*, p. 101.
33. Cited in Bleackley, *Life of John Wilkes*, p. 261.
34. John Calcraft to William Pitt the Elder, 24 March 1771, in William Stanhope Taylor and John Henry Pringle (eds), *Correspondence of William Pitt, Earl of Chatham* (London: John Murray, 1840), vol. 4, p. 123.
35. Bleackley, *Life of John Wilkes*, p. 263.
36. Almon, *The Correspondence of the Late John Wilkes*, vol. 3, p. 121.
37. Horace Twiss, *The Public and Private Life of Lord Chancellor Eldon, with Selections from his Correspondence* (London: John Murray, 1844), vol. 2, p. 356.
38. Walpole, *Memoirs of the Reign of King George III*, vol. 3, p. 30.

39. Ninetta S. Jucker (ed.), *The Jenkinson Papers, 1760–1766* (London: Macmillan & Co. Ltd, 1949), p. 147.
40. Horace Walpole, *Memoirs of the Reign of King George II*, ed. by John Brooke (New Haven and London: Yale University Press, 1985), vol. 2, p. 118.
41. Walpole, *Memoirs of the Reign of King George III*, vol. 3, pp. 130–1.
42. Paget Toynbee (ed.), *The Letters of Horace Walpole, Fourth Earl of Orford* (Oxford: Clarendon Press, 1904), vol. 7, pp. 105–6n.
43. Horace Walpole to Horace Mann, 19 March 1767, in Lewis, *Horace Walpole's Correspondence*, vol. 22, p. 498.
44. Lewis Namier, *Charles Townshend* (London: Macmillan & Co. Ltd, 1964), p. 166.
45. Ibid., p. 187.
46. Benjamin Franklin to Joseph Galloway, 9 January 1769, in Ellen Cohn, et al. (eds), *The Franklin Papers*; https://franklinpapers.org/ [accessed January–July 2025].
47. Hutchinson Letters, 20 January 1769, in ibid.
48. Horace Walpole to Horace Mann, 27 September 1767, in Lewis, *Horace Walpole's Correspondence*, vol. 22, p. 551.
49. Cited in Namier, 'Huske, John', *HP*, 1754–1790.
50. Patrick Henry, cited in James D. Hart, *The Oxford Companion to American Literature*, 6th edn (Oxford: Oxford University Press, 1995), p. 286.

Chapter Seven: The Revolting Stage (1775–1806)

1. Nathaniel Wraxall, *Historical Memoirs of His Own Time* (London: Richard Bentley, 1836), vol. 4, p. 490.
2. *The Parliamentary Register; Or, History of the Proceedings and Debates of the House of Commons* (London: John Stockdale, 1802), vol. 15, p. 17.
3. Horace Walpole to Horace Mann, 5 June 1780 in Lewis, *Horace Walpole's Correspondence*, vol. 25, pp. 52–3.
4. *The London Chronicle*, 1–3 June 1780, vol. 47, p. 536.
5. Horace Walpole to Horace Mann, 5 June 1780, in Lewis, *Horace Walpole's Correspondence*, vol. 25, p. 53.
6. Horace Walpole, *The Last Journals of Horace Walpole*, ed. by John Doran and A. Francis Steuart (London: The Bodley Head, 1910), vol. 2, p. 306.
7. Wraxall, *Historical Memoirs*, vol. 1, pp. 363–4.
8. Horace Walpole to Horace Mann, 5 June 1780, in Lewis, *Horace Walpole's Correspondence*, vol. 25, p. 54.
9. Ibid., p. 55.
10. Horace Walpole to Lady Ossory, 8 June 1780, in Lewis, *Horace Walpole's Correspondence*, vol. 33, pp. 186–92.
11. Ibid.
12. *The London Chronicle*, 8–10 June, vol. 47, p. 553.

Endnotes

13. Horace Walpole to Horace Mann, 5 June 1780, in Lewis, *Horace Walpole's Correspondence*, vol. 25, p. 53; Cobbett, *State Trials*, vol. 21, pp. 486–7.
14. Wraxall, *Historical Memoirs*, vol. 1, p. 367.
15. W. K. Firminger (ed.), 'The Letters of Mr Richard Barwell', 184–209, in *Bengal Past and Present* 8 (1914), p. 203.
16. Dalrymple, *The Anarchy*, p. 76.
17. Ibid., p. 70.
18. Cited in ibid., p. 240.
19. Ibid., p. 233.
20. Edmund Burke to William Baker, 22 June 1784, in Edmund Burke, *The Correspondence of Edmund Burke* (Cambridge: Cambridge University Press, 1965), vol. 5, p. 154.
21. Dalrymple, *The Anarchy*, p. 216.
22. Burke, *Works*, vol. 6, pp. 92–7.
23. Henry Frederick Thompson, *The Intrigues of a Nabob: Or, Bengal the Fittest Soil for the Growth of Lust, Injustice and Dishonesty* (1780), p. 14.
24. Ibid.
25. Alfred Spencer (ed.), *Memoirs of William Hickey* (London: Hurst & Blackett, Ltd, c.1924), vol. 2, p. 308.
26. Eleanor Minto (ed.), *Life and Letters of Sir Gilbert Elliot, First Earl of Minto* (London: Longmans, Green, and Co., 1874), vol. 1, pp. 123–4.
27. Richard Brinsley Sheridan, *The Rivals*, ed. by Elizabeth Duthie (London: A & C Black, 1979), III. 25 (p. 62).
28. Charles Burnley, cited in Suzanne Aspden, 'Linley, Elizabeth Ann', in *DNB*.
29. Horace Walpole to Lady Ossory, 16 March 1773, in Lewis, *Horace Walpole's Correspondence*, vol. 32, p. 106; Thomas Moore, *Memoirs of the life of the Right Honourable Richard Brinsley Sheridan* (London: Longman, Rees, etc., 1826), vol. 2, p. 141.
30. *Sheridaniana, or, Anecdotes of the life of Richard Brinsley Sheridan; his table talk and bons mots* (London: Henry Colburn, 1826), pp. 9–48.
31. Moore, *Memoirs of . . . Richard Brinsley Sheridan*, vol. 1, p. 80.
32. *St James's Chronicle*, 4 July 1772, cited in ibid., vol. 1, p. 92.
33. *Sheridaniana*, pp. 290–1.
34. Ibid., p. 266.
35. Ibid., pp. 174–5.
36. Ibid., p. 151.
37. Ibid., p. 206.
38. Whitbread to Grey, 16 June 1808, cited in R. G. Thorne, 'Sheridan, Richard Brinsley', *HP*, 1790–1820.

39. *Sheridaniana*, p. 216.
40. *Hansard*, Commons, 6 April 1893.
41. *Sheridaniana*, pp. 244–6.
42. H. G. Bennet to Thomas Creevey, 12 July 1816, in Thomas Creevey, *The Creevey Papers*, ed. by Herbert Maxwell (London: John Murray, 1904), vol. 1, p. 257.
43. Leslie Mitchell, 'Fox, Charles James', *DNB*.
44. L. G. Mitchell, *Charles James Fox* (London: Penguin, 1992), p. 11.
45. Joseph Parkes and Herman Merivale (eds), *Memoirs of Sir Philip Francis* (London: Longmans, Green, and Co., 1867), vol. 2, p. 446.
46. Horace Walpole to Horace Mann, 11 January 1774, in Lewis, *Horace Walpole's Correspondence*, vol. 23, p. 542.
47. Mitchell, *Charles James Fox*, p. 102.
48. Lord Ilchester, 'Some Pages Drawn from the Last Journals of Horace Walpole', 449–59, in Dorothy Miner (ed.), *Studies in Art and Literature for Belle da Costa Greene* (Princeton, NJ: Princeton University Press, 1954), p. 456.
49. Mitchell, *Charles James Fox*, p. 130.
50. Charles James Fox, *The Speeches of the Right Honourable Charles James Fox, in the House of Commons* (London: Longman, Hurst, Rees, Orme and Brown, 1815), vol. 5, p. 397.
51. Mitchell, *Charles James Fox*, p. 201.
52. Ibid., p. 230.
53. Margaret E. Poole Sandford, *Thomas Poole and His Friends* (London: Macmillan and Co., 1888), vol. 2, p. 160.
54. Leslie Mitchell, 'Fox, Charles James', *DNB*.

Chapter Eight: Officers and No Gentlemen (1802–32)

1. *Abolition of Slavery Act 1833* (3 & 4 William 4 c.73) (London: HMSO).
2. A. Aspinall (ed.), *The Later Correspondence of George III* (Cambridge: Cambridge University Press, 1968), vol. 4, p. 615.
3. William Bagwell, *A plain statement of facts relative to Sir Eyre Coote* (London: Sherwood, Neely and Jones, 1816), pp. 35–43.
4. Ibid., p. 27.
5. *The Late Elections: An Impartial Statement of All Proceedings* (London, 1818), p. 7.
6. Andrew Cochrane Johnstone, *Defence of the Honourable Andrew Cochrane Johnstone; Including a View of the Evidence Produced on His Trial* (London: J. Barfield, 1805), p. 6.
7. Ibid., p. 5.
8. *Niles' Weekly Register*, 16 September 1815, vol. 9, p. 46.

9. James Atlay, *The Trial of Lord Cochrane before Lord Ellenborough* (London: Smith, Elder, & Co., 1897), p. 7.
10. Ibid., pp. 8–9.
11. Ibid., p. 14.
12. Ibid.
13. *The Times*, 22 February 1814.
14. Thomas Cochrane, *The Autobiography of a Seaman* (London: Richard Bentley, 1860), vol. 1, pp. 104–5.
15. Cochrane, *Autobiography*, vol. 2, pp. 171–80.
16. *Hansard*, Commons, 6 June 1811.
17. Thomas Barnes Cochrane and Henry Richard Fox Bourne, *The Life of Thomas, Lord Cochrane, Tenth Earl of Dundonald* (London: Richard Bentley, 1869), vol. 1, p. 54.
18. Ibid., vol. 1, p. 57.
19. Ibid., vol. 1, p. 59.
20. Ibid., vol. 1, p. 70.
21. Cochrane, *Autobiography*, vol. 2, p. 399.
22. Hansard, *Parliamentary Debates from the Year 1803 to the Present Time* (London: T. C. Hansard, 1803–20), vol. 35, pp. 81–2.
23. John Gore (ed.), *Creevey* (London: John Murray, 1948), p. 119n.
24. Cited in Dalrymple, *The Anarchy*, p. 382.
25. *Cobbett's Political Register*, 25 October 1806.
26. 18 March 1807, *CJ*.
27. *The Gentleman's Magazine and Historical Review* 78 (1808), vol. 1, p. 373.
28. J. Ann Hone, *For the Cause of Truth: Radicalism in London, 1796–1821* (Oxford: Clarendon Press, 1982), p. 325.
29. David R. Fisher, 'Pole Tylney Long Wellesley, Hon. William', *HP*, 1820–1832.
30. William Beckford, *Life at Fonthill, 1807–1822: With Interludes in Paris and London*, ed. by Boyd Alexander (London: Rupert Hart-Davis, 1957), p. 137.
31. *The Annual Register, or a View of the History, Politics, and Literature, of the Year 1827*, 69 (London: Baldwin and Craddock, 1828), 'Chronicle', p. 303.
32. Ibid., pp. 300–10.
33. *The Gentleman's Magazine and Historical Review* 203 (1857), p. 216.

Chapter Nine: Full Steam Ahead (1832–67)
1. James O'Shea, *Prince of Swindlers: John Sadleir MP, 1813–1856* (Dublin: Geography Publications, 1999), p. 53.
2. John Francis, *A History of the English Railway* (London: Longman, Brown, Green & Longmans, 1851), vol. 2, p. 219.

3. Brian Bailey, *George Hudson: The Rise and Fall of the Railway King* (Stroud: Alan Sutton Publishing Limited, 1995), p. 93.
4. Cited in ibid., p. 88.
5. Ibid., p. 152.
6. John Henry Whyte, *The Independent Irish Party, 1850–9* (Oxford: Oxford University Press, 1958), p. 5.
7. O'Shea, *Prince of Swindlers*, p. 74.
8. *Tablet*, 11 February 1854.
9. O'Shea, *Prince of Swindlers*, p. 401.
10. *Carlow Sentinel*, 23 February 1856.
11. *The Times*, 18 February 1856.
12. David Morier Evans, *Facts, Failures and Frauds: Revelations, Financial, Mercantile, Criminal* (London: Groombridge & Sons, 1859), pp. 252–3.
13. O'Shea, *Prince of Swindlers*, p. 366.
14. Ibid., p. 423.
15. Matthias McDonnell Bodkin, *Recollections of an Irish Judge* (New York: Dodd, Mead and Company, 1915), p. 10.
16. Ibid., p. 8.
17. Ibid., p. 7.
18. Ibid., p. 8.
19. Ibid., pp. 8–9.
20. Ibid., p. 11.
21. Romola Davenport, 'Mortality, Migration and Epidemiological Change in English Cities, 1600–1870', 37–49, in *International Journal of Paleopathology* 34 (2021).
22. Cormac Ó Gráda, *Ireland: A New Economic History, 1780–1939* (Oxford: Clarendon Press, 1994), p. 213.
23. Ibid., p. 214.
24. Seán Donnelly, 'A Piping MP: Joseph Myles McDonnell (1796–1872), Doo Castle, Ballaghadereen, County Mayo', in *The Seán Reid Society Journal*, vol. 1 (1999); http://www.seanreidsociety.org/index.html [accessed February 2025].
25. *Morning Post*, 2 April 1836.
26. Augustus Wathen, *Proceedings of the General Court Martial upon the Trial of Captain Wathen* (London: Roake and Varty, 1834), p. 265.
27. Cecil Woodham-Smith, *The Reason Why* (New York: Barnes & Noble Books, 1953), p. 60.
28. Saul David, *The Homicidal Earl: The Life of Lord Cardigan* (London: Little, Brown and Company, 1997), p. 157.
29. *Morning Chronicle*, 17 September 1840.

30. Ibid., 4 September 1840.
31. James Thomas Brudenell, *The Trial of James Thomas Earl of Cardigan: Before the Right Honourable the House of Peers* (London: William Brodie Gurney, Joseph Gurney, And Thomas Gurney, 1841), p. 18.
32. Ibid., p. 122.
33. *The Times*, 17 February 1841.
34. Ibid., 18 February 1841.
35. *Hansard*, Commons, 13 May 1841.
36. William Howard Russell, *The Great War with Russia* (London: George Routledge & Sons, Limited, 1895), p. 118.
37. David, *The Homicidal Earl*, p. 330.
38. Francis Duberly, *Mrs Duberly's War: Journal and Letters from the Crimea, 1854–6*, ed. by Christine Kelly (Oxford: Oxford University Press, 2007), pp. 33–4.
39. Alfred Tennyson, 'The Charge of the Light Brigade', in *The Poems of Alfred, Lord Tennyson* (Oxford: Oxford University Press, 1929), pp. 199–200.
40. J. W. Wightman, 'One of the "Six Hundred" on the Balaclava Charge', 850–63, in *Nineteenth Century* 31 (1892), pp. 853–6.

Chapter Ten: 'Rule by Virtue' (1867–1910)
1. Sarah Bradford, *Disraeli* (New York: Stein and Day, 1982), p. 85.
2. Benjamin Disraeli, *Vivian Grey* (London: Routledge, Warnes and Routledge, 1859), p. 19.
3. Bradford, *Disraeli*, p. 87
4. Ibid., p. 32.
5. Disraeli to Benjamin Austen, 18 November 1830 (103) in Benjamin Disraeli, *Benjamin Disraeli Letters* (Toronto: University of Toronto Press, 1982), vol. 1, p. 173.
6. Nathaniel Parker Willis, *Pencillings by the Way: Written during Some Years of Residence and Travel in Europe* (New York: Charles Scrivener, 1852), pp. 491–3.
7. Benjamin Disraeli, *Tancred* (London: Longmans Green, and Co., 1871), p. 370; Bradford, *Disraeli*, p. 88.
8. *Manchester Times*, 19 June 1858.
9. *Morning Chronicle*, 15 July 1858.
10. Ibid.
11. Bradford, *Disraeli*, p. 51.
12. Hay, *Mr and Mrs Disraeli*, p. 221.
13. William Fraser, *Disraeli and His Day* (London: Kegan Paul, Trench, Trübner & Co. Ltd, 1891), p. 52.

Endnotes

14. *Hansard*, Commons, 17 March 1845; Benjamin Disraeli, *Coningsby; Or the New Generation* (London: Henry Colburn, 1844), pp. 210–11.
15. University College London, *Legacies of British Slavery*; https://www.ucl.ac.uk/lbs/person/view/8961 [accessed 21 March 2025]
16. Roy Jenkins, *Gladstone: A Biography* (London: Macmillan, 1995), p. 43.
17. Kenneth Harris, *Attlee* (New York: W.W. Norton & Company, 1982), p. 525.
18. 18 May 1848, William E. Gladstone, *The Gladstone Diaries*, ed. by M. R. D. Foot and H. C. G. Matthew (Oxford: Clarendon Press, 1968–94), vol. 4, p. 37.
19. J. F. Burns, 'From Whoredom to Evangelism: The story of Mrs. Thistlethwayte (nee Laura Bell, who was a native of Glenavy)', in *Lisburn Historical Society* 2 (1979).
20. Wilde's attraction was the inverse to his own age: the older he became, the younger he liked his women. Burns, 'From Whoredom to Evangelism'.
21. Ibid.
22. Francis C. Burnand, *Records and Reminiscences, Personal and General* (London: Methuen & Co., 1904), vol. 1, p. 237.
23. Burns, 'From Whoredom to Evangelism'.
24. London, Imperial War Museum, WMR-107115.
25. S. M. Ellis (ed.), *A Mid-Victorian Pepys: The Letters and Memoirs of Sir William Hardman* (New York: George H. Doran Company, 1923), p. 192; Mary Jeune, *Memories of Fifty Years* (London: Edward Arnold, 1910), p. 44.
26. H. C. G. Matthew, *Gladstone: 1809–1874* (Oxford: Clarendon Press, 1986), p. 238.
27. Gladstone, *Diaries*, vol. 12, p. lxxxi.
28. 1 July 1852, 30 and 31 March 1851, ibid., vol. 4, pp. 440, 319.
29. 20 January 1854, ibid., vol. 4, p. 586.
30. 22 April 1849, ibid., vol. 4, pp. 116–17.
31. George W. E. Russell, *Portraits of the Seventies* (London: T. Fisher Unwin Ltd., 1916), p. 53.
32. 10 May 1853, Gladstone, *Diaries*, vol. 4, p. 525.
33. Evelyn Ashley, 'Mr Gladstone: Fragments of Personal Reminiscences', 536–40, in *National Review* (June 1898), p. 540.
34. H. C. G. Matthew, *Gladstone: 1875–1898* (Oxford: Clarendon Press, 1995), p. 378n.
35. Claire Hirshfield, 'Labouchere, Truth and the Uses of Antisemitism', 134–42, in *Victorian Periodicals Review* 26 (1993), p. 135.
36. See, for example, Hesketh Pearson, *Labby: The Life and Character of Henry Labouchère* (London: Hamish Hamilton, 1936), p. 18.
37. Ibid., p. 31.
38. Ibid., p. 43.
39. Jenkins, *Gladstone*, p. 501.

40. Cannadine, *Victorious Century*, p. 267; J. R. Seeley, *The Expansion of England* (London: Macmillan & Co., Limited, 1900), p. 8.
41. Cited in Paul H. Emden, *Randlords* (London: Hodder & Stoughton, 1935), p. 311.
42. Eveleigh Nash, *Nash's War Manual* (London: Eveleigh Nash, 1914), p. 309.
43. John Laband, 'Elizabeth van Heyningen: The Concentration Camps of the Anglo-Boer War: A Social History', in *The American Historical Review* 120 (2015), p. 760.
44. Matthew, *Gladstone: 1875–1898*, p. 375.
45. Pearson, *Labby*, pp. 119–21.
46. Emden, *Randlords*, p. 166.
47. Ibid.; Henry Hess, 'The stock-jobbing of Henry Labouchere', in *The African Critic* (1897), supplement, p. v.
48. Ibid.
49. Most biographies argue differently. This is based on misdating the Hess article and a rather hazy memory contained in a memoir (T. M. Healy, *Letters and Leaders of My Day* (London: Thornton Butterworth Ltd., ?1928), vol. 1, p. 309).
50. Hirshfield, 'Labouchere, Truth and the Uses of Antisemitism', pp. 141–2.

Chapter Eleven: Led by Donkeys (1910–45)

1. *The Times*, 20 May 1910.
2. Niall Ferguson, *The Pity of War* (London: Allen Lane, 1998), p. 293.
3. Peter Rowland, *David Lloyd George: A Biography* (New York: Macmillan, 1975), p. 321.
4. Cited in ibid., p. 321.
5. Cited in ibid., p. 324.
6. George Riddell, *More Pages from My Diary, 1908–1914* (London: Country Life Ltd, 1934), p. 152.
7. Richard Lloyd George, *My Father, Lloyd George* (New York: Crown Publishers Inc., 1961), p. 12.
8. Ibid., p. 42.
9. Ibid., p. 222.
10. Vernon Bogdanor, review of Ian Ivatt, 'The Financial Affairs of David Lloyd George', in *Journal of Liberal History* 106 (2020), pp. 47–8.
11. Cited in Rowland, *David Lloyd George*, p. 135.
12. G. R. Isaacs, *Rufus Isaacs, first marquess of Reading* (London: Hutchinson & Co., 1948), p. 11.
13. Ibid., pp. 23–4.
14. Richard Lloyd George, *My Father*, p. 135.

15. G. R. Searle, *Corruption in British Politics, 1895–1930* (Oxford: Clarendon Press, 1987), p. 37.
16. Rowland, *David Lloyd George*, p. 263.
17. *Hansard*, Commons, 11 October 1912.
18. *Hansard*, Commons, 19 June 1913; Searle, *Corruption in British Politics*, p. 183.
19. *Hansard*, Commons, 19 June 1913.
20. Searle, *Corruption in British Politics*, pp. 145–6.
21. Ibid., p. 353.
22. *The Times*, 16 February 1927.
23. *Hansard*, Lords, 17 July 1922.
24. *Hansard*, Commons, 17 July 1922.
25. Richard Lloyd George, *My Father, Lloyd George*, pp. 215–16.
26. Robert Skidelsky, *Oswald Mosley* (New York: Holt, Rinehart and Wilson, 1975), p. 182.
27. Oswald Mosley, *My Life* (London: Thomas Nelson and Sons Ltd, 1968), p. 262.
28. James Lees-Milne, *Another Self* (New York: Coward-McCann, Inc., 1970), p. 97.
29. *London Daily News*, 5 October 1936.
30. Ibid.
31. Stephen Dorril, *Blackshirt: Sir Oswald Mosley and British Fascism* (London: Penguin, 2006), p. 390.
32. *London Daily News*, 5 October 1936.
33. Wensley Clarkson, *Hit 'Em Hard: Jack Spot, King of the Underworld* (London: HarperCollins, 2002), pp. 33–7.
34. Skidelsky, *Oswald Mosley*, p. 405.
35. *London Daily News*, 5 October 1936.
36. David Lloyd George, 'Unrest in Europe', in *Sunday Pictorial*, 24 June 1934.
37. Albert Sylvester, *The Real Lloyd George* (London: Cassell and Company Ltd, 1947), p. 202.
38. TNA CAB 23/95/42.
39. Cited in Bernard Wasserstein, *The Secret Lives of Trebitsch Lincoln* (London: Yale University Press, 1988), p. 41.
40. I. T. T. Lincoln, *Revelations of an International Spy* (New York: Robert M. McBride & Company, 1916), p. 235.
41. Ibid., pp. 237–9.
42. Hugh Cleland Hoy, *40 O.B.; or How the War Was Won* (London: Hutchinson & Co. Ltd, 1932), p. 124.
43. Ibid., p. 125.
44. Lincoln, *Revelations of an International Spy*, p. 273.
45. Wasserstein, *The Secret Lives of Trebitsch Lincoln*, p. 105.

46. 'Trebitsch-Lincoln Is Reported Dead', *New York Times*, 9 October 1943.
47. 'Ex-Spy Warns World of Buddhist Wrath', *New York Times*, 20 December 1939.
48. Cited in Wasserstein, *The Secret Lives of Trebitsch Lincoln*, p. 275.
49. Ibid., p. 277.
50. Ibid., p. 284.
51. Bernard Wasserstein, 'Lincoln, Ignatius Timotheus Trebitsch [formerly Ignácz Trebitsch; name in religion Chao Kung]', *DNB*.
52. Tim Bouverie, *Allies at War: The Politics of Defeating Hitler* (London: The Bodley Head, 2025), p. xiii.

Epilogue
1. Francis Fukuyama, *The Origins of Political Order* (London: Profile Books Ltd, 2012), p. 139.
2. Pearson, *Labby*, p. 156.
3. Johnson and Cole, *Commons Debates 1628*, vol. 2, p. 3.
4. William Lovett, *The People's Charter: With the Address to the Radical Reformers of Great Britain and Ireland, and a Brief Sketch of its Origin* (London: C. H. Elt and C. Fox, 1848).

Bibliography

Archive sources
TNA, CAB   London, The National Archives, Cabinet Minutes
TNA, PROB   London, The National Archives, Probate Records
WMR   London, Imperial War Museum, War Memorials Register

Printed primary sources
Abolition of Slavery Act 1833 (3 & 4 William 4 c.73) (London: HMSO)
'An Account of the Misfortunes of Mrs Erskine of Grange, Commonly Known as Lady Grange', 333–9, in *The Edinburgh Magazine and Literary Miscellany, Being a New Series of the Scots Magazine*, 1 (November 1817)
Almon, John (ed.), *The Correspondence of the Late John Wilkes* (London: Richard Phillips, 1805), 5 vols
———, *The New Foundling Hospital for Wit* (London, 1768–1772), 4 vols
The Annual Register, or a View of the History, Politics, and Literature, of the Year (London, 1828–58)
Ashley, Evelyn, 'Mr Gladstone: Fragments of Personal Reminiscences', 536–40, in *National Review* (June 1898)
Aspinall, A. (ed.), *Mrs Jordan and Her Family* (London: Arthur Baker, 1951)
———, *The Later Correspondence of George III* (Cambridge: Cambridge University Press, 1968), 5 vols
Aubrey, John, *Brief Lives*, ed. by Andrew Clark (Oxford: Clarendon Press, 1898), 2 vols
Bagwell, William, *A plain statement of facts relative to Sir Eyre Coote* (London: Sherwood, Neely and Jones, 1816)
Balfour, Jabez Spencer, *My Prison Life* (London: Chapman and Hall Ltd., 1907)
Barrington, Jonah, *Personal Sketches of His Own Time*, 3rd edn (London: George Routledge and Sons, 1869), 2 vols
Beckford, William, *Life at Fonthill, 1807–1822: With Interludes in Paris and London*, ed. by Boyd Alexander (London: Rupert Hart-Davis, 1957)
Berry, James, *Tales of the West of Ireland*, ed. by Gertrude M. Horgan (Dublin: Dolmen Press Ltd, 1966)
Blunt, Wilfrid Scawen, *My Diaries: Being a Personal Narrative of Events 1888–1914* (London: Martin Secker, 1932)

Boswell, James, *Boswell on the Grand Tour: Italy, Corsica, and France, 1765–1766*, ed. by Frank Brady and Frederick A. Pottle (Surrey: Windmill Press, 1955)

Boyer, Abel, *The History of King William III* (London: A. Roper, 1702), 3 vols

Boyle, Robert, *A Transcription of Robert Boyle's Weather Diary 1684-6*, ed. by Richard Cornes; https://figshare.com/articles/dataset/A_Transcription_of_Robert_Boyle_s_Weather_Diary_1684-6/7011743 [accessed on 17 July 2025]

Brown, Beatrice Curtis (ed.), *The Letters and Diplomatic Instructions of Queen Anne* (New York: Funk & Wagnalls, 1968)

Brudenell, James Thomas, *The Trial of James Thomas Earl of Cardigan: Before the Right Honourable the House of Peers* (London: William Brodie Gurney, Joseph Gurney, And Thomas Gurney, 1841)

Burke, Edmund, *The Works of the Right Honourable Edmund Burke* (London: F. C. and J. Rivington, 1801–13), 12 vols

―――, *The Correspondence of Edmund Burke* (Cambridge: Cambridge University Press, 1958–78), 10 vols

Burnand, Francis C., *Records and Reminiscences, Personal and General* (London: Methuen & Co., 1904), 2 vols

Burnet, Gilbert, *Bishop Burnet's History of His Own Time* (Oxford: Clarendon Press, 1833), 6 vols

Carey, Robert, *Memoirs of Robert Cary, Earl of Monmouth* (Edinburgh: Archibald Constable and Co., 1808)

Carleton, Dudley, *Letters from and to Sir Dudley Carleton . . . During His Embassy in Holland, From January 1615/16, To December 1620*, 2nd edn (London, 1775)

Carlow Sentinel (1856)

Carlyle, Alexander, *Autobiography of the Rev. Dr Alexander Carlyle, Minister of Inveresk*, 2nd edn (Edinburgh and London: William Blackwood and Sons, 1860)

Carte, Thomas (ed.), *A Collection of Original Letters and Papers, Concerning the Affairs of England, from the Year 1641 to 1660* (London, 1739), 2 vols

Cary, Henry (ed.), *Memorials of the Great Civil War in England, from 1646 to 1652* (London: Henry Colburn, 1842)

Clark, James G. (ed.), *The Chronica Maiora of Thomas Walsingham (1376–1422)* (Suffolk: Boydell, 2005)

Cobbett, William (ed.), *Cobbett's Complete Collection of State Trials* (London: Hansard, 1809–26), 33 vols

―――, *Cobbett's Parliamentary History of England* (London: Hansard, 1806–20), 36 vols

——, *Cobbett's Political Register* (London, 1802–36)
Cochrane, Thomas, *The Autobiography of a Seaman* (London: Richard Bentley, 1860), 2 vols
Cochrane, Thomas Barnes, and Henry Richard Fox Bourne, *The Life of Thomas, Lord Cochrane, Tenth Earl of Dundonald* (London: Richard Bentley, 1869), 2 vols
Cohn, Ellen, et al. (eds), *The Franklin Papers*; https://franklinpapers.org/ [accessed January–July 2025]
Coke, Roger, *A Detection of the Court and State of England* (London: Andrew Bell, 1697)
A Continuation of the True Narration of the Most Observable Passages in and about Plymouth, from January 26 1643 till this present . . . (London, 1644)
Cooper, William Durrant (ed.), *Savile Correspondence* (London: Camden Society, 1858)
Coxe, William (ed.), *Memoirs of the Life and Administration of Sir Robert Walpole, Earl of Orford* (London: T. Cadell, Jun., and W. Davies, 1798), 3 vols
Creevey, Thomas, *The Creevey Papers*, ed. by Herbert Maxwell (London: John Murray, 1904), 2 vols
Defoe, Daniel, *The villainy of stock-jobbers detected, and the causes of the late run upon the bank and bankers discovered and considered* (London, 1701)
——, *The Anatomy of Exchange-Alley: Or a System of Stock-Jobbing*, 2nd edn (London: E. Smith, 1719)
——, *The Commentator*, nos 1–74 (London, 1720)
——, *A Tour through the Whole Island of Great Britain*, ed. by Pat Rogers (Exeter: Webb & Bower, 1989)
Devon, Frederick (ed.), *Issues of the Exchequer; Being a Collection of Payments Made out of His Majesty's Revenue, from King Henry III to King Henry VI Inclusive* (London: J. Murray, 1837)
Disraeli, Benjamin, *Coningsby; Or the New Generation* (London: Henry Colburn, 1844)
——, *Sybil; Or, the Two Nations* (London: Henry Colburn, 1845)
——, *Vivian Grey* (London: Routledge, Warnes and Routledge, 1859)
——, *Tancred* (London: Longmans Green, and Co., 1871)
——, *Benjamin Disraeli Letters* (Toronto: University of Toronto Press, 1982), 10 vols
Dobbs, Francis, *A letter to the Right Honourable Lord North, on his Propositions in Favour of Ireland* (Dublin: M. Mills, 1780)
Duberly, Francis, *Mrs Duberly's War: Journal and Letters from the Crimea, 1854–6*, ed. by Christine Kelly (Oxford: Oxford University Press, 2007)

Examiner, The (London, 1838)

Fielding, Henry, *The Covent Garden Journal*, ed. by Gerald Edward Jensen (New Haven: Yale University Press, 1915)

Firminger, W. K. (ed.), 'The Letters of Mr Richard Barwell', in *Bengal Past and Present*, vols 8–18 (1914–19)

Firth, C. H. (ed.), *Scotland and the Protectorate: Letters and Papers Relating to the Military Government of Scotland from January 1654 to June 1659*, for the Scottish History Society, 31 (Edinburgh: Edinburgh University Press, 1899)

Ford, Mark (ed.), *London: A History in Verse* (Cambridge, MA, and London: The Belknap Press of Harvard University Press, 2012)

Fox, Charles James, *The Speeches of the Right Honourable Charles James Fox, in the House of Commons* (London: Longman, Hurst, Rees, Orme and Brown, 1815), 6 vols

Gardiner, Dorothy (ed.), *The Oxinden Letters, 1607–1642* (London: Constable & Co., 1933)

Gardiner, Samuel Rawson (ed.), *Parliamentary Debates of 1610, Edited from the Notes of a Member of the House of Commons* (London: Camden Society, 1862)

——, *Debates in the House of Commons in 1625* (London: Camden Society, 1873)

Gee, Henry (ed.), *Documents Illustrative of English Church History* (London: Macmillan, 1910)

Gentleman's Magazine and Historical Review, The (London, 1731–1922)

Given-Wilson, Christopher (ed.), *Parliament Rolls of Medieval England, 1275–1504: Henry IV, 1399–1413* (Suffolk: Boydell Press, 2005) [CD-ROM]

Gladstone, William E., *The Gladstone Diaries*, ed. by M. R. D. Foot and H. C. G. Matthew (Oxford: Clarendon Press, 1968–94), 14 vols

——, *The Prime Ministers' Papers: W.E. Gladstone, 1: Autobiographica* (London: HMSO, 1971)

Gore, John (ed.), *Creevey* (London: John Murray, 1948)

Green, Mary Anne Everett, (ed.), *Calendar of State Papers Domestic: James I, 1611–1618* (London: HMSO, 1858), British History Online; http://www.british-history.ac.uk/cal-state-papers/domestic/jas1/1611-18 [accessed January 2023–June 2025]

Grenville, Richard, *A letter written by Sir Richard Grenville (under his own hand) to an honourable person in the city of London, concerning the affairs of the west* (London, 1646)

Gronow, R. H., *The Reminiscences and Recollections of Captain Gronow*, ed. by Joseph Grego (London: John C. Nimmo, 1892), 2 vols

Hall, Edward, *Hall's Chronicle, Containing the History of England . . .* (London: J Johnston et al, 1809)

Hall, Richard, *The Life of Fisher*, ed. by Ronald Bayne (London: Early English Text Society by H. Milford, Oxford University Press, 1921)

Hansard (London: HMSO, 1803–1945)

———, *Parliamentary Debates from the Year 1803 to the Present Time* (London: T. C. Hansard, 1803–20), 41 vols

Hardman, William, *A Mid-Victorian Pepys: The Letters and Memoirs of Sir William Hardman*, ed. by S. M. Ellis (London: C. Palmer, 1923)

Healy, T. M., *Letters and Leaders of My Day* (London: Thornton Butterworth Ltd., ?1928), 2 vols

Hector, L. C. (Leonard Charles), and Barbara F. Harvey, *The Westminster Chronicle, 1381–1394* (Oxford: Clarendon Press, 1982)

Henderson, Frances (ed.), *The Clarke Papers: Further Selections from the Papers of William Clarke* (Cambridge: Camden Society by Cambridge University Press, 2005)

Hess, Henry, 'The stock-jobbing of Henry Labouchere', in *The African Critic* (1897)

Historical Manuscripts Commission, *The Manuscripts of the Earl Cowper* (London: HMSO, 1888–9)

———, *The Manuscripts of the Duke of Beaufort . . . and Others* (London: HMSO, 1891)

———, *Report on the Manuscripts of His Grace the Duke of Portland Preserved at Welbeck Abbey* (London: HMSO, 1891–1931), 10 vols

———, *The Manuscripts of the Earl of Buckinghamshire, et al* (London: HMSO, 1895)

———, *The Manuscripts of the Earl of Carlisle* (London: HMSO, 1897)

———, *Report on the Manuscripts of the Marquess of Lothian* (London: HMSO, 1905)

———, *Report on Manuscripts in Various Collections*, vol. 8 (London: HMSO, 1913)

House of Commons, *The Several Reports of the Committee of Secrecy to the Honourable House of Commons, Relating to the Late South Sea Directors, &c* (London: A. Moore, 1721)

House of Lords, *The History and Proceedings of the House of Lords from the Restoration in 1660 to the Present Time* (London: Ebenezer Timberland, 1842–4), 8 vols

Hoy, Hugh Cleland, *40 O.B.; or How the War Was Won* (London: Hutchinson & Co. Ltd, 1932)

Hutcheson, Archibald, *Some Calculations Relating to the Proposals Made by the South Sea Company and the Bank of England to the House of Commons* (London, 1720)

Hyde, Edward *The History of the Rebellion and Civil Wars in Ireland*, 3rd edn (London: T. Cooper, 1740)

———, *The History of the Rebellion and Civil Wars in England, Begun in the Year 1641*, ed. by W. Dunn Macray (Oxford: Clarendon Press, 1888), 6 vols

Ilchester, Lord, 'Some Pages Drawn from the Last Journals of Horace Walpole', 449–59, in Dorothy Miner (ed.), *Studies in Art and Literature for Belle da Costa Greene* (Princeton, NJ: Princeton University Press, 1954)

Inderwick, F. A. (ed.), *A Calendar of the Inner Temple Records* (London: Masters of the Bench, 1898)

Jackson, Catherine (ed.), *The Bath Archives: A Further Selection from the Diaries and Letters of Sir George Jackson, KCH, from 1809 to 1816* (London: Richard Bentley and Son, 1873), 2 vols

Jeune, Mary, *Memories of Fifty Years* (London: Edward Arnold, 1910)

John Bull (London, 1906)

Johnson, Robert C., and Maija Jansson Cole, *Commons Debates 1628* (London: Yale University Press, 1977–83), 6 vols

Johnstone, Andrew Cochrane, *Defence of the Honourable Andrew Cochrane Johnstone; Including a View of the Evidence Produced on His Trial* (London: J. Barfield, 1805)

Journal of the House of Commons (London: HMSO, 1802), British History Online; http://www.british-history.ac.uk/commons-jrnl/ [accessed January 2023–June 2025]

Journal of the House of Lords (London: HMSO, 1767–1830), British History Online; https://www.british-history.ac.uk/series/house-lords-journals [accessed January 2023–June 2025]

Jucker, Ninetta S. (ed.), *The Jenkinson Papers, 1760–1766* (London: Macmillan & Co. Ltd, 1949)

Kaleidoscopiana Wiltoniensia (London, 1818)

Kenyon, J. P. (ed.), *The Stuart Constitution 1603–1688: Documentary and Commentary* (Cambridge: Cambridge University Press, 1966)

King Charles his speech made upon the scaffold at Whitehall-Gate, immediately before his execution, on Tuesday the 30 of Jan. 1648 (London, 1649)

Knyvett, Thomas, *The Knyvett Letters* (London: Constable & Co Ltd., 1949)

The Late Elections: An Impartial Statement of All Proceedings (London, 1818)

Lee, Maurice (ed.), *Dudley Carleton to John Chamberlain, 1603–1624: Jacobean Letters* (New Jersey: Rutgers University Press, 1972)

Lees-Milne, James, *Another Self* (New York: Coward-McCann, Inc., 1970)

Bibliography

Letters and Papers, Foreign and Domestic, Henry VIII, ed. by J. S. Brewer, James Gairdner and R. H. Brodie (London, 1880–1920), 28 vols

Lewis, W. S. (ed.), *The Yale Edition of Horace Walpole's Correspondence* (New Haven: Yale University Press, 1937–83), 48 vols

Lincoln, I. T. T., *Revelations of an International Spy* (New York: Robert M. McBride & Company, 1916)

Lloyd George, David, 'Unrest in Europe', in *Sunday Pictorial*, 24 June 1934

London Chronicle, The (London, 1765–1823)

London Gazette, The (London, 1665–1945)

Lorrain, Paul, *The ordinary of Newgate his account of the behaviour, confessions, and dying-words of Captain William Kidd, and other pirates, that were executed at the Execution-Dock in Wapping, on Friday May 23. 1701* (London: E. Mallet, 1701)

Lovett, William, *The People's Charter: With the Address to the Radical Reformers of Great Britain and Ireland, and a Brief Sketch of its Origin* (London: C. H. Elt and C. Fox, 1848)

Lowe, D. M. (ed.), *Gibbon's Journal to January 28th, 1763* (New York: W. W. Norton and Company, 1929)

Loy Smith, George, *A Victorian RSM: From India to the Crimea* (Winchester: Costello, 1987)

Ludlow, Edmund, *The Memoirs of Edmund Ludlow*, ed. by C. H. Firth (Oxford: Clarendon Press, 1894), 2 vols

Luttrell, Narcissus, *A Brief Historical Relation of State Affairs from September 1678 to April 1714* (Oxford: Oxford University Press, 1857), 6 vols

Lytton, Edward Robert Bulwer, *The Life, Letters and Literary Remains of Edward Bulwer, Lord Lytton* (New York: Harper & Brothers, 1884), 2 vols

Lytton, Rosina Bulwer, *A Blighted Life: A True Story* (London: The London Publishing Office, 1880)

Macky, Spring, *Memoirs of the Secret Services of John Macky, Esq* (London, 1733)

Manchester Times (Manchester, 1828–1922)

Margoliouth, H. M. and Legouis, Pierr-e (eds), *The Poems and Letters of Andrew Marvell*, 3rd edn (Oxford: Oxford University Press, 1971), vol. 1

Marvell, Andrew, *Flagellum Parliamentarium*, ed. by N. H. Nicolas (London: J. B. Nichols, 1827)

Maxwell Lyte, H. C. (ed.), *Calendar of Close Rolls, Richard II* (London: HMSO, 1921–5), vols 3–5, *British History Online*; https://www.british-history.ac.uk/series/calendar-close-rolls-richard-ii [accessed January 2023–June 2025]

McClure, Norman Egbert (ed.), *The Letters of John Chamberlain* (Philadelphia: The American Philosophical Society, 1939), 2 vols

McGowan, A. P. (ed.), *The Jacobean Commissions of Enquiry, 1608 and 1618* (London: Navy Records Society, 1971)
Mercurius publicus: comprising the sum of forraign intelligence . . . 29 (London, 12–19 July 1660)
Minto, Eleanor (ed.), *Life and Letters of Sir Gilbert Elliot, First Earl of Minto* (London: Longmans, Green, and Co., 1874), 3 vols
Montagu, Basil (ed.), *The Works of Francis Bacon* (Philadelphia: A. Hart, 1852)
Montagu, Mary Wortley, *The Complete Letters of Lady Mary Wortley Montagu*, ed. by Robert Halsband (Oxford: Clarendon Press, 1965–7), 3 vols
Moritz, Carl P., *Travels in England in 1782* (London: Cassell & Company Limited, 1886)
Morning Chronicle (and London Advertiser) (London, 1769–1862)
Morning Post (London, 1772–1937)
Mosley, Oswald, *My Life* (London: Thomas Nelson and Sons Ltd, 1968)
Murray, John, *Memorials of John Murray of Broughton, Sometimes Secretary to Prince Charles Edward, 1740–1747*, ed. by Robert Fitzroy Bell (Edinburgh: Scottish History Society, 1898)
New York Times (New York, 1851–1947)
Nicolson, Harold, *Diaries and Letters, 1930–1939*, ed. by Nigel Nicolson (London: Collins, 1966)
Niles' Weekly Register (Maryland, 1815)
'The Nine Worthies' in *Notes and Queries*, 2nd series, vol. 1 (1856), 25
Notestein, Wallace, et al (eds), *Commons Debates 1621* (New Haven: Yale University Press, 1935), 7 vols
Pamphlets and Leaflets for 1922, Being the Publications for the Year of the Liberal Publication Department (London: The Liberal Publication Department, 1923)
Parkes, Joseph, and Herman Merivale (eds), *Memoirs of Sir Philip Francis* (London: Longmans, Green, and Co., 1867), 2 vols
The Parliamentary Register; Or, History of the Proceedings and Debates of the House of Commons (London: John Stockdale, 1802), 17 vols
Pepys, Samuel, *The Diary of Samuel Pepys*, ed. by R. C. Latham and W. Matthews (London: HarperCollins, 2016), 9 vols
Pope, Alexander, *The Works of Alexander Pope, Esq.*, ed. by William Roscoe (London: Longman, Brown and Co., 1847)
Proceedings of the General Court Martial in the Trial of Major John Gordon (London: E. Lloyd, 1804)
Reresby, John, *Memoirs of Sr John Reresby: The Complete Text and a Selection from his Letters*, ed. by Andrew Browning, 2nd edn (London: Royal Historical Society, 1991)

Bibliography

Riddell, George, *Lord Riddell's War Diary, 1914–1918* (London: Ivor Nicholson & Watson Limited, 1933)

——, *More Pages from My Diary, 1908–1914* (London: Country Life Ltd, 1934)

Rushworth, John, *Historical Collections of Private Passages of State* (London: D. Browne, 1721)

Russell, George W. E., *Portraits of the Seventies* (London: T. Fisher Unwin Ltd., 1916)

Russell, William Howard, *The Great War with Russia* (London: George Routledge & Sons Limited, 1895)

Sandford, Francis, *The History of the Coronation of the Most High, Most Mighty, and Most Excellent Monarch, James II* (London, 1687)

Seitz, Don C. (ed.), *The Tryal of Capt. William Kidd* (New York: Rufus Rockwell Wilson, Inc., 1936)

Sheridan, Richard Brinsley, *The Letters of Richard Brinsley Sheridan*, ed. by Cecil Price (Oxford: Oxford University Press, 1966), 3 vols

——, *The Rivals*, ed. by Elizabeth Duthie (London: A & C Black, 1979)

Sinclair, John, *Memoirs of the Insurrection in Scotland in 1715*, ed. by Walter Scott (Edinburgh, 1858)

Spalding Club, *The Miscellany of the Spalding Club*, vol. 3 (Aberdeen: Spalding Club, 1846)

Spedding, James, *The Letters and Life of Francis Bacon* (London: Longmans, Green, Reader and Dyer, 1861–74)

Spencer, Alfred (ed.), *Memoirs of William Hickey* (London: Hurst & Blackett, Ltd, 1913–25), 4 vols

St James's Chronicle, 1214, 8–10 December 1768 (London, 1768)

Stamp, A. E. (ed.), *Calendar of Close Rolls, Henry IV* (London: HMSO, 1927), vol. 2, *British History Online*; https://www.british-history.ac.uk/series/calendar-close-rolls-henry-iv [accessed January 2023–June 2025]

Stevens, John, *The Journal of John Stevens*, ed. by Robert H. Murray (Oxford: Clarendon Press, 1912)

Tablet, The (Dublin, 1854)

Taylor, William Stanhope, and John Henry Pringle (eds), *Correspondence of William Pitt, Earl of Chatham* (London: John Murray, 1838–40), 4 vols

Temple, Richard Grenville, and George Grenville, *The Grenville Papers, Being the Correspondence of Richard Grenville Earl Temple, K.G., and the Right Hon George Grenville*, ed. by William James Smith (London: John Murray, 1852–3), 4 vols

Temple Bar (London, 1886)

Tennyson, Alfred, *The Poems of Alfred, Lord Tennyson* (Oxford: Oxford University Press, 1929)

Thompson, Henry Frederick, *The Intrigues of a Nabob: Or, Bengal the Fittest Soil for the Growth of Lust, Injustice and Dishonesty* (1780)

Thurloe, John, *A Collection of the State Papers of John Thurloe*, ed. by Thomas Birch (London: Fletcher Gyles, 1742), 7 vols

Times, The (London, 1785–1945)

Toynbee, Paget, *The Letters of Horace Walpole, Fourth Earl of Orford* (Oxford: Clarendon Press, 1903–18), 16 vols

—— , 'Horace Walpole's Journals of Visits to Country Seats, &c', 9–80, in *The Volume of the Walpole Society* 16 (1927–8)

Treglown, Jeremy (ed.), *The Letters of John Wilmot, Earl of Rochester* (Oxford: Basil Blackwell, 1980)

Twiss, Horace, *The Public and Private Life of Lord Chancellor Eldon, with Selections from his Correspondence* (London: John Murray, 1844), 3 vols

Tyrwhitt, Thomas (ed.), *The Proceedings and Debates of the House of Commons in 1620 and 1621* (Oxford: Clarendon, 1766)

Vane, Charles William (ed.), *Correspondence, Despatches and Other Papers of Viscount Castlereagh* (London: John Murray, 1848–53), 12 vols

Vernon, James, *Letters Illustrative of the Reign of William III*, ed. by G. P. R. James (London: Henry Colburn, 1841), 3 vols

Walpole, Horace, *The Last Journals of Horace Walpole*, ed. by John Doran and A. Francis Steuart (London: The Bodley Head, 1910), 2 vols

—— , *Memoirs of the Reign of King George II*, ed. by John Brooke (New Haven and London: Yale University Press, 1985), 3 vols

—— , *Memoirs of the Reign of King George III*, ed. by Derek Jarrett (New Haven and London: Yale University Press, 2000), 4 vols

Ward, Ned, *The London Spy Compleat* (London: Casanova Society, 1924)

Warrand, Duncan (ed.), *More Culloden Papers* (Inverness: Robert Carruthers & Sons, 1923–30), 5 vols

Wathen, Augustus, *Proceedings of the General Court Martial upon the Trial of Captain Wathen* (London: Roake and Varty, 1834)

Watkin, A. E. (ed.), *Absalom Watkin: Extracts from His Journal, 1814–1856* (London: T. Fisher Unwin Ltd, 1920)

Weldon, Anthony, *The Court and Character of King James* (London: J. Collins, 1651)

Wellesley, William Pole Tylney Long, *Two Letters to the Right Hon. Lord Eldon, Lord Chancellor* (London: John Miller, 1827)

Wemyss, David, *A Short Account of the Affairs of Scotland in the Years 1744, 1745, 1746* (Edinburgh: David Douglas, 1907)

Whitelocke, Bulstrode, *Memorials of the English Affairs: Or, an Historical Account of What Passed from the Beginning of the Reign of King Charles the*

First, to King Charles the Second His Happy Restoration (London: Nathaniel Ponder, 1682)

Wightman, J. W., 'One of the "Six Hundred" on the Balaclava Charge', 850–63, in *Nineteenth Century* 31 (1892)

Wilkes, John, *John Wilkes, Patriot: An Unfinished Autobiography*, ed. by R. Des Habits (Harrow: William F. Taylor, 1888)

——, *The North Briton*, nos 1–46 (New York: AMS Press Inc, 1976)

Williams, Benjamin (ed.), *Chronique de la traïson et mort de Richart Deux roy d'Engleterre* (London: Bentley, Wilson & Fley, 1846)

Willis, Nathaniel Parker, *Pencillings by the Way: Written during Some Years of Residence and Travel in Europe* (New York: Charles Scrivener, 1852)

Wood, Anthony, *Athenæ Oxonienses*, vol. 2, 2nd edn (London: Knaplock, Midwinter and Tonson, 1721)

——, *The Life and Times of Anthony Wood*, ed. by Andrew Clark (Oxford: Clarendon Press, 1891), 3 vols

Wraxall, Nathaniel, *Historical Memoirs of His Own Time* (London: Richard Bentley, 1836), 4 vols

Secondary sources

Arnold, F. H., 'Memoirs of Mrs. Oldfield', 83–98, in *Sussex Archaeological Collections*, 38 (1892)

Atlay, James, *The Trial of Lord Cochrane before Lord Ellenborough* (London: Smith, Elder, & Co., 1897)

Bailey, Brian, *George Hudson: The Rise and Fall of the Railway King* (Stroud: Alan Sutton Publishing Limited, 1995)

Bailey, Mark F., 'The 1844 Railway Act: A Violation of Laissez-Faire Political Economy?', 7–24, in *History of Economic Ideas* 12 (2004)

Ball, S., 'MP of the Month: Joseph Myles McDonnell, thwarted bagpiper', *The Victorian Commons*; https://victoriancommons.wordpress.com/2014/02/19/mp-of-the-month-joseph-myles-mcdonnell-thwarted-bagpiper/ [accessed March 2024–March 2025]

Bank of England, *A Millennium of Macroeconomic Data for the UK* (2024); https://www.bankofengland.co.uk/-/media/boe/files/statistics/research-datasets/a-millennium-of-macroeconomic-data-for-the-uk.xlsx [accessed November 2024]

'The Barwell Family', 184–7, in *Bengal Past and Present* 26 (1923)

Black, Jeremy, *The Hanoverians: The History of a Dynasty* (London: Hambledon and London, 2004)

Blanning, Tim, *George I* (London: Penguin, 2017)

Bleackley, Horace, *Life of John Wilkes* (London: Bodley Head, 1917)

Bibliography

Bodkin, Matthias McDonnell, *Recollections of an Irish Judge* (New York: Dodd, Mead and Company, 1915)

Bogdanor, Vernon, 'Ian Ivatt: *The Financial Affairs of David Lloyd George*', in *Journal of Liberal History* 106 (2020)

Bonomi, Patricia U., *A Factious People: Politics and Society in Colonial New York* (New York and London: Columbia University Press, 1971)

Boswell, James, *The Life of Samuel Johnson*, ed. by Roger Ingpen (Bath: George Bayntun, 1925), 2 vols

Bouverie, Tim, *Allies at War: The Politics of Defeating Hitler* (London: The Bodley Head, 2025)

Boyce, D. George, *Nineteenth Century Ireland: The Search for Stability* (Dublin: Gill and Macmillan Ltd., 1990)

Boyer, Allen D. (ed.), *Law, Liberty and Parliament: Selected Essays on the Writings of Sir Edward Coke* (Indianapolis: Liberty Fund, 2004)

Bradford, Sarah, *Disraeli* (New York: Stein and Day, 1982)

Browne, James, *A History of the Highlands and of the Highland Clans* (Glasgow: A. Fullarton, 1840), 4 vols

Bryant, Chris, *Parliament: The Biography* (London: Transworld Publishers, 2015), 2 vols

Burns, J. F., 'From Whoredom to Evangelism: The story of Mrs. Thistlethwayte (nee Laura Bell, who was a native of Glenavy)', in *Lisburn Historical Society* 2 (1979)

Busteed, H. E., *Echoes from Old Calcutta* (London: W. Thackery & Co., 1908)

Cannadine, David, *Victorious Century: The United Kingdom 1800–1906* (New York: Viking, 2017)

Carswell, John, *The Old Cause: Three Biographical Studies in Whiggism* (London: Cresset Press, 1954)

———, *The South Sea Bubble* (Stroud: Alan Sutton, 1993)

Cash, Arthur H., *John Wilkes: The Scandalous Father of Civil Liberty* (New Haven and London: Yale University Press, 2006)

Chambers, William, and Robert Chambers, 'Story of Lady Grange', in *Chambers's Journal of Popular Literature, Science, and Art* 551 (1874)

Clark, J. Kent, *Whig's Progress: Wharton Between Revolutions* (London: Associated University Presses, 2004)

Clarkson, Wensley, *Hit 'Em Hard: Jack Spot, King of the Underworld* (London: HarperCollins, 2002)

Cleary, E. J., *The Building Society Movement* (London: Elek Books, 1965)

Cleave Books, 'Calculator of Units of Alcohol (UK Only)'; http://www.cleavebooks.co.uk/scol/ccalcoh2.htm [accessed September 2024]

Bibliography

Cornes, Richard, 'Robert Boyle's Weather Journal for the Year 1685', *Natural Environment Research Council*; https://nora.nerc.ac.uk/id/eprint/524879/1/cornes_weather.pdf [accessed 17 July 2005]

Coulthard, Sally, *Fowl Play* (London: Head of Zeus, 2022)

Crowley, Aleister, *The Book of the Law* (1904)

Cunningham, Peter, *The Story of Nell Gwyn*, ed. by Henry B. Wheatley (London: W. W. Gibbins, 1892)

Cust, Lionel, and Sidney Colvin (eds), *History of the Society of Dilettanti* (London: Macmillan and Co., 1914)

Dale, Bryan, *The Good Lord Wharton: His Family, Life, and Bible Charity* (London: The Congregational Union of England and Wales, 1906)

Dalrymple, William, *The Anarchy: The Relentless Rise of the East India Company* (London: Bloomsbury, 2019)

Dashwood, Francis, *The Dashwoods of West Wycombe* (London: Aurum Press Limited, 1987)

Davenport, Romola, 'Mortality, Migration and Epidemiological Change in English Cities, 1600–1870', 37–49, in *International Journal of Paleopathology* 34 (2021)

David, Saul, *The Homicidal Earl: The Life of Lord Cardigan* (London: Little, Brown and Company, 1997)

Donnelly, Seán, 'A Piping MP: Joseph Myles McDonnell (1796–1872), Doo Castle, Ballaghadereen, County Mayo', in *The Seán Reid Society Journal*, vol. 1 (1999); http://www.seanreidsociety.org/index.html [accessed February 2025]

Dorril, Stephen, *Blackshirt: Sir Oswald Mosley and British Fascism* (London: Penguin, 2006)

Echard, Laurence, *The History of England, from the Restoration of King Charles the Second to the Conclusion of the Reign of King James the Second* (London: Jacob Tonson, 1718), 3 vols

Emden, Paul H., *Randlords* (London: Hodder & Stoughton, 1935)

Evans, David Morier, *Facts, Failures and Frauds: Revelations, Financial, Mercantile, Criminal* (London: Groombridge & Sons, 1859)

Ferguson, Niall, *The Pity of War* (London: Allen Lane, 1998)

Firth, Charles, *The Regimental History of Cromwell's Army* (Oxford: Clarendon Press, 1940)

Fox, Charles James, *A History of the Early Part of the Reign of James the Second* (London: William Miller, 1808)

Fox-Strangways, Giles Stephen Holland, *Henry Fox, First Lord Holland, His Family and Relations* (London: John Murray, 1920), 2 vols

Francis, John, *A History of the English Railway* (London: Longman, Brown, Green & Longmans, 1851), 2 vols

Fraser, William, *Disraeli and His Day* (London: Kegan Paul, Trench, Trübner & Co. Ltd, 1891

Fukuyama, Francis, *The Origins of Political Order* (London: Profile Books Ltd, 2012)

Gardiner, Samuel Rawson, 'On Four Letters from Lord Bacon to Christian IV of Denmark', 219–69, in *Archaeologia* 41 (1867)

Gibson, Carrie, *Empire's Crossroad: A New History of the Caribbean* (London: Macmillan, 2014)

Gillespie, Raymond, *Seventeenth-Century Ireland: Making Ireland Modern* (Dublin: Gill & Macmillan Ltd, 2006)

Gosh, Suresh Chandra, 'The Social Condition of the British Community in Bengal, 1757–1800', unpub. thesis, University of London (1966)

Grant, I. F., *The Macleods: A History of a Clan, 1200–1956* (London: Faber & Faber, 1959)

Granville, George, *The Genuine Works in Verse and Prose* (London: J. Tonson, 1736)

Granville, Roger, *The King's General in the West: The Life of Sir Richard Granville, Bart., 1600–1659* (London: J. Lane, 1908)

Gregg, Edward, *Queen Anne* (New Haven & London: Yale University Press, 2001)

Grego, Joseph, *A History of Parliamentary Elections and Electioneering in the Old Days: Showing the State of Political Parties and Party Warfare at the Hustings and in the House of Commons from the Stuarts to Queen Victoria* (London: Chatto & Windus, 1886)

Harris, Kenneth, *Attlee* (New York: W. W. Norton & Company, 1982)

Hart, James D., *The Oxford Companion to American Literature*, 6th edn (Oxford: Oxford University Press, 1995)

Hay, Daisy, *Mr and Mrs Disraeli: A Strange Romance* (London: Chatto & Windus, 2015)

Haywood, Ian, and John Seed (eds), *The Gordon Riots: Politics, Culture and Insurrection in Late Eighteenth-Century Britain* (Cambridge: Cambridge University Press, 2012)

Hickman, Katie, *Courtesans* (London: HarperCollins, 2003)

Hinde, Wendy, *Castlereagh* (London: Collins, 1981)

Hirshfield, Claire, 'Labouchere, Truth and the Uses of Antisemitism', 134–42, in *Victorian Periodicals Review* 26 (1993)

History of Parliament Trust; https://www.historyofparliamentonline.org/ [accessed January 2023–June 2025]

Bibliography

Hone, J. Ann, *For the Cause of Truth: Radicalism in London, 1796–1821* (Oxford: Clarendon Press, 1982)

Honychurch, Lennox, *The Dominica Story: A History of the Island* (London: Macmillan, 1995)

Howitz, Henry, *Parliament, Policy and Politics in the Reign of William III* (Manchester: Manchester University Press, 1977)

Hoyle, R. W., *The Pilgrimage of Grace and the Politics of the 1530s* (Oxford: Oxford University Press, 2001)

——, 'The Fortunes of the Tempest Family of Bracewell and Bowling in the Sixteenth Century', 169–89, in *Yorkshire Archaeological Journal* 74 (2002)

Hughes, Andy K., *A History of Political Scandals: Sex, Sleaze and Spin* (Barnsley: Pen & Sword, 2013)

Hutton, Ronald, *Charles II: King of England, Scotland and Ireland* (Oxford: Oxford University Press, 1989)

——, *Oliver Cromwell: Commander in Chief* (London: Yale University Press, 2024)

Isaacs, G. R., *Rufus Isaacs, First Marquess of Reading* (London: Hutchinson & Co., 1948)

Ivatt, Ian, *The Financial Affairs of David Lloyd George* (Cardiff: Welsh Academic Press, 2019)

Jardine, Lisa, and Alan Stewart, *Hostage to Fortune: The Troubled Life of Sir Francis Bacon* (New York: Hill and Wang, 1998)

Jenkins, Roy, *Gladstone: A Biography* (London: Macmillan, 1995)

Jeremy, David J. (ed.), *Dictionary of Business Biography* (London: Butterworths, 1984), 5 vols

Johnson, Samuel, *Lives of the English Poets*, ed. by Arthur Waugh (Oxford: Oxford University Press, 1926

Jones, Clyve (ed.), *A Short History of Parliament: England, Great Britain, the United Kingdom, Ireland and Scotland* (Suffolk: Boydell, 2012)

Keates, Jonathan, *William III & Mary II: Partners in Revolution* (London: Penguin, 2018)

Keay, Anna, *The Restless Republic: Britain without a Crown* (London: William Collins, 2022)

Kelly, Linda, *Richard Brinsley Sheridan: A Life* (London: Sinclair-Stevenson, 1997)

Kemp, Betty, *Sir Francis Dashwood: An Eighteenth-Century Independent* (London: Macmillan, 1967)

King James Bible

Knight, Roger, *Britain against Napoleon: The Organization of Victory, 1793–1815* (London: Penguin Books, 2013)

Laband, John, 'Elizabeth van Heyningen: The Concentration Camps of the Anglo-Boer War: A Social History', in *The American Historical Review*, 120 (2015)

Laing, David, 'An Episode in the life of Mrs Rachel Erskine, Lady Grange', 593–608, in *Proceedings of Society of Antiquaries of Scotland*, 11 (1876)

Leder, Lawrence H., 'Robert Livingston's Voyage to England, 1695', 16–38, in *New York History*, 36 (1955)

Lehmberg, Stanford E., *The Reformation Parliament, 1529–1536* (Cambridge: Cambridge University Press, 1970)

Levenson, Thomas, *Money for Nothing: The South Sea Bubble and the Invention of Modern Capitalism* (London: Head of Zeus, 2020)

Lloyd George, Richard, *My Father, Lloyd George* (New York: Crown Publishers Inc., 1961)

Longueville, Thomas, *The Curious Case of Lady Purbeck: A Scandal of the XVIIth Century* (London: Longmans, Green, and Co., 1909)

Lord, Evelyn, *The Hell-Fire Clubs: Sex, Satanism and Secret Societies* (New Haven and London: Yale University Press, 2008)

Luthman, Johanna, *Love, Madness and Scandal: The Life of Frances Coke Villiers, Viscountess Purbeck* (Oxford: Oxford University Press, 2017)

Lysons, Daniel, *An Historical Account of those Parishes in the County of Middlesex, Which Are Not Described in the Environs of London* (London: T. Cadwell Jr and W. Davies, 1800)

Macaulay, Thomas Babington, *The Essays of Lord Macaulay: Earl of Chatham*, ed. by H. W. C. Davis (London: William Heinemann, 1908)

Marquis, Samuel, *Captain Kidd: A True Story of Treasure and Betrayal* (New York: Diversion Books, 2025)

Matthew, H. C. G., *Gladstone: 1809–1874* (Oxford: Clarendon Press, 1986)

——, *Gladstone: 1875–1898* (Oxford: Clarendon Press, 1995)

Measuring Wealth; https://www.measuringworth.com/calculators/ukcompare/ [accessed January 2023–June 2025]

Meisel, Joseph S., 'The Importance of Being Serious: The Unexplored Connection Between Gladstone and Humour', 278–300, in *History* 84 (1999)

Miller, Amos C., *Sir Richard Grenville of the Civil War* (London: Phillimore, 1979)

Mitchell, L. G., *Charles James Fox* (London: Penguin, 1992)

Monypenny, William Flavelle, *The Life of Benjamin Disraeli, Earl of Beaconsfield* (New York: Macmillan, 1929)

Moore, Thomas, *Memoirs of the life of the Right Honourable Richard Brinsley Sheridan* (London: Longman, Rees, etc., 1826)

Mountfield, David, *The Railway Barons* (New York: W. W. Norton & Company Inc., 1979)

Namier, Lewis, *The Structure of Politics at the Accession of George III*, 2nd edn (London: Macmillan & Co. Ltd, 1963)

——, *Charles Townshend* (London: Macmillan & Co. Ltd, 1964)

Nash, Eveleigh, *Nash's War Manual* (London: Eveleigh Nash, 1914)

Norsworthy, Laura, *The Lady of Bleeding Heart Yard: Lady Elizabeth Hatton, 1578–1646* (London: John Murray, 1935)

Ó Gráda, Cormac, *Ireland: A New Economic History, 1780–1939* (Oxford: Clarendon Press, 1994)

Oldmixon, John, *Memoirs of the Life of the Most Noble Thomas Late Marquess of Wharton* (London: J. Roberts, 1715)

——, *Memoirs of the Life of John Lord Somers* (London: J. Roberts, 1716)

O'Shea, James, *Prince of Swindlers: John Sadleir MP, 1813–1856* (Dublin: Geography Publications, 1999)

Oxford Dictionary of National Biography; https://www.oxforddnb.com/ [accessed January 2023–June 2025]

Parris, Matthew, *Great Parliamentary Scandals: Five Centuries of Calumny, Smear and Innuendo* (London: Robson, 2004)

Payling, Simon, '"Am I not your uncle?": John of Gaunt, the murder of Friar Latimer and the Salisbury Parliament of 1384', *History of Parliament*; https://historyofparliament.com/2022/03/08/salisbury-parliament-of-1384/ [accessed 25 April 2024]

Pearson, Hesketh, *Labby: The Life and Character of Henry Labouchère* (London: Hamish Hamilton, 1936)

Pettigrew, William A., *Freedom's Debt: The Royal African Company and the Politics of the Atlantic Slave Trade, 1672–1752* (Chapel Hill: University of North Carolina Press, 2013)

Phillips, Charles James, *History of the Sackville Family* (London: Cassell, 1930)

Pincus, Steven, *1688: The First Modern Revolution* (London and New Haven: Yale University Press, 2009)

Pinto, Vivian de Sola, *Sir Charles Sedley* (London: Constable and Company, 1927)

Plumb, J. H., *Sir Robert Walpole* (London: The Cresset Press, 1956–60), 2 vols

Prestwich, Menna, *Cranfield: Politics and Profits under the Early Stuarts* (Oxford: Clarendon Press, 1966)

Pugh, R. H., (ed.), *Victoria History of the County of Essex*, vol. 6 (London: Institute of Historical Research by Oxford University Press)

Reece, Henry, *The Army in Cromwellian England, 1649–1660* (Oxford: Oxford University Press, 2013)

―――, *The Fall: Last Days of the English Republic* (New Haven and London: Yale University Press, 2024)
Riding, Jacqueline, *Jacobites: A New History of the '45 Rebellion* (London: Bloomsbury, 2016)
Ridley, Jane, *The Young Disraeli* (London: Sinclair-Stevenson, 1995)
Ritchie, Robert C., *Captain Kidd and the War against the Pirates* (Cambridge, MA, and London: Harvard University Press, 1986)
Roberts, S. K., 'Alehouses, brewing, and government under the early Stuarts', 45–71, in *Southern History* 2 (1980)
Rowland, Peter, *David Lloyd George: A Biography* (New York: Macmillan, 1975)
Russell, Conrad, *The Crisis of Parliaments: English History, 1509–1660* (Oxford: Oxford University Press, 1971)
―――, 'Why Did Charles I Call the Long Parliament?', 375–83, in *History* 69 (1984)
Sackville-West, Robert, *Inheritance: The Story of Knole and the Sackvilles* (London: Bloomsbury, 2010)
Sackville-West, Vita, *Knole and the Sackvilles* (New York: George H. Doran Company, 1922)
Sandford, Margaret E. Poole, *Thomas Poole and His Friends* (London: Macmillan and Co., 1888), 2 vols
Saul, Nigel, *Richard II* (London: Yale University Press, 1997)
Searle, G. R., *Corruption in British Politics, 1895–1930* (Oxford: Clarendon Press, 1987)
Seeley, J. R., *The Expansion of England* (London: Macmillan & Co., Limited, 1900)
Seton-Watson, R. W., 'The Strange Story of Lady Grange', 12–24, in *History* 16 (1931)
Shakespeare, William, *The Complete Works*, ed. by Stanley Wells and Gary Taylor (Oxford: Oxford University Press, 1988)
Sharpe, Kevin, *The Personal Rule of Charles I* (London: Yale University Press, 1992)
Sheffield, Gary, *The Somme* (London: Cassell, 2003)
Sheridaniana, or, Anecdotes of the life of Richard Brinsley Sheridan; his table talk and bons mots (London: Henry Colburn, 1826)
Skidelsky, Robert, *Oswald Mosley* (New York: Holt, Rinehart and Wilson, 1975)
Smith, David L., and Patrick Little, *Parliaments and Politics During the Cromwellian Protectorate* (Cambridge: Cambridge University Press, 2007)
Smith, R. B., *Land and Politics in the England of Henry VIII: The West Riding of Yorkshire, 1530–1546* (Oxford: Clarendon Press, 1970)
Stoyle, Mark, 'The Honour of General Monck', in *History Today* 43 (1993)

Strong, Roy, *Coronation: A History of Kingship and the British Monarchy* (London: HarperCollins, 2005)
Sylvester, Albert, *The Real Lloyd George* (London: Cassell and Company Ltd, 1947)
Szechi, Daniel, *1715: The Great Jacobite Rebellion* (New Haven and London: Yale University Press, 2006)
Thomas, Donald, *Cochrane: Britain's Last Sea-King* (London: Star, 1980)
Thomas, Peter D. G., *The House of Commons in the Eighteenth Century* (Oxford: Clarendon Press, 1971)
———, *British Politics and the Stamp Act Crisis: The First Phase of the American Revolution, 1763–1767* (Oxford: Clarendon Press, 1975)
———, *The Townshend Duties Crisis: The Second Phase of the American Revolution, 1767–1773* (Oxford: Oxford University Press, 1987)
———, *Tea Party to Independence: The Third Phase of the American Revolution, 1773–1776* (Oxford: Clarendon Press, 1991)
———, *John Wilkes: A Friend to Liberty* (Oxford: Clarendon Press, 1996)
Tuck, Anthony, *Richard II and the English Nobility* (New York: St Martin's Press, 1974)
University College London, *Legacies of British Slavery*; https://www.ucl.ac.uk/lbs/ [accessed October 2024–March 2025]
Wake, Joan, *The Brudenells of Deene* (London: Cassell and Company, 1953)
Walvin, James, *Black Ivory: A History of British Slavery* (London: HarperCollins, 1992)
Wasserstein, Bernard, *The Secret Lives of Trebitsch Lincoln* (London: Yale University Press, 1988)
Watt, Douglas, *The Price of Scotland: Darien, Union and the Wealth of Nations* (Edinburgh: Luath Press Limited, 2024)
West, Shearer, 'Wilkes's Squint: Synecdochic Physiognomy and Political Identity in Eighteenth-Century Print Culture', 65–84, in *Eighteenth-Century Studies* 33 (1999)
Whyte, John Henry, *The Independent Irish Party, 1850–9* (Oxford: Oxford University Press, 1958)
Wilson, Charles, *Anglo-Dutch Commerce and Finance in the Eighteenth Century* (Cambridge: Cambridge University Press, 1966)
Wilson, John Harold, *The Court Wits of the Restoration* (New York: Octagon Books Inc., 1967)
Wilson, Peter H., *The Thirty Years War: Europe's Tragedy* (Cambridge, MA: Harvard University Press, 2009)
Womersley, David, *James II: The Last Catholic King* (London: Penguin, 2019)

Woodham-Smith, Cecil, *The Reason Why* (New York: Barnes & Noble Books, 1953)

Worden, Blair, *The English Civil Wars, 1640–1660* (London: Weidenfeld & Nicolson, 2009)

Wyndham, Maud, *Chronicles of the Eighteenth Century, Founded on the Correspondence of Sir Thomas Lyttelton and His Family* (Boston: Houghton Mifflin Company, 1924), 2 vols

Index

A
absolutism 3
Abolition of Slavery Act (1833) 169
Abolition of the Slave Trade Act (1807) 163
abolitionism 152, 162–63, 169, 180–81, 215–16
Act of Indemnity and Oblivion (1660) 50
Act of Settlement (1701) 69, 93
Acts of Union (1707) 92, 195–96
Admiralty Court 81–82, 172–76
adultery 183–84
    Adultery Act (1650) 46
Aislabie, John 97, 100–1
American Revolutionary War (1775–83) 135–38, 162
Anglicanism *see* Church of England; Protestantism
Anglo-Scottish war (1650–52) 47–48
Anne (Queen of England) 92–93, 96
anti-Catholicism 76–77, 140
    Act of Settlement (1701) 93
    anti-Catholic riots 141–43
    succession 69, 93
antisemitism 229–30, 242
assault and kidnap 4
    Belasyse 64
    Cochrane 170
    Coke 21
    Erskine 110
    Macleod 110
    Sackville 64
    Stanhope 101–2
    Wharton, Tom 73

Avery, Henry 86
Axtell, Daniel 37–38, 41–44, 50–51

B
Bacon, Sir Francis 11–14, 15–16, 17–18, 44
Bank of England 82, 97, 103, 142
bankruptcy 229
    East India Company 136–37
    Fox 156
    Hess 229
    Lincoln 247
    Lincoln 247
    Sadleir 195
    Savile 68
    South Sea Bubble 103
    Wilkes 127
bans from state or Court positions
    Bacon 13
    financial interests 188
    Mompesson 17
    Wharton, Tom 75
    see also reputation
'Barebones' Parliament 47
Barons, Anna 45
Barwell, Richard 146–48
Batten, Sir William 55–56
Battle of Cable Street (1936) 242–45
Battle of the Boyne (1690) 83, 115
Battle of Waterloo (1815) 177–78
Battyn, Nicholas 44–46
Belasyse, Sir Henry 64–66, 69
Bell, Laura 216–20
    relationship with Gladstone 220
Bence, John 79, 80–81

Index

bigamy 46–47, 66–67
Bingham, George Charles, Lord Lucan 204
Black Bottle affair 200
blackmail
    Erskine 104–5
    Gladstone 221
    Pepys 57
blasphemy 61, 119, 120, 124–25
Bligh, Mrs 182–84
Boer Wars
    First Boer War (1880–81) 226
    Second Boer War (1899–1902) 226–27
Bonnie Prince Charlie 112–14
Boyne, Battle of the (1690) 83, 115
brawling in Parliament 23, 141–42
bribery and corruption 11
    Bacon 12–14
    Cochrane 172–73
    Coote 165
    East India Company 86
    land disputes 12–13
    Mompesson 15–16
    Pepys 55–56
    Villiers 15–16
British South Africa Company 226, 229–30
British Union of Fascists 242
Brudenell, James Thomas, Earl of Cardigan 199–208
buccaneering 87
Bulwer-Lytton, Sir Edward 211–12
Bulwer-Lytton, Lady Rosina 212–13

C

Cable Street, Battle of (1936) 242–45
Californian Gold Rush (1853) 224
Calvinism 24–25, 120
canals 186–87
Cape Colony 226
Carey, Sir Robert 9–11
Carr, Robert 64
Catholic Emancipation Act (1829) 194

Catholicism
    Act of Settlement (1701) 69, 93
    Catholic Emancipation Act (1829) 194
    Catholic Relief Act (1778) 140–41
    Catholicisation of the Church of England 29
    Elizabethan religious settlement 24–25
    Exclusion Crisis 70
    Gordon Riots (1780) 140–44
    Ireland 32, 41, 82–83, 153, 192, 194, 195–96, 221–22
    James VII and II 72, 76–77, 82, 120–21
    political emancipation 143
    Restoration 68–70
Cavaliers and Roundheads 33–36, 41
    see also English Civil War
Chamberlain, Neville 245–46
charge of the Light Brigade (1854) 204–8
Charles I 18, 23–25
    Personal Rule 25
    trial and execution 37–41, 43–44, 50
    Scotland 29–30
Charles II 41, 47–48, 50–51, 55, 56–57, 58, 77
Chartism 186, 214
Chiesley, Rachel 103–5
Church of England 76–77
    Catholicisation 29
    Charles I reforms 24
Churchill, Winston 241
Clarges, Anne 46–47, 50
Cochrane, Lord Thomas 169–78
Cochrane-Johnstone, Andrew James 166–69
Coke, Clement 22–25
Coke, Sir Edward 18–21
Culpeper, John, Lord Culpeper 35
Colonel Pride's Purge 37, 49
colonialism 55, 85, 87, 91, 163, 170, 198, 224–25, 232
    American colonies 135–38
    South African territories 226

Index

Colony of Natal 226
Common Prayer Book 51
communism 240, 242, 245, 252
Company of Scotland Trading to Africa
    and the Indies 91
Coote, Richard Earl of Bellomont 85–90
Coote, Sir Eyre 162–66
Corn Laws 181, 191–92, 195–96, 214
corruption *see* bribery and corruption
courts martial 171
    Axtell 42
    Brudenell 199, 200, 204
    Cochrane 171
    Cochrane-Johnstone 167
Courtenay, Sir Philip 1–2
Craggs, James 102–3
Crimean War (1854) 204–8, 219
Cromwell, Oliver 37, 42–44, 46, 48
Cromwell, Richard 44
cronyism 178–79
Culloden, Battle of (1746) 114–15
Curzon, Lady Cynthia Blanche 241
Cutteford, George 29, 33

D

Dashwood, Sir Francis 121–22
debauchery 37–38, 58–59, 60–63, 66–68,
    82–83, 103, 155
  see also drunkenness/drinking;
    promiscuity; sexual activity; sexual
    impropriety
debt
    Brudenell 208
    Carey 9
    Cochrane 180
    Cochrane-Johnstone 169
    Coke 25
    Disraeli 211, 214
    Fox 156–57
    Gladstone 219–20
    Grenville 29
    Hudson 190–91
    Lincoln 246, 247
    Lloyd-George 237

    Macleod 110–11, 115
    McDonnell 197–98
    Monck 44–45
    Paull 179, 180
    Pole 182
    Rich 81
    Sackville 67
    Sadleir 192–94
    Savile 68
    Sheridan 153–54
    Wharton, Philip 120–21
    Wilkes 131
Defoe, Daniel 79, 100
Demerara rebellion (1823) 169
diplomatic postings
    Labouchère 224–25
    Walpole 103
    Wellesley 179–80
Disraeli, Benjamin 210–14
dissolution of Parliament 3, 23–24, 31
divine right to rule 10–11
domestic abuse 29
    Coke and Lady Hatton 18–21
    Grenville and Mary Howard 29, 33
    Pole and Catherine Tylney Long
        182–84
drunkenness/drinking
    Fox 158–59
    Hudson 190
    Sheridan 153–54
    McDonnell 196–98
  see also debauchery
Dryden, John 65
duels and duelling 6, 64
    Barwell 146
    Brudenell 201–3
    Coke 22
    Disraeli 210
    Labouchère 224
    Lloyd George 236
    Paull 178–79, 180
    Porter 66
    Savile 59
    Sheridan 151

Index

duels and duelling (continued)
    Sinclair 92
    Slingsby 35
    Talbot 123–24
    Wharton, Henry 75–76
    Wilkes 123–24, 125

E
East India Company 86, 87, 91, 97–98, 102, 135, 136–37, 144, 179, 201–2
Easter Rising (1916) 232–33
Edward VII 232
Edward VIII 246
electoral interference 14
    Huske 133
    James VII and II 73, 73–74
    Reform Acts 238–39
    Sadleir 192
    Savile 68
    Wharton, Tom 73–75
    Wilkes 130–33
electoral reform 153–54, 177–78, 178–79, 181–82
    Great Reform Act (1832) 186
    Reform Acts 238–39
Elizabeth I 9, 10, 14
Elizabethan religious settlement (1559) 24–25
embezzlement 14, 15, 169
    Cochrane-Johnstone 168–69
    Company of Scotland 91
    Fox 155–56, 157
    Hudson 190–91
English Civil War (1642–52)
    Axtell 37
    Bacon 18
    Grenville 36
    Monck 46, 48
entrapment 15–16
Erskine, James, Lord Grange 103–10
espionage 33, 247–51
Exclusion Crisis 70
extortion 1, 5–6, 16, 146, 191
extra-marital affairs *see* adultery

F
Farro, James 81
fascism 230
    Battle of Cable Street 242–45
female suffrage 229, 234
Fenian uprising (1867) 221–22
The 'Fifteen', 93–94
fines 13, 15–16, 18
First Bishops' 'War' (1639) 29–30
First Boer War (1880–81) 226
First English Civil War (1642–49) 29, 32–36, 39
First World War 233–34, 247–48
Fitzgerald, Lord Edward 154
Forbes Duncan 112–13
forgery 97–98, 192–93, 247
Fox, Charles James 69, 155–59
Fox, Henry, Lord Holland 155–56
Francis, Philip 145
Franklin, Benjamin 122–23
fraud 97
    Cochrane 173
    Cochrane-Johnstone 167–68, 169
    Huske 133, 138
    Lloyd-George 236, 239
    Mompesson 15–16
    Sadleir 193, 194–95
free-traders 85
Freemasonry 120–21

G
gambling 87, 96
    Barwell 147–48
    Carey 9–10
    Fox 155–57
    McLeod 115
    Paull 179, 180
    Wharton, Philip 120
Garrick, David 152
General Strike (1926) 240
George I 93–94, 96, 101
George II 94, 101–2
George III 123, 132–33, 155, 157–58
George IV 155

Index

George V 232
Gerard, John 11
Gerard, Thomas 11
Gibbon, Edward 119
Gladstone, Herbert 238–39
Gladstone, William Ewart 215–22, 227
   president of the Board of Trade 188
   Railway Regulation Act 188
Glencoe Massacre 82
Glorious Revolution (1688) 82, 120–21, 157–58
Good Old Cause 43–44, 50
Gordon, Major General Charles George 225
Gordon, Lord George 140–44
Gordon Riots (1780) 141–43
Great Reform Act (1832) 186, 210–11, 238
Great War *see* First World War
Grenville, Sir Richard 28–36
Guy, Thomas 99–100

H
Haitian Revolution (1791) 163
Hastings, Warren 145–46
Hatton, Lady Elizabeth 18–21
Henry IV 2
Heveningham, Henry 81
Hitler, Adolf 242, 245–46, 250–51
Hogarth, William 123
homosexuality 210
honours/peerages sale of 11, 238–39
Howard, Mary 28–29, 36
Hudson, George 186–91
Huske, John 133–34, 136–38
Hutcheson, Archibald 99

I
impeachment 17, 23, 32, 90, 145, 180
imprisonment 2, 6, 23–24, 69–70, 92, 111
   Barwell 146
   Cochrane 173–74
   Craggs 102–3
   Gordon 144

Hess 229
Lincoln 249–50
Monck 46
Sheridan 152–53
Wilkes 128–30
in absentia trials 17, 127
India 144–46
   Brudenell 199–200
Indian Rebellion (1857) 201–2
Industrial Revolution
   manufacturing 198–99
   railways 188–91
   steam 198–99
insider trading
   East India Company 102
   Marconi Scandal 236–38
   stock-market manipulation 226–27, 236
   railways 188–91
intimidation 20–21, 137, 165
investment
   mining 211
   railways 188–91, 211
   see also financial misdealings; insider trading; stock market
Ireland
   Axtell 41–42
   Catholicism 32, 41, 82–83, 153, 192, 194, 195–96, 221–22
   Easter Rising (1916) 232–33
   Fenian uprising (1867) 221–22
   Grenville 32–33
   home rule 222, 232–33
   Irish Rebellion (1641) 32–33
   James VII and II 82–83
   McDonnell 195–98
   potato famine (1845–52) 191–92
   Sadleir brothers 191–95
   Sheridan 153–54
   siege of Carrickfergus (1689) 82–83
   Wharton, Henry 82–83
   William and Mary 84
Irish Coercion Bill 195–96
Irish home rule 222, 232–33

Index

Irish potato famine (1845–52) 191–92
Isaacs, Rufus 236–38

J
Jacobite rebellions (1715–45) 103
    Bonnie Prince Charlie 112–14
    Culloden, Battle of 114–15
    Erskine 104–10
    Macleod 110–12
Jamaica 162–63, 164
Jamaican slave revolt (1760) 163–64
James VI and I 5, 9–10
    accession as king of England 10–11
    divine right to rule 10–11
James VII and II 72–73
    'abdication', 82
James VIII and III 93, 112–13
Jameson, Dr Leander Starr 226
Jameson Raid 226
Jeffreys, Sir George (Hanging Judge Jeffries) 73
Johnson, Dr Samuel 119–20

K
Keynesianism 241
Kidd, William 84–90
knighthoods in exchange for loyalty 10–11, 238–39
Knights of Saint Francis of Wycombe 121–23, 125
Korean War (1950–53) 252
Kynaston, Edward 63

L
Labouchère, Henry 222–30
labour movement 240–41
land disputes 11, 12, 16–18, 83
    see also plunder and land theft
libel
    Bacon 14
    Cochrane 171
    Disraeli 210
    Gladstone 222, 222–23
    Labouchère 227, 229

North Briton 123–27, 133
    seditious libel 76–77
    Truth 222–23
    Wilkes 124–25, 127
Lincoln, Ignatius Timotheus Trebitsch 246–51
Linley, Elizabeth 148–49
Lloyd George, David 234–40, 245
Long Parliament (1640–60) 31–32, 49–51
Lydford Law 34

M
McDonnell, Joseph Myles 195–98
Macleod, Norman 110–12
Malta 170, 172, 174–76
manslaughter 64
Marconi Scandal (1912) 236–38
marriage for advancement 18–21
Martin, Samuel 125–26
Mary II 76–77
    see also William and Mary
Mathews, Mr 149–51
Medmenham Monks 121–23, 125
military commissions 43
    purchase 80–81, 200
military inquiries 166
    see also courts martial
Mompesson, Giles 14–18
Monck, George 44–51
Morrison, Sir Charles 22–23
Mosley Sir Oswald 240–41
    Battle of Cable Street 242–45
murder and attempted murder
    Axtell 42–43
    Belasyse 64
    Brudenell 200–1
    Monck 44–46
    Sackville 64
mutinies and mutineers 84–87, 158, 162–63, 167, 218

N
Napoleon I (Napoleon Bonapart) 177, 178
Napoleon III (Louis Napoleon) 213, 219

Index

Napoleonic Wars (1803–15) 158, 162, 163, 167–69, 169–70, 176
national debt, 82, 97–99
Navy blockades 137–38, 171–72
Nazism 229–30, 250–51
 see also fascism
Nelson, Horatio 162
nepotism 11, 14–15, 178–79
New Model Army 35–36, 37
Newton, Sir Issac 99

O

Oates, Titus 69–70
Opium Wars (1839–42/1856–60) 225

P

parliamentary privilege 124–25, 127, 131
patents
 Marconi 237
 Mompesson 15–17
 patent trolling 15–17
patronage 14–15, 68, 79, 86–88, 133, 210–11
Paull, James 178–80
Peace of Amiens (1802) 158
Penn, Sir William 55–56
Penn, William 68
Pepys, Samuel 54–59
Percy, Elizabeth, Lady Northumberland 59–60
perjury 70, 89, 229
Peterloo Massacre (1819) 181–82
Petition of Right 23–24
pirates and piracy 84–90
plunder and land theft 142–43
 Cochrane 174
 Grenville 33–34, 36
 Irish Catholics 70
Pole Tylney Long Wellesley, William 180–81
Poor Law system 192
Pope, Alexander 124–25
Porter, Tom 64–65
Potter, Thomas 122–25

press-gangs 170
Pride's Purge 37, 49
prisoners of war 34–35
privateering 84–87, 90
Privy Council 3, 9–10, 11, 19, 21, 30, 69, 83, 92, 143
profiteering 239
promiscuity 133–34
 Disraeli 210–12
 Gladstone 216, 220–213, 216–20
 Lloyd George 235–27
 Pepys 57–58
 Pole 183–84
 Savile 59–60
 Wilkes 127–28
prostitutes and prostitution 120
 Disraeli 211
 Gladstone 216
 rescue of prostitutes 216
Protestantism 10, 69
 Act of Settlement (1701) 93
 Calvinism 24–25, 120
 'Catholicisation' of the Church of England and State 29, 76–77, 82
 Ireland 32, 41–42, 221–22

R

rail travel 186–91
Railway Regulation Act (1844) 188
Reform Act (1867) 238
Reformation 24, 67
Representation of the People Act (1884) 238
representative democracy 3–4
reputation 94, 149, 163
 Bacon 13, 14
 Brudenell 202
 Carey 10
 Dashwood 121
 Disraeli 213
 Grenville 36
 Kidd 84, 90
 Labouchère 228
 Macleod 110

Index

reputation (continued)
    Medmenham Monks 121–22
    Mompesson 17
    Monck 46
    Wilkes 132
Restoration 49, 56–57, 66, 68–69
Reynolds, John 200
Reynolds, Richard 200
Rhodes, Cecil 226, 229–30
Rich, Sir Robert 79–82
Richard II 1
riots and rioting 131–32
    Battle of Cable Street (1936) 242–45
    Gordon Riots (1780) 140–44
road travel 186–87
Royal African Company 110–11
Rump 37–38, 43–44, 48–51

S

Sackville, Charles, Lord Buckhurst 58–59, 60–61, 64
Sadleir, James 191, 194–95
Sadleir, John 191, 192–95
Savile, Henry 59–60, 67–68
Schaw, Hugh 92
Schaw, Sir John 92
Scotland
    Acts of Union (1707) 92, 195–96
    Carey 9–11
    Company of Scotland Trading to Africa and the Indies 91
    Monck 47–49
    Scottish imperialism 91
    union of the crowns of Scotland and England 5
Scottish Darien Company *see* Company of Scotland Trading to Africa and the Indies; Scotland
Second Anglo-Dutch War (1665–67) 55
Second Boer War (1899–1902) 226–27
Second English Civil War (1648) 37
Second World War 5, 252
    Mosley 240–45
    Nazism 229–30, 250–51

sedition 76, 105, 123–27, 132, 158, 181–82
    see also libel; treason
Sedley, Sir Charles 60–63, 66–67
sexual activity 29, 138
    see also promiscuity
sexually transmitted disease 156, 211
Sheridan, Richard Brinsley 148–55
Short Parliament (1640) 30–31
siege of Carrickfergus (1689) 82–83
Sinclair, John 92–94
Sino-Japanese War (1937–45) 250
slavers and slave trade
    abolitionism 152, 162–63
    Cochrane-Johnstone 166–69
    Coote 162–66
    Macleod 110–11
Slingsby, Sir Henry 35
smuggling 137, 146, 167–68
Society of Dilettanti 121–22
South Africa 226, 228–30
South Sea Company 97–100
Stanhope, Charles 101–2
Stevenson, Frances 235–36
stock market
    fraud 236
    manipulation 188–91, 226–27, 236
    railways 188–91, 211
    South Sea Bubble 97–100
    speculation 193, 227
    stock-jobbing 86
Stuart, Charles Edward *see* Charles I
Suez Canal 225
sugar trade 84, 166, 193
suicide
    John Sadleir 193–94
systemic dishonesty and corruption 253–55

T

Talbot, Sir John 123–24
taxes 3, 14, 37–38, 158, 239
    American Revolutionary War 135–37, 144
    Company of Scotland 91

Index

Forced Loan 23–24
Good Old Cause 43–44
import tax 24
Intolerable Acts 137–38
Personal Rule 25
tea trade 136–37
theft 6, 176, 246
   highwaymen 64
Third English Civil War *see* Anglo-Scottish war
Thirty Years' War (1618–48) 28, 46
Titanic 236–37
tobacco trade 84
torture 1, 42–43
Tower of London, imprisonment in 13, 23, 46
Townshend, Charles 133–35, 136–38
trade
   slavers and slave trade 110–11, 162–66, 166–69
   sugar trade 84, 166, 193
   tea trade 136–37
transportation 43, 176
Transvaal 226
treason/plotting 10, 31, 77
   Act of Indemnity and Oblivion 50
   Erskine 104–5
   Jacobite rebellion 103, 112–15
Trim Law 32–33, 34, 41
Tuckett, Harvey 201–2
turnpikes and toll roads 186–87
Tylney Long, Catherine 182–83

U

union of the crowns of Scotland and England (1603) 5
universal male suffrage 186

V

Villiers, Sir Edward 15, 17–18
Villiers, George 15–16
Villiers, John 20

W

Walpole, Horace 121, 135
Walpole, Sir Robert 101–2
War of the Seventh Coalition (1815) 177
Wars of the Three Kingdoms (1639–53)
   English Civil War (1642–52) 18, 36, 37, 46, 48
   Anglo-Scottish war (1650–52) 47–48
   First English Civil War (1642–49) 29, 32–36, 39
   Second English Civil War (1648) 37
   First Bishops' 'War' (1639) 29–30
   Irish Rebellion (1641) 32–33
   Long Parliament (1640–60) 31–32, 49–51
   Short Parliament (1640) 30–31
Waterloo, Battle of (1815) 177–78
Wellesley, Arthur, Duke of Wellington 162, 179–80, 183
Wellesley, Richard 179–80
Wellesley, William *see* Pole Tylney Long Wellesley, William
West Indies 162–63
Wharton, Henry 75–76, 82–83
Wharton, Philip 120–21
Wharton, Thomas 73–77, 83
Wilberforce, William 152
Wilkes, John 118–20, 123–33, 138, 157
William and Mary 77–78, 82
William III (William of Orange) 77–80, 82–83, 84, 86, 92
   see also William and Mary
William IV 154, 182
worker rights 214–15
   labour movement 240–41
workhouses 192
   see also Poor Law system
Wyndham Lewis, Mary Anne 213–14